# New Economic Thinking and Real Estate

# New Economic Thinking and Real Estate

Danny Myers

WILEY Blackwell

This edition first published 2016
© 2016 by John Wiley & Sons, Ltd.

*Registered Office*
John Wiley & Sons, Ltd, The Atrium, Southern Gate, Chichester, West Sussex, PO19 8SQ, United Kingdom.

*Editorial Offices*
9600 Garsington Road, Oxford, OX4 2DQ, United Kingdom.
The Atrium, Southern Gate, Chichester, West Sussex, PO19 8SQ, United Kingdom.

For details of our global editorial offices, for customer services and for information about how to apply for permission to reuse the copyright material in this book please see our website at www.wiley.com/wiley-blackwell.

*Library of Congress Cataloging-in-Publication Data*

Names: Myers, Danny, author.
Title: New economic thinking and real estate / Danny Myers.
Description: Hoboken : Wiley-Blackwell, 2016. | Includes bibliographical references and index.
Identifiers: LCCN 2016004467 (print) | LCCN 2016023019 (ebook) | ISBN 9781119048756 (paperback) |
    ISBN 9781119048732 (pdf) | ISBN 9781119048749 (epub)
Subjects: LCSH: Real estate development–Economic aspects. | Construction industry. |
    BISAC: BUSINESS & ECONOMICS / Real Estate.
Classification: LCC HD1390 .M945 2016 (print) | LCC HD1390 (ebook) | DDC 333.33–dc23
LC record available at https://lccn.loc.gov/2016004467

A catalogue record for this book is available from the British Library.

Wiley also publishes its books in a variety of electronic formats. Some content that appears in print may not be available in electronic books.

Cover image: Getty Images © Hong Li

Set in 10/12pt Sabon by SPi Global, Pondicherry, India
Printed and bound in Malaysia by Vivar Printing Sdn Bhd

1   2016

# Contents

# Foreword

A new form of economic thinking began to emerge in 2008, prompted by the unforeseen financial crisis that had stumbled banks across America and Europe. This catastrophic event also served to accelerate the ongoing academic debate about the relevance of some aspects of the mainstream economics curriculum, which had been simmering across Europe since the turn of the century. As Professor of Economics Diane Coyle (2012) perceptively observed: it was patently obvious that a chasm existed between 'the interesting questions of real-world problems and the workhorse economics being taught to students'. In other words, the financial crisis had highlighted a tension that existed between those who taught traditional, orthodox, neo-classical economics, and those making the case for a modern, heterodox, new economics.

No longer were the scientific methods offered by econometric (mathematical) approaches, or the precision of marginal returns, or economic models based on historical data, held up as sacrosanct. The modern challenge for economists was to make sure that their work is set in a real-world context; that the data and logic used confirms the current circumstances; and lastly, but by no means least important, that the growing scale and complexity of financial markets and products is acknowledged as a key part of economic analysis. As students of this text will discover, rather surprisingly, much of this appears to be in sharp contrast to the established approaches taught by many mainstream economists.

*New economic thinking* benefits from this debate as it seeks to establish the virtues of a modern approach to economic analysis. In a good number of chapters, this simply involves reiterating basic economic principles; improving the practical grasp of managing and using data; and recognising the importance of the financial sector to the broader economy. In short, what is identified is a selective approach, and content that blends with the times and resonates with the current graduate community as they search for jobs in difficult times.

Another unique feature of this text is its emphasis on the importance of real estate. Far too often, property is overlooked by mainstream texts but, given that many of the risks that banks accept when they provide loans are secured by property (be it residential or commercial), it can no longer be left out of the subject. In fact, real estate assets are too often the 'window dressing' and the 'noise' that confuses the analysis of so many locked into the mind-set of neo-classicism.

*New economic thinking*, therefore, brings into sharp focus the importance of property, finance and data handling as central tenets to comprehending today's economy. Furthermore, to enhance the approach several links to the internet are included as hyperlinks in the eBook and webnotes in the paperback.

The picture we end up presenting is not particularly neat and tidy with answers to closed questions based on tried and tested theory. Instead, we present a view that is slightly more complex in order to develop insight into the practical tools available to economists and enable answers to the open-ended questions that will inevitably arise during your professional career. This is not stated to provide some kind of excuse not to study economics, but to highlight why those who seek to *understand* the world of real estate need to embrace the language and methodology of 21st century economics.

# Introduction: Setting the Scene

This book is designed to provide an introduction to the role of the economy in understanding real estate. To make it topical, the Great Recession that ran across much of Europe from 2008 to 2014 is used to provide the story line, and a defining set of data is outlined in Table I.1, below. This recessionary saga presents a fascinating set of events that not only allows a broad review of modern economics, but also captures the state of play within the real estate profession. Ironically, the financial crisis that triggered the period of Great Recession took everyone by surprise, and there was no consensus about the solutions. Consequently, the debate over the options ranged far and wide; For example, should a government respond by reducing the national deficit or increasing it? Would lower rates of interest stimulate economic recovery or suppress it? Should welfare benefits be maintained or cut? Does economic inequality damage or encourage economic growth? Should depositors in failed banks be protected or face big losses?

Obviously, these policy options will make more sense once you have completed your studies – but do not expect to be given definite answers. Economics is clearly not that kind of subject, and the supporters of the new approach are keen to dispel the myth that economics is a science analogous to physics; hence, it should not be expected to produce universal, timeless, truths. Indeed, it is important to introduce economics as a social science that deals with human behaviour. As a consequence, at best it can be expected to provide guidelines, ideas, models and predictions – but not hard and fast rules.

The text was primarily conceived for those studying surveying or real estate management, as the RICS regard comprehension of business economics as an essential prerequisite for anyone graduating into a profession relating to property. However, a parallel market also exists among those studying finance and business. In fact, anyone interested in the economics profession's response to the challenges presented by the marked reductions to the pace of economic growth; the systemic

*New Economic Thinking and Real Estate*, First Edition. Danny Myers.
© 2016 John Wiley & Sons, Ltd. Published 2016 by John Wiley & Sons, Ltd.

**Table I.1**   Gross Domestic Product, European Union (28 countries). Millions of Euro

| 2008 | 2009 | 2010 | 2011 | 2012 | 2013 | 2014 |
|------|------|------|------|------|------|------|
| 12,325,878 | 11,781,797 | 12,030,439 | 12,240,116 | 12,179,168 | 12,199,435 | 12,365,418 |

*Note*: Data expressed in constant 2005 prices.
*Source*: OECD Statistics, December, 2015.

financial failures that haunted economies worldwide; and a desire to acknowledge and comprehend the multitude of real estate questions that arise from its use as an asset for investment, security for loans, development and ownership, should find the content informative.

*New economic thinking* is pertinent for three reasons. Firstly, it introduces some of the academic debate that occurred following the credit crises that prevailed in most high income countries following the collapse of Lehman Brothers in September 2008 – the now-notorious Wall Street investment bank. Secondly, the text highlights the uncontested ideas that have endured the crisis and continue to be central to economic discourse. In this sense, it cherry-picks, from the 250-year history of economic ideas, the tools and concepts that have survived the test of time. Thirdly, it places a strong focus on the relationships that exist between real estate markets and the broader economy.

This third feature is most important, as 'property' or 'real estate' is rarely addressed by mainstream texts. For example, if you look up 'real estate' in the index of an introductory economics textbook (such as Mankiw (2014), or Samuelson and Nordhaus (2010)), you will find real exchange rates, real GDP, real interest rates, real variables, and even reality versus perception – but no real estate. Under 'housing', you might find references to the consumer price index (CPI), to rent control and, possibly, even business cycles and forecasting – but certainly nothing on commercial property. Yet, each and every year, commercial and retail developments are, in value terms, the biggest sectors within real estate. Similarly, macroeconomics data miners, working for agencies forecasting economic activity, are also prone generally to overlook the broad range of real estate activity, apart from the occasional reference to housing. However, as we highlight in this text, *all* real estate is of central importance to understanding and forecasting fluctuations in the general levels of economic activity.

Recognising which property to proceed with for development, occupation or investment purposes is based on good timing and an ability to interpret economic activity. In fact, the principal reason for showing an interest in a property will depend upon the precise market it is being traded in and, inevitably, these are dynamic markets in which economic conditions (rates of return, finance costs and values, etc.) frequently fluctuate. Thus, compiling valuation and investment reports should not be regarded as crude mathematical processes that can be learnt by rote; professional surveyors also need to be able to draw upon market information and economic data to form an overall evaluation.

Studying this text, therefore, should help you to develop an intuitive judgement of property markets and enable you to provide sound advice to clients with financial interest in property assets. It will provide confidence in reading economic indicators and identifying trends, and give the ability to understand the role of property in an economic context. Such skills should avoid the embarrassment of the next generation of economists, financiers, surveyors and estate managers having to spectate during subsequent recessions like innocent bystanders. As the high-powered American Financial Crisis Inquiry Commission (FCIC), which Congress set up in 2009 to examine the causes of the financial and economic crisis in the United States, concluded, 'the crisis was avoidable'.

To be precise, the FCIC (2011) clearly confirmed that the mess left by the crisis was the result of: 'a series of ill-advised and poorly executed decisions, inactions and serious misjudgements'. Warning signs were ignored and misunderstandings prevailed. This text sets out to clarify these findings and, more importantly, to prepare the property world to be sharper next time round. As the commission wisely stated, 'The greatest tragedy would be to accept the refrain that no one could have seen this coming and thus nothing could have been done. If we accept this notion, it will happen again' (FCIC, 2011: xxviii).

So do not be fooled; economic cycles will continue to fluctuate between good and bad times, and an upheaval on the scale of 2008 could even be repeated. However, by rehearsing some of the economic logic – the tell-tell signs – that formed the backdrop to this almighty crash, we could benefit from the lessons learnt, and stand a far better chance to stay ahead of the market in the future.

## The storyline

The crisis that began in the American housing market during 2007 rapidly impacted on the economies and financial systems of Europe and beyond from 2008 onwards. The data (see Table I.1) detailing the impact reveals a sorrowful tale. Total economic activity across the 28 EU countries had contracted between 2008 and 2013 by €126 billion. In 2014, there were some signs of recovery, and the EU countries as group made €40 billion more than they had in 2008. Regardless of the sluggish recovery that had begun, recessionary problems rumbled on in Greece, Holland, Italy, Portugal, and Spain throughout 2014/15.

From 2009 to 2012, the global financial system slid further into disrepute, business communities became disorganised, and neighbourhoods were destroyed. The repercussions of the economic downturn were all encapsulating. They were certainly far wider and deeper than anything that went before, and the economy is predicted to remain below par in certain parts of Europe until 2016. With the Great Depression of the 1930s, recovery took four years; in some cases, however, it looks as though the Great Recession could take twice as long to return to the pre-recession level of 2008.

This period of economic decline and instability, contrasts sharply with the relative calm steady economic growth that had prevailed since 1995. Furthermore, a recovery from this low point would require a different regulatory approach to the risks involved in funding the large amounts of loans awarded by the world's banks and financial institutions for commercial property development, residential mortgages and so on.

In a nutshell, what had happened in the run-up to the financial crisis was that the relatively free flow of finance from banks to property owners had led to what commentators called a 'credit bubble' which, in turn, fuelled a bubble in property prices. Typically, the term 'economic bubble' – like an actual bubble – is used to capture the price of something rising continually upwards, becoming more and more fragile the higher it gets. They tend to be driven by herd-like behaviour, where people share a common interest in a specific type of commodity and cause its price to rise far beyond any intrinsic value the commodity in question might actually have.

In effect, the term 'bubble' is used to capture the idea of a speculative asset being constantly transacted and bid up in price – inflating, and inflating, until it eventually bursts. Famous bubbles include the price of black tulips, which had been the subject of a bubble in Holland in the 17th century; the value of British South Sea stock, whose bubble inflated and burst in 1720; and the more recent dotcom bubble in internet company shares that burst in March 2000, causing more than $7 trillion dollars to be wiped off the market value.

The Great Recession bubble, however, represents the biggest of them all. House prices and mortgage-backed securities (credit allowances given on residential and commercial property) both inflated at unbelievable rates from 2002 to 2007, a good deal further and faster than any forecaster could imagine. In fact, the two bubbles ran in tandem, as house prices and mortgage-related credit (in the form of various mortgage-backed securities) followed one another in an upwards spiral (the consequences of this residential investment frenzy were amplified by the global reach of these bubbles, as they were experienced more or less simultaneously across many countries, the prime examples being the USA, Australia, Ireland, South Africa, Spain and the UK).

The bottom line was that for many years, and certainly since the beginning of the 'noughties', the risk of mortgage default had diminished to the tiniest amount and, backed by ever-spiralling house prices, money was lent (mortgaged) and re-lent (re-mortgaged) to millions of people, including those on exceptionally low incomes – the phrases 'sub-prime', 'junk' and 'toxic lending' were coined in retrospect. For nearly a decade, the financial world had progressed securely and happily, until the inevitable happened – the bubble burst and the excessive concentrations of mortgage-related risk were splattered across the financial counters at banks across the world. This financial earthquake was difficult to foresee, and is still rather difficult to account for, but more will be explained in Part B. The point is that a housing bubble had begun to leak here and there in 2007, and eventually burst across the world economies in 2008 – not with a pop but an almighty crash – as property (unlike black tulips) affects everybody.

The world began to experience the worst recession since the 1930s – but this one would prove to be more protracted and difficult to resolve. Economists had not seen it coming and were dumbfounded and undermined in suggesting solutions. Thousands of customers of all major banks and related organisations had simultaneously defaulted on loans, to the tune of several trillion, and this had led to the bursting of an another bubble, in which the people struggling to pay debts sold property assets which were rapidly falling in price. This incredible breakdown in the financial system had serious worldwide implications for employment, productivity, welfare, prices and the importance of real estate as an asset class. As the press coverage at the time portrayed it: the credit crisis had sucked the life out of the economy. It sent shockwaves across each economic system, and there were relatively few markets across the globe that were not affected.

The key lesson that can be learnt from the global crisis of 2008 is that no economy can live beyond its means in perpetuity. In other words, unless the assets of a business, a bank or a household are sufficient to cover the liabilities of that business, bank or household, in time the balance sheet will go out of kilter – become imbalanced, turn insolvent, end up bankrupt – *kaput* – whatever you want to call it. The double whammy that was dealt to the financial system and the economy in 2008 was caused by two bubbles bursting more or less simultaneously. This raises the question: why did no one see this coming? Some preliminary answers to the house price bubble are outlined below, while questions relating to the bubble in mortgage backed securities will be put on hold until we examine financial systems in Part B.

## Hindsight is a wonderful thing

The Halifax price index, shown in Figure I.1, has been calculated for over 30 years, and it provides evidence of two housing bubbles. The first, relatively small, bubble commenced in 1986 and burst in 1989, leaving a significant number of people in a position of negative equity (where a mortgage is greater than the value of the related house). The second bubble, which is central to the story being relayed, commenced in 2000 and burst in 2007. In fact, during this period, house prices actually soared rapidly, by an astounding 130% in real terms (that is, relative to inflation) before crashing down.

This is all so easy to see and comment on in hindsight, but few managed to call it as it happened. In their defence, the low mortgage interest rates made house

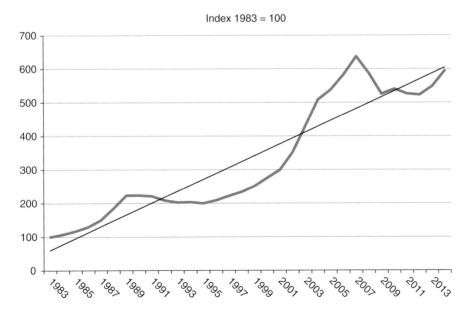

Index 1983 = 100

**Figure I.1**    UK house prices, 1983 to 2014.
*Source*: Adapted from Halifax house price index, 2015.

price rises seem perfectly logical at the time. Furthermore, the Halifax is only one of several house price indices, and the others were not going up as quickly (the discrepancies between data measuring the same phenomenon will be dealt with in Chapter 8, where we review various statistical indicators used to monitor economic activity).

The more reliable data to forecast from looks at trends in housing construction – namely, housing starts, and these are portrayed in Figure I.2. From these data, it is clear that housing is a boom-and-bust industry and, more specifically, a decline in residential investment is often one of the first indicators to reveal that a recession is about to occur. In fact, the data suggests that housing starts began to decline from 2004 onwards, whereas industrial production did not begin its nose-dive until 2008. The logic behind this data set is that builders usually commence with the construction of residential property when they are confident that it can be quickly sold on completion. If the economic climate changes, they might delay progressing the project until conditions become more favourable; no one wants to incur the cost of construction until they are confident that sales will follow on pretty quickly after completion. Consequently, during a recession, it might be possible to count a large number of foundations, but any other signs of activity to complete the work are non-existent. As a result, housing starts will increase in number when the economy is on the up, and slow considerably when the economy is on the way down.

Comparing the data in Figures I.1 and I.2 highlights an important contrast. Housing starts data demonstrates more volatility (in the sense that it is more sensitive to changes in circumstances), whereas house price data is less responsive to changes in economic conditions (in the sense that they tend to be 'sticky downwards'). Thus, whenever an economy experiences a decline in demand, the volume of sales adjusts more sharply than the prices. Furthermore, with a decline

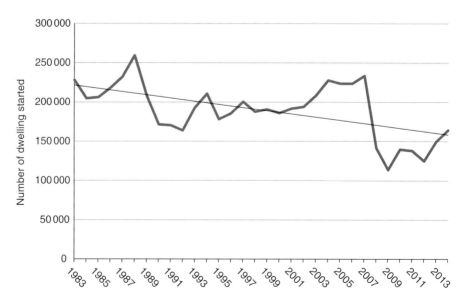

**Figure I.2**   UK housing starts 1983 to 2014.
*Source*: Adapted from Housing Statistics, Live Table 211, 2015.

in sales volume comes a decline in jobs in construction, finance, surveying and real estate agencies. Hence, when demand reduced as it did in 2008, it was quickly followed by a marked decline in the number of starts. In short, housing starts provide a better forecasting indicator than house prices.

## The writing on the wall

By now the message should be clear. This book is designed to help students develop an intuitive ability to interpret economic indicators and acquire the confidence to assess property markets. As such, it is divided into three parts, namely:

A   Resource choices
B   Financial systems
C   Measuring and forecasting

### Part A: Resource choices

This part deals with many of the traditional basic microeconomic principles, outlining the ways that resources tend to be allocated in private property markets. As budding economists might expect, a significant part of the exposition here is concerned with the determinants of supply and demand. However, we also emphasise that markets evolve and, to a large extent, are culturally derived. We therefore seek to explain, as plainly as possible, the position of man-made markets that deal with property in today's dominantly capitalist world.

In many introductory texts, two model systems of resource allocation are rehearsed – the centrally planned and the free market economy. These economic models are simplified representations of two different systems, but neither extreme exists in a pure form. In practice, modern economic systems are far more complex. We propose, therefore, to cut to the chase and emphasise that free private market decisions exist alongside centralised legislation and control. In some ways, this approach suggests that the typical textbook world of 'free markets' is a myth.

The intention of Part A, therefore, is to demonstrate how investors in property continually face choices that are constrained and refined by government and other cultural interventions. Resource choice is often compromised by social and political controls that limit what market participants can or cannot do. If people cannot do the things that they find most profitable, they lose the incentive to invest and innovate. To use examples presented by Ha-Joon Chang (2011) in his critique of capitalism: if the government seeks to keep privately rented accommodation at an affordable level and put a cap on rents, landlords lose the incentive to maintain their properties or build new ones. Or, if the government restricts the kinds of financial products that can be sold, two contracting parties that may both have benefited from innovative transactions that fulfil their idiosyncratic needs cannot reap the potential gains of free contract. Thus, we present a case that those interested in property and finance are less 'free to choose' than conventional mainstream economic titles might suggest.

## Part B: Financial Systems

Part B seeks to emphasise the importance of the financial sector to make sense of the broader macroeconomic scene. In an introductory text comprising eight main chapters, having three of them allocated to central banks, monetary policy, financial products and the performance of related markets, etc. may seem imbalanced. However, the received wisdom is that the financial crisis of 2008 and the subsequent Great Recession raised serious questions about neoclassical economics, and financial systems are a central part of the story.

An important section of Part B reviews the recently conceived flow of funds model as a means of understanding the determinants of economic growth and the likelihood of entering into future debt-fuelled recessions. As such, it introduces the relationships between the real economy and the financial system – or, to be more precise, the relationship between the stock of financial assets and real sector assets (actual economic output).

This relatively new approach goes some way to explaining why so few surveyors and traditionally trained economists could manage to forecast, or even to anticipate, the recession of 2008 as, in their day, no distinction was drawn between the financial sector and the real economy. It is only since the emergence of the Great Recession that explicit modelling of the financial sector alongside the real economy has gained credence as an important aspect of macroeconomic analysis that needs to be studied by budding economists and surveyors. To paraphrase the Harvard economist Benjamin Friedman (2009: 42): 'an important question – which few seemed interested in addressing before the onset of the 2008 credit crisis – is what fraction of an economy's total returns are absorbed up front by the financial industry and the real estate sector.

The new paradigm puts investment – particularly for commercial and residential real estate – at the centre of the analysis. It focuses on the debt and cash flow, emphasising how 'risks' and 'uncertainty' tend to make economic systems unstable and difficult to forecast. This fresh approach rejects the static equilibrium methodology of mainstream economics as irrelevant in analysing property assets, and plays up the importance of understanding how investment is financed and debts managed to determine the state of the macroeconomy.

## Part C: Measuring and Forecasting

Without doubt, being able to manage, use and interpret data is a vital skill for surveyors (and economists) to develop. The appraisals that clients request need to demonstrate an economic awareness. There is an expected level of detail relating to: the relative costs and benefits arising from the proposed investment; the implications of the interest rates paid on borrowed funds; the relevant tax measures; the prevailing market conditions; the legislative constraints imposed by planning policy and building regulations; and the end user requirements.

As such, there are many indicators of economic change to explore, ranging from the formal to the ridiculously informal: from levels of business investment, the availability of credit and the number of cranes that can be counted on the skyline, to the sales of men's underpants [1] and the membership numbers of the National

Pawnbrokers Association [2]. What to take notice of and how to read it is a subtle art, and it is well worth following up at least one or two data series, to begin to appreciate the level of rigour and accuracy portrayed. Unfortunately, there is no one sovereign set of data that gives all the clues; interpreting the bigger picture relies upon piecing together several bits of information.

Part C of the text, therefore, focuses on several sets of data, outlining the various ways and means used to measure and forecast economic progress. For example, the processes used to capture the scale of economic growth, inequality, inflation, unemployment, and international trade are all reviewed. Part C also highlights the difficulty of managing and forecasting an economy, as well as playing up the need for professionals working in the property world to acquire an economic vocabu-lary. With this in mind, it should be noted that the key terms, shown in bold in the text, are defined in the glossary at the back of the book.

**Introduction**

# Part A
# Resource Choices

*New Economic Thinking and Real Estate*, First Edition. Danny Myers.
© 2016 John Wiley & Sons, Ltd. Published 2016 by John Wiley & Sons, Ltd.

# Chapter 1
# Basic Economic Principles

As the introduction and forward implied, the global financial crisis and subsequent recession raised some serious questions about the validity of mainstream economics and, in particular, its approach to the integration of financial systems and its unshakable belief in market forces and forecasting. As a result, those influenced by the new approach can be excused from being trained to comprehend elegant algebra or to manipulate large complicated mathematical sets and algorithms. This textbook is simply designed to introduce economics that will help the reader to understand the current business markets and government policies that operate in the real world, with specific reference to decisions to develop, own or invest in property.

As Professor Robert Lucas (2009), was keen to point out in defence of the subject: 'One thing we are not going to have, now or ever, is a set of models that forecasts sudden falls in the value of financial assets, like the declines that followed the failure of Lehman Brothers in September 2008. This is nothing new. It has been known for more than 40 years and is one of the main implications of the **efficient market hypothesis,** which states that the price of a financial asset reflects all relevant, *generally available information.* If an economist had a formula that could reliably forecast crises a week in advance, then that formula would become part of *generally available information* and prices would fall a week earlier!'

In other words, Professor Lucas highlights that the economic world is far more complex than the physical world, as it is influenced by our beliefs about it, and this information is generally signalled through market prices. He does not seek to demean the discipline – he is aware of its limitations, but respectful of its insights.

As Chapter 3 and others in this text emphasise, market prices incorporate much information, but the intriguing aspect of the analysis is that they do not necessarily convey *all* information accurately, completely or transparently. There is room for

*New Economic Thinking and Real Estate*, First Edition. Danny Myers.
© 2016 John Wiley & Sons, Ltd. Published 2016 by John Wiley & Sons, Ltd.

differences of opinion and different perceptions of an uncertain future, as the art of interpretation and forecasting depends on intuition. Economics cannot be learnt by rote or by following hard and fast rules. It should certainly not be regarded as a narrow mathematical discipline, related solely to a study of costs or valuations that produce definite answers. Indeed, economics is a far broader subject than many anticipate, and an important aim of this chapter is to demonstrate that the core principles continue to influence the work of those engaged in finance, business, real estate and politics

## Definition of economics

As Lionel Robbins's (1932) classic statement captured it in his famous book on the *Nature and Significance of Economic Science* (published more than 80 years ago): 'Economics is the science which studies human behaviour as a relationship between ends and scarce means which have alternative uses'. Thus, entrepreneurs – and that includes property developers – must learn to manage scarce resources. This simple-sounding idea, however, is far more complex than it first appears. Many of the world's resources are finite, yet people have infinite wants. We are, in effect, faced with a two-pronged problem: at any point in time there is a fixed stock of resources, set against many wants. This problem is formally referred to as **scarcity**. In an attempt to reconcile this problem, economists emphasise that people must make careful choices – choices about what is made, how it is made, and for whom it is made; or, in terms of property, choices about what investments are made, how they may be constructed, and whether they should be developed for rent or purchase.

Intriguingly, the challenges facing the surveying profession have been presented in a similar way. As the Royal Institution of Chartered Surveyors (RICS) points out in their publicity blurb: the world is already overpopulated (growing at a rate of about 240 000 people a day) and everyone needs to be fed and housed – yet the earth's resources are not infinite! According to the RICS, part of the solution to scarcity lies in the sustainable use of land and maximising the long term value of all kinds of property. Therefore, they highlight that the choices we make affect not only how we live today, but how others will live in the future.

What determines these choices are financial rewards, as every resource has an alternative use and, therefore, an alternative source of income. As economists like to emphasise, choosing one thing inevitably requires giving up something else. In making a choice, an alternative opportunity is missed. To highlight this dilemma, economists refer to the concept of **opportunity cost** – where the value of the foregone alternative becomes the focus of the decision. In other words, economics emphasises how every want that ends up being satisfied results in some other want, or wants, remaining unsatisfied.

To take a simple example, if a specific plot of land is used for residential purposes, it cannot also be used as farmland. This means that an important part of understanding property in an economic context involves recognising that we have to decide on the alternative uses made of the fixed amount of land available. This choice is informed by the level of returns paid and the risks involved. Unfortunately, social and environmental returns, and the greater wider good, are often overlooked.

In a nutshell, a key objective of economics is about achieving economic efficiency for the benefit of the greater good – or, to use a commonly quoted nautical metaphor, first used by John F Kennedy more than 50 years ago – to raise the tide that lifts all boats. The Great Recession, however, complicated this straightforward idea as the economy ebbed towards lower levels of economic activity and greater numbers of unemployed. By 2015, serious ethical and political questions ruled the day, such as: should we continue to allow self-interest and self-regulation to allocate resources; or should we recognise that social justice requires that we put an end to society's excessive greed for profit and growth? Part of the new thinking highlighted that we cannot all be flooded with money at the same time. Extending the analogy the impact of the great recession has been somewhat selective – lifting a few gorgeous yachts, but leaving many smaller boats struggling to stay afloat.

To express the same sentiment in a political guise: to what extent should the taxpayer be expected to fund spending on public services, particularly those that effect the welfare of the typical man in the street? These dilemmas are currently being played out in all sectors of the economy and are exemplified by policy debates relating to the size of the state, and in resource decisions relating to property and housing. In terms of new economic thinking, an over-reliance on efficient markets and rational expectations should be avoided. As Kaletsky (2010: 181) pointed out: 'The dream of creating a market system with no economic role for government ended on September 15, 2008'.

To sum up, then, about what constitutes the subject matter of economics. It appears that it emerges from questions about money, consumption, work, technology, markets, government policies – and, in the broadest sense, how things are produced. Sometimes there is also a concern about the ways that the incomes generated are distributed, although this has been largely overlooked for the last 200 years, since the work of David Ricardo.

Finally, to close this introductory section, it should be remembered that by defining economics in terms of its core principles, or subject matter, we are avoiding the debate about a preferred methodology. Remember, all we are trying to achieve is insight into a complex machine with many moving parts; we are not seeking universal truths or constant proof.

## Resources (or factors of production)

Resources can be defined as the inputs used in the production of those things that we desire. Economists tend to refer to these resources as **factors of production**, to emphasise that, to produce any good or service, various factors need to be combined. Therefore, the total quantity, or stock, of resources that an economy has determines what can be produced. To construct real estate, for example, labour is required to develop a plot of land, and plant and equipment, which may be hired or bought, is required to facilitate the process. To put it another way, land and labour are always combined with manufactured resources to produce the things that are demanded.

When introducing property economics to groups of students, I often ask them to pause for thought and think of anything that can be produced without the involvement of these factors. The most common responses relate to ideas, thoughts, and decisions, and these answers enable me to distinguish economics from philosophy, psychology and business. The most intriguing answers to the question are suggestions relating to some 'virtual' activity based on digital technology – but these clearly still require people, equipment and a location to function from. In economic terms, they depend, like all economic goods, on using land, labour and capital to exist.

For property economists, these technology-based activities are actually most interesting, as they change the nature of demand for real estate. Nowadays, the conventional High Street retailer competes with online sales from stocks held in huge warehouses; businesses increasingly outsource activities to call centres; and financial transactions are mostly completed electronically via the internet, a mobile phone or a tablet computer. The development of the so-called **new economy** does not change the basic economic problem of allocating limited resources between competing ends – but, as we explain, particularly in Chapters 3 and 8, it does change the nature of markets and the nature of employment.

## Natural resources

**Land** is the natural resource we think of most often, and the production of any good or service is dependent on its existence; property is a prime example, as obviously each unit requires a 'site' or a 'location' (and the requisite planning permission). To date, however, there has been a limited economic analysis of the supply of land as, in a purely theoretical sense, it is ultimately fixed in supply and completely immobile (rural land cannot get up and move to seek better opportunities in urban areas). Land exists regardless of financial reward; its earnings are determined entirely by demand!

In the jargon of economics, the quantity of present and future available supply is completely inelastic with respect to price. This has several economic implications; to take one current example, over the years London has experienced continual growth and the demands for property has increased, to the extent that more and more development is now going on underground. For instance, during 2013, 3000 applications were made for basements (Allen, 2013). In short, economic change has created new patterns of demand for land use in London – but the actual amount of land has not changed.

The urban centres of China are undergoing similar pressure, as a period of unprecedented growth rapidly increases the demands for property in cities such as Beijing and Shanghai. Again, economic change has created new patterns of demand for land use and property in China – but the actual amount of Chinese land has not changed. Similarly, pressures of demand for retail premises on Fifth Avenue near Central Park in New York account for the astronomic levels of rent in the area. For example, in June 2015, it was reported that tenants were paying in the region of $3,500 per square foot – to reiterate, £2,250 for one square foot of sales floor (i.e. £24,300 per square metre) – making it the most expensive retail space in the world.

In the long run, which may be defined as the period of time that firms need to adjust to price changes, it is the level of rent that signals changes to land use.

In effect, rent (or price) allocates the use of land between buildings and other uses. It identifies what becomes used for transport infrastructure, for agriculture, for commercial and residential use, and so on. As with every resource bought and sold in competitive markets, the highest reward determines its current use. In other words, the value of land is derived from its end use; the higher the value, the higher the rent.

For example, some land is extremely fertile and commands its best value when used for agriculture, while other land is incapable of growing anything in its natural state, and reaps far more value as development land. In other instances, the planning legislation may act as a constraint – especially in Britain, where the town and country planners proceed from a premise that much of the nation's land should be protected from development and retained as 'Green Belt'.

Of all the factors of production, parcels of land and their location is of key importance, and students of this text should not be misled by those traditional economists who regard land markets to be of secondary importance, on the basis that its quality and quantity are relatively fixed! This is part of the intrigue of the economics of real estate. Land cannot simply transfer to Luxembourg for tax reasons.

Indeed, the limited supply of land presents an interesting dynamic to the property world, and this is added to by central and local government planning policy that specifies what can be built and where. It certainly explains the problem of securing affordable accommodation, and leads to high-density living in many parts of the world. The continual demands made on a nation's fixed stock of land lead to continual price rises, and this in turn can have a negative impact on the quality and size of built structures. Interestingly, a UK government report, set up to examine how the supply of new homes is influenced by the nature and structure of the building industry, concluded that after the cost of land is taken into account, 'the returns to housebuilders for investing in quality barely justify the effort' (Callcutt, 2007: 8).

In other words, in order to maintain profit margins, builders will try to squeeze all other areas of their product, reducing spend on design, putting pressure on input costs, and trying to minimise the amount of land that is used (by maximising densities). The result is a string of disparaging remarks that refer to 'shoe box Britain' (RIBA, 2011), where people live in 'rabbit hutches on plots the size of postage stamps' (Evans, 1991), in 'identikit houses designed at Lego land' (Shapps, 2011).

### Human resources

In order to produce anything, a human resource must be used. That human resource consists of the productive contributions of **labour** made by individuals who work, such as architects, estate agents, project managers, surveyors and construction workers. Whenever labour acquires training, the potential contribution to productive output increases; in other words, there is an improvement in **human capital**. A relevant example is the effect that good trained management can have on the efficiency of a whole project. Finally, there is another type of human resource; namely, entrepreneurial ability.

The **entrepreneur** is associated with the founding of new businesses, or the introduction of new products and techniques. However, it means more than that. It also encompasses taking risks (possibly losing large sums of wealth on new ventures), inventing new methods of making existing goods, and generally experimenting with any type of new thinking that could lead to a monetary benefit. Without entrepreneurs, businesses would find it difficult to survive and property would not be developed. The entrepreneur is a scarce human resource, as not everyone is willing to take risks or has the ability to make successful business decisions.

Interestingly, over the past 10 or 20 years, there have been a significant number of academic papers analysing how the demand for human resources has changed due to advances in information and communication technology (ICT). The literature reviews the remarkable innovations that technology, the World Wide Web and intelligent machines can deliver, and raises the debate on whether the digital revolution will cause a mass destruction or creation of jobs. In the early part of the 21st Century, as we experience the outcomes of the first wave of these developments, it seems that the digital revolution has opened up a significant divide between skilled and less skilled labour. It appears that the demand for creative and abstract thinkers has increased for a fortunate minority, while many others are left relatively underemployed and poorly paid, carrying out menial, routine, and manual tasks. A further consequence of ICT, therefore, is its association with a widening inequality of income and wealth, and this is another core principal that needs to be considered in an economics course in a post-crisis world. Hence, inequality is discussed further in the *food for thought* section at the close of this chapter.

## Manufactured resources

When any form of labour or entrepreneurial skill is applied to land for agricultural or development purposes, something else is used. It may be a plough, a tractor or a cement mixer. In short, land and labour are always combined with manufactured resources to produce the things that are in demand. In the neoclassical approach, the term 'capital' is, in fact, solely dedicated to mechanical or physical items that can be paired with labour. This notion of capital supports the use of a 'production function' (a mathematical ratio) that links the respective output of each factor. In textbook language, therefore, manufactured resources are usually referred to as capital, and include things such as machines, buildings and tools.

A problem with this standard presentation of factor resources is that each unit of capital and labour (and land when it is discussed) tend to be treated as equal. Obviously, this is far too simple, as each unit of capital or labour has unique qualities, so they should not be discussed as 'homogeneous blobs'. They are certainly not infinitely substitutable from one production process to another, and it seems a sweeping generalisation to simply present each firm as a 'black box' that transforms homogenous factors of production into output. Equally, entrepreneurs (the ultimate decision makers composing the firm) are not credited with any real talent or importance in the classic view of production.

Neoclassical economics presents a non-complex view of the world and, in effect, oversimplifies economic reality. To some extent, this weakness justifies the need for specialisms such as real estate economics. It also accounts for the work on productivity that has emerged since the 2008 recession as, during these years, we witnessed more and more labour being successively added to the production process, but economic growth did not increase by anyway near the same proportion – productivity per head actually declined. To express this in UK statistics, 1.8 million new jobs were created between 2011 and 2014, but 75% of these were part-time, and often of a low skilled nature. As a consequence, the increased employment did not generate a proportionate increase in economic activity. This new characteristic of slow growth running alongside improving levels of employment was also experienced in several other countries.

## Income and wealth

Strictly speaking, a distinction should be drawn between these two related ideas. Income is a *flow* concept that is closely associated with annual salaries and wages, whereas wealth is a *stock* concept, associated with accumulated assets built up over time. Thus, a discussion of the distribution of income is not precisely the same thing as a discussion of the distribution of wealth.

Income changes with output and in some senses, this determines its distribution. The classic economists divided income between the different factors of production and, in many ways, the neoclassical economists that followed them continued with this tradition. Thus, a basic introductory principle is that incomes are distributed between the owners of factors of production – namely, labour generates wages, land owners receive rent, the return to the ownership of capital is interest, and entrepreneurs get profits. Hence, all workers, all landlords and all capitalists are kind of lumped together and, as a general principle, the distribution of income is seen to reflect these broad factor categories – although there is no reason to divide the income between them equally. However, in today's world, it would make more sense to look beyond these broad categories and understand why rents are higher in some areas than others, and why some jobs are paid better than others.

In fact, the distribution of income is a good example of where the neoclassical approach is questionable. Mainstream economists always trust that the market will determine the correct level of reward for each specific type of factor but, without some central government determining a minimum wage level, making welfare payments and collecting taxation (especially on inherited wealth and high incomes), there could be unacceptable levels of inequality. As Paul Samuelson (2010: 333), the author of the largest selling economic textbook, remarked: 'Today most high-income countries face the prospect of rising tax burdens to finance health and retirement programs as well as income support for poor families'.

In plain English, governments regard it as some kind of necessary duty to redistribute income in order to keep the market working, maintain welfare, and avoid social unrest. The standard theoretical approach becomes even more worrying when we turn our attention to problems of inequality of wealth.

As stated above, wealth is all about stock, and it can be built up in families, over time, especially if it is allowed to pass freely from one generation to the next. The classic example is land and property that is inherited and forms large family estates. Therefore, do not be confused – stocks of wealth are not just about shares in a company; lots of things can be included as stock. An economist's definition of wealth would typically fall into two categories: *non-human wealth* – which would include tangible objects that people own and frequently trade, such as buildings, houses, machinery, land, cars and works of art; and *human wealth* – which involves the intangible skills, talents, knowledge and initiative that people offer to a nation. The total of human and non-human wealth gives a nation its capital stock (note that the terms 'wealth' and 'capital' are often used interchangeably).

To sharpen the contrast between these two related concepts, following the financial crisis, the nation's wealth immediately tumbled in value (whereas incomes hardly budged). In fact, it was recorded that, in general terms, the typical household's net worth (i.e. its assets minus its debts) plummeted by approximately 12% in 2008. This decline would be largely attributed to the significant fall in house values, as housing wealth makes up approximately 50% of a typical household's assets.

Recently, another definition of wealth has been introduced into the literature that is derived from an important new treatise on 'capital' (Piketty, 2014). This new definition of wealth conflates physical capital equipment with all forms of money. In these new terms, wealth is defined by personal assets such as land, houses, property, stocks and shares and personal savings, but excludes 'human capital,' and 'fixed capital' (such as machines). The main thrust of Piketty's research was to estimate the current market value of wealth and identify how it was distributed across the population.

The research by Thomas Piketty (2014) confirmed that wealth is much more unequally distributed than income – so, while a division of society into those who own things and those who work for a living is overly simplistic, it is not totally off-base. In the United States, for example, 5% of households own a majority of the wealth while the bottom 40% has negative wealth due to debts. Piketty (2014) demonstrates that, in rich countries, the growth of incomes is generally between 1–2% a year, while the rate of return on wealth averages about 4–5% a year. Thus, those who draw their income from capital outstrip wage earners. The relevance of this question of inequality is picked up again in the *food for thought* section at the close of this chapter.

## Investment

In mainstream economic texts, the property sector is not usually referred to. It does, however, represent a major form of investment – directly, as residential or commercial property, and indirectly, via institutional funds and instruments. When companies spend money in this way, it is formally referred to as capital expenditure – and informally as 'capex'.

From a purely economic perspective, **investment** refers to additions to productive capacity – activity that makes use of resources today in such a way that they allow for greater production in the future. For example, when a business puts funds into new equipment or develops a new factory, it is making an investment to increase its capacity in the future.

Following the Great Recession, one of the immediate aims of central banks was to suppress interest rates, in order to encourage all types of investment to increase jobs and economic growth. However, due to uncertainty about demand and the risk of weak returns, capital expenditure fell across the Eurozone and emerging economies. In fact, there appeared to be something of a chicken-and-egg problem. Without a strong global recovery, companies would not spend more but, because they did not spend more, there continued to be no recovery.

Two further bits of jargon used to distinguish between types of investment are 'net' and 'replacement'. Replacement investment corresponds to depreciation, and is determined by the rate at which capital wears out, while net investment represents new additions to capital stock. The former is relatively constant, as it is determined by time, but the latter is related to changes in economic activity.

In terms of property investment, these two categories can be associated with the repair and maintenance of existing property assets, and new additions to property being let or sold for the first time. This distinction is useful, as it serves to explain why the property sector is prone to fluctuate more than other sectors. Investment expenditure on maintenance and repairs will be fairly constant, whereas new additions will be one-offs to support expected changes to overall activity. For example, if a retail or manufacturing group manages £100 million pounds worth of property assets, they may spend each year, say, 5%, on maintenance (£5,000,000). If economic activity in their sector rises, however, they will need both to maintain their existing property and to increase their capacity for sales or manufacture by adding to the stock of property assets.

This example might be easier to understand from the converse position, where economic activity decreases and, as a result, the firm release or sells some of its property stock; in effect, it can meet the present level of demand with zero property investment. As a consequence, property investment tends to alter with greater amplitude than other sectors. It certainly helps to explain the large swings in capital expenditure that are recorded in national accounts.

From a pure property perspective, it is useful to add one final twist to these traditional economic interpretations of investment to include two distinct types of developer; those who create built environment assets for investment clients, and those who develop property for their own purposes; sometimes distinguished by the phrases **investor-developer** and **trader-developer**.

These two terms help to clarify the surveyor's role in investment decisions, as they confirm a need to understand property assets as a means of generating income flows in the future. In short, investment in property must always be seen as an opportunity cost. This is because the relative returns made on other investments, such as government bonds, company shares or general business activities, might be more profitable. In other words, it is not possible to understand property in isolation; it is essential to recognise that it competes as an investment with other assets. Interactions between property markets and the broader economy are discussed in more detail in Parts B and C.

## Property in a resource context

For the last 20-odd years, a part of my work has been associated with the *Estates Gazette* (for example, *see* Myers, 2006). The *Estates Gazette* is a weekly professional magazine where much of the commercial property and land coming to the market is advertised and property related news is reviewed. It somehow manages to continue to run as a relatively small independent business, even though it has been part of the Reed Elsevier group since 1991. The publisher-author relationship that I experienced highlighted the contrast between academic writing and journalistic commentary. By its very nature, the *Estates Gazette* relies on capturing sound bites that reflect what is happening in a specific sector at a specific time – with understandably slightly less emphasis on what might happen in the future. By comparison, a specialised textbook on property economics attempts to:

- tease out synergies;
- make connections between concepts and theories;
- create a framework to assess future trends;
- encourage a methodological and analytical approach; and
- help to develop certain skills, perspective and confidence.

It is arguable whether these two approaches are complimentary. In fact, Professor Skidelsky (2010: xi) goes so far as to admit in his preface that: 'once I had started writing in January 2009 I stopped reading the newspapers on a daily basis to avoid filling my mind with "noise".'

A distinct advantage, however, of the *Estates Gazette* relationship was that it effectively framed what surveyors do. In the words of its editor, its business is to inform those who 'fund, develop, hold, buy, sell, invest, value, manage and give professional and legal advice on offices, shops, industrial property, tenanted homes and new build apartments' (see Bill, 2013: 83). Interestingly, this definition includes every type of property market except for second-hand residential property – which is an interesting omission, as residential valuation is a part of a surveyor's work. Evidently, those involved in these types of activity have a crucial need to understand what is going on in an economy – not only because economic activity takes place in offices, shops, factories, and warehouses, but largely because businessmen tend to respect and trust a surveyor's judgment when taking up new risks. In short, surveyors need to be able to interpret the nature of the current economic backdrop and to be able to give advice on future prospects.

In fairness, a weekly magazine cannot be expected to perform such a rigorous task; this is not stated to demean the role of the *Estates Gazette*, but merely to recognise its place in some kind of educational hierarchy. First and foremost, professional magazines provide a tool of communication, and at best they provide a documentary record of what has happened over the years. For example, the extracts in the next section are used to pick up the storyline and portray what appeared to be happening in the run-up to the Great Recession.

*Evidence of a sector slowly sliding into an abyss*

The *Estates Gazette*, like most journalistic teams, missed forecasting the Great Recession; in fact, their reportage highlighted how the sector appeared to be coasting along, regardless of the occasional alarm bell being set off. For example, in May 2005, the Bank of England flagged up the worrying amount of commercial property debt that was building up in the system. According to their records, outstanding loans awarded to fund commercial development had jumped from £76 billion in 2002 to £122 billion in 2005, representing a 60% increase in three years. Potentially more worrying was the fact that this amounted to at least 10% of total bank lending – coincidentally, the precise percentage that had been reached before the cyclical busts of 1973 and 1991. The Bank of England presented this as a warning, but it fell on deaf ears.

Some commentary on the increase in the size of loan books was flagged up by the *Estates Gazette* in June 2005, as follows: 'There is a collective madness at work here: a madness driven by a desire for market share, a madness rooted in bankers' bonus systems that reward the volume of money lent rather than the performance of the loan. Will this madness evaporate? Eventually, yes. But the sheer weight of money bearing down on the sector, and the prospect of lower interest rates, mean sanity may return later rather than sooner....'

Ten months later, a similar message was signalled by Hank Paulson, the boss of commercial bank Goldman Sachs, who warned the industry to be cautious over loans made to the property sector. The *Estate Gazette* captured the mood with the following editorial comment: 'Is the world going crackers ...? Yields have fallen so low it is more profitable to stick the money into an e-saver account, which currently yields 5.05%. Will capital values continue to rise? Nobody, frankly, has a clue. But it does not require much detective work to discover the prime driver: the lending banks. Only when they curb their enthusiasm for property will the acceleration of values slow. Right now, there is not a sign of that happening' (*Estates Gazette*, 22/4/06)

As we now know, the madness intensified and the boom continued for another year. By 2007, the entire market was engulfed in loans secured by various financial instruments – that formed part of the shadow banking network, which is described in Chapter 5. Bankers appeared to be desperate to lend, and investors in property resources behaved as if the party could go on forever.

But then a period of panic struck the international financial markets, and the Great Recession commenced. Problems became apparent, in Britain, in September 2007, when Northern Rock (Britain's fifth-biggest mortgage lender before it was sold off and rebranded as Virgin money) was granted emergency funding by the Bank of England after finding itself unable to secure loans from elsewhere. This was the first run on a British bank for more than a century, and it set alarm bells ringing in financial markets. Within a year, the whole deck of cards across the financial system of Europe and America had begun to collapse. Uncertainty spread, loan defaults increased, liquidity evaporated, and central banks were called upon to throw financial lifelines to keep many institutions afloat. The overriding problem was that banks had insufficient capital to meet their obligations, and a significant number of banks and mortgage lenders were forced into protective mergers, nationalisation, and even bankruptcy.

Regardless, the *Estate Gazette* continued to maintain its relatively upbeat and optimistic tone, as the following editorial published in November 2008 suggests: '… the consensus forecast from a group of valuers is that the peak-to-trough drop in values will be between 45 and 50 per cent. This alarming number relies on the already known fall of almost 25% between the summer of 2007 and September 2008 …. In one very bleak sense this is good news … Best to write down the value of the loan, extend the terms and hang on in there and hope … Every single bank is 'kitchen sinking' down the price of real estate loans. The welcome 1.5% drop in interest rates on Thursday may break the fall … The odd brave buyer can be spotted bargain hunting.'

Obviously a key question is, how does one gain the confidence to know when to call the top or bottom of a market? Hopefully, this textbook will provide some answers, enabling future surveyors to be able to broadly judge the current economic scene and to give reliable advice on future economic prospects.

## The unique characteristics of property markets

Slowly, it should be dawning on you why transactions in property related resources warrant a separate economic approach. This is largely because each property is characterised by unique qualities, and these need to be acknowledged before we go much further into our study of property economics. They relate to properties being difficult and protracted to transact, as they differ so much from one to the next (i.e. they are not 'homogenous'). This can make them difficult to express in value terms. Moreover, they are never traded in prices or ways that can be handled by a retailer, and each unit will quite commonly exceed six-figure numbers. Property also has the problem that it tends to depreciate over long time periods, and when the going gets tough, it can prove to be irritatingly illiquid. If these introductory remarks do not immediately make sense, it may help to preview the opening sections to Chapter 3 on property markets, where students can gain a better understanding of markets and the unique characteristics of property before venturing any further.

## The scarcest resource

As presented above, mainstream economists introduce the subject as being about the allocation of scarce resources. Of these, the most important relationships presented as analysed appear to be between labour and capital. There is a distinctly worrying aspect about this traditional approach – namely, the interpretation of capital. The term is used in established introductions of economics to refer to machines, tools and instruments, which businesses need to produce goods and services. It *does not include* money, shares, mortgage backed securities, or loans that enable businesses to buy fixed and working capital. Strictly speaking, therefore, financial capital *is not* a factor of production!

As we shall see in subsequent chapters, this oversight is a marked limitation to understanding the essence of the key attributes of a modern market based system. As Liza Minelli and Joel Gray neatly remind us in the film of the musical *Cabaret*, 'money makes the world go around'. Without financial resources, businesses cannot do anything. It is the essential oil that enables transactions to take place. Indeed, it was a shortage of available funds that prolonged the Great Recession across so many sectors for so many years. Without financial support, entrepreneurs cannot produce anything. This is as evident in communities that want to buy, sell, rent, or develop real estate, as in any other economic community. Without access to a supply of funds, economies dry up and nothing can happen.

## History of economic thought

An aim of this chapter is to explain what modern real estate economics is about so, apart from identifying some basic concepts, the methods employed by economists also need to be reviewed. The methodology of an academic discipline says a lot about the nature of that subject. In general terms, economics is a social science and it attempts to adopt the same kind of value-free approach as other sciences. However, it cannot arrive at universal truths analogous to those in physics and chemistry. Unlike things that are studied by natural scientists, economists are concerned with a study of human behaviour, and that is inevitably complicated by the fact that people have free will, imagination, emotions and a tendency to follow trends. Therefore, when economists use the terms 'models', 'theories' or 'laws', they do so in a broad, generic, sense to promote intuitive, insightful, and instinctive ways of thinking.

It is important to remember, therefore, that there is no one all-embracing economic theory, or method, that can explain everything better than others. Indeed, new economics does not aim to dismantle neoclassical thinking, but simply to put it into context and acknowledge the relevance and value of other schools of economic thought. To make the best of what the subject has to offer, the student should not be brainwashed by one approach but offered the opportunity to experience a plethora of ways forward. This text aims to lay down guides and principles as a means of understanding complex economic systems in the 21st Century, and this entails adapting a pluralist approach that draws on 250 years of economic thought and its associated methodological tools.

The reason that we appear to be stating the obvious is because many economists had become locked in a time warp. Up until 2008, academic and government economists, governors of Central Banks and businessmen, including real estate surveyors, were all under the influence of one dominant academic paradigm – **neoclassical economics**. It was as if they had a monopoly over the way that economics was taught. This was a great handicap, as they had overestimated the ability of the free market to self-correct. Neoclassical theorists worked from the premise that resource allocation – ownership, production, consumption, transactions and all that economics entails – was determined by individuals. In other words, the preferred *'modus operandi'* of mainstream economists was to treat people in isolation from one another, working from an assumption that competitive economic behaviour is selfish and rational. Following this logic to its natural conclusion, economic analysis boils down to a simple rule: there is only one representative agent making economic decisions – the 'rational economic being' – and such beings act in their best interests and know what they are doing, so leave them alone to get on with it.

The caricature of this generalised pleasure-seeking rational individual lends itself to another important characteristic of neoclassical thinking, and that is a belief in **modelling**. These scientific economic frameworks are often fed with data to reach conclusions and forecasts. It was assumed by lecturers that students can begin to understand how an economic system works (be it competition, the macro economy, normal profits, price equilibrium, or whatever) when they have a reference point – a model – that represents the system in question. Economic models can take on various forms, such as verbal statements, numerical tables, and graphs and even mathematical equations, although there is some question if these really have any predictive validity. As Lanchester (2014: 49) cynically remarked: 'In economics, models are spoken of as being made of physics when in truth they are "Lego".' In other words, economic models have a provisional and tentative quality and, significantly from an academic position, can be revised, reformulated, and rebuilt.

It seems surprising that this view of the world had prevailed for so long, as not only was it somewhat mechanistic, but it also led to a general blindness to the type of catastrophic failure that could occur in market economies. In fact, some critics went as far as suggesting that neoclassical thinking had become out of sync with the complex global systems that had evolved in the 21st Century. As Ronald Coase (1991) had observed in his Nobel Prize lecture, neoclassical theories were better suited to the analysis of 'individuals exchanging nuts and berries on the edge of the forest'. This might seem a little disparaging but, for many years, markets were regarded as inherently stable, enabling exchanges of manufactured products, real estate, stocks, and other financial assets at just the right price. There was nothing in the neoclassical model to suggest the possibility of the kind of global collapse that happened in 2008.

Neoclassical approaches had not been rigorously questioned since the last great recession – the depression of the 1930s – when John Maynard Keynes sought to explain how there could be huge amounts of spare capacity in an economy, such as unemployed workers and idle factories, when markets are supposed to equate supply and demand.

Keynes's model of the economy emphasised that one person's spending is another's income, and that the level of demand across a whole economy would not necessarily be sufficient to support full employment of resources in an economy. Indeed, he made a case for government intervention – to use its spending to pump up the level of demand by increasing the amount of income available to the public.

To paraphrase his argument: what might appear to be perfectly rational for the isolated individual can be economically destructive for an economy. To clarify this, Keynes introduced the idea of the 'fallacy of composition', which was a complicated way of highlighting that what applies in one case does not necessarily apply when repeated by everybody. In other words, behaviour which may seem perfectly rational for the individual in isolation can be economically destructive if pursued by society as a whole.

A good example of such a fallacy is saving. If an individual saves more, they will increase their consumption opportunities in the future. However, if everyone saves more, there will be less current spending, and firms will produce less; the outcome will be a rundown in national income, output, and employment. If, in these circumstances, the government, too, tries to 'save' more, by cutting down its own spending, this will make things even worse. Eventually, the economy will come to rest in a state of stable equilibrium that is well below its potential of production. This seeming irony of higher saving leading to lower national income was referred to by Keynes as 'the paradox of thrift'.

The policy implications of Keynesian theory distinguished that the general principles on which an economy must be run are totally different from those that apply to a household or a business. This was an enormous step change, as his advice to governments experiencing a recession was to increase – not reduce – their spending, even if this adds to its deficit. The important objective is to offset the decline of private spending and kickstart a failing economy. Interestingly the IMF, in its *World Economic Outlook* (2014), advocated substantially increased public infrastructure investment. The Italian government subsequently heeded this advice with several expansionary budget measures. Understandably, this alarmed the neoclassical economists but delighted the Keynesians. At the time of the budget announcement, Italy had debts of 138% of GDP, but it was hoped that by expanding the economy with tax cuts and increased spending, the debt would actually reduce.

So Keynes was one of the first to effectively redefine the approach and model adopted by economists. He single-handedly moved the focus onto managing the whole economy – making the case that an economy is different from the sum total of its parts. Thus, what makes sense at the household level does not necessarily make sense at the national level. In terms of economic discourse, the macroeconomic system was identified as a separate entity. As a result, the performance of each economy is now measured by GDP, and managed and manipulated by central bankers and central government (as outlined in Chapters 5 and 7, respectively). In short, the Keynesian approach broadened the economic debate.

## The new behaviourism

The financial crisis, however, gave added impetus to those who questioned the neoclassical approach. Newer thinking began to gain credence. In particular, many began to explore alternatives to economic models based on the idea of manageable and predictable behaviour. The idea that people gather all the information they need, carefully weigh up all the costs and benefits and then decide what is best is challenged by this new approach. In the new jargon of the behaviourist school, people are not always 'deliberative'; they often reach decisions in a split-second, by simply drawing on what comes effortlessly to mind – as the behaviourist puts it, 'automatically'.

In other words, people evaluate day-to-day economic decisions quickly and intuitively, and the process cannot be switched on and off. To paraphrase the ideas of a leading behaviourist: operation of the automatic system involves no sense of intentional control, but it is the 'secret author' of many of the choices and judgments that people make (Kahneman, 2011). Behaviourists are not trying to suggest that people are incapable of careful analysis; they simply recognise that, in many instances, people seem to act spontaneously on gut reaction, using just a small part of the relevant information to make a decision.

This new approach emphasises that people are subject to peer pressure, herding, fear and greed. Hence, decisions about choices and how people respond to policy depend on how the options are framed, and their context. In a nutshell, people do not always respond to policy and other economic phenomena in rational ways. People can, and do, make incorrect judgements as they base their decisions on gut instincts, since they are – in a phrase – 'irrational, illogical, and selfless'.

As marketing strategy informs us, people are increasingly interconnected affected by fashion, peer pressure, social, business and media networks, and these influences are as important as individual motives. Therefore, economists should give up trying to optimise all decisions and be satisfied with general rules of thumb that indicate trends and insight. As a consequence individuals can easily be misled and can make inappropriate decisions. They could, for example, buy property when it is at its peak; and sell, for one reason or another, when it is at its lowest point. In short, investors, consumers, producers do not always act according to the text image of rational economic man. The new approach attempts to understand society, warts and all, from the point of individuals interacting with others in society.

In 2010, the UK Government set up the Behaviour Insights Team (or the Nudge unit, as it is more commonly referred to) to investigate how behavioural economics could be used to improve policy. It has had a profound effect on the way in which Whitehall interacts with the people it is governing. By subtly changing the processes, forms and language used by Government, it has achieved outcomes that are in the 'public good' and save money. In fact, in 2014, the OECD published an international review of the initial applications of behavioural economics, stating more than 60 examples of new regulatory policy from a number of OECD countries – in particular, the USA, Denmark, Australia and the UK (see Lunn, 2014 [1]).

Finally, for another excellent summary of behavioural economics and examples of their work, see the *World Development Report* (2015) [2]. This annual publication from the World Bank took the inspired decision in 2015 to follow how the emergence of behaviourism could affect the policy of development. The timing of these two international institutional publications confirms that the era for a behavioural approach has begun. We exemplify and consider their contribution further at various points in the text but, in particular, in the *food for thought* section of Chapter 3.

## So where do we go from here?

This quick tour of methodology has highlighted the alternatives that economists are currently faced with. Commencing with the (neo)-classic trust in the market, based on rational, competing individuals seeking to maximise pleasure and profits, through the Keynesian model that makes a case for government intervention to achieve the goals of society as whole, to the behavioural school that adopts a distinctive psychological approach to economic decision-making; challenging the processes, forms and language conventionally used to achieve macro objectives and alter market behaviour.

As a result, students today have the benefit of being able to draw from a range of methods, some of which have been in development for more than 200 years, plus a particularly rich range of official data that governments have been collecting in one way or another for the greater part of a century. The modern economists' toolbox, therefore, includes models, simulations, experiments, econometrics, and the use of statistical data to confirm theories and test analysis, policy and forecasts. Indeed, it is important to note that new thinking does not dismiss mathematical or quantitative approaches *per se*. Numerical-based analysis still has an important place in economics; the only thing is that it should not be regarded as 'the be-all and end-all'. In short, a recurring feature of each school of thought is that they endorse statistical evidence. In many cases, the evidence provides the starting point to build a hunch and gain reassurance to act on instincts. For example, any client willing to accept a surveyor's 'gut' feeling will feel more confident if it is also backed by data. The two are complimentary.

## Food for thought: The problems of inequality

The purpose of these closing sections is to reiterate the important points discussed in the chapter, and to raise related issues and questions. For example, in reviewing Chapter 1, it should be clear that the basic principles of neoclassical economics are very much concerned with production, and this raises some immediate challenges about the associated distribution of income and wealth.

In the neoclassical tradition, inequality formed an inherent part of the free market, as it was assumed that the incentive to better oneself would always drive an economy forwards. However, the enormous economic growth achieved in free markets has left many people out of the equation. The irony is that through the process of economic growth, the offer of the opportunity to get richer has been handsomely achieved by a fortunate few, and has left a worryingly large number without the resources to take advantage of the goods and services produced. This is particularly pronounced between the highest income and lowest income countries, where the average GDP *per capita* differs by a factor greater than twenty (adjusted for inflation and the lower cost of living in the countries concerned – the basis of such adjustments is explained in Chapter 8).

The bottom line is that there are more than one billion people – 14% of the world's population – still trying to exist on less than $1.25 per day. But income inequality is also marked within the so called high income nations; for example, in the 34 OECD countries [3], income inequality has reached unprecedented levels. In these high-income countries, the average income of the richest 10% of the population is now about ten times that of the poorest 10%, as opposed to seven times 25 years ago (World Bank Group, 2015). The significance of this problem has begun to challenge the conventional economic order, and to raise some gritty new questions – such as, should reducing inequality become a macroeconomic goal?

The World Bank added a further subtle twist to the debate when it recently focused its attention to the poorest 40% in low and lower-middle income countries, the premise being that a society as a whole is more likely to improve if it can increase the income of the least well off. In other words, while it might be arguable that inequality is undesirable, poverty is a greater evil, as the well-being of households in the bottom 40% remains so much lower than households in the top 60%. Hence, when the central concern of a society is welfare, income growth for the bottom 40% is a far better goal than plainly seeking to reduce inequality *per se* (World Bank, 2013; World Bank Group, 2015).

### Are all men naturally created unequal?

The core principles outlined in this chapter convey a general impression that the neoclassical curriculum is all about laws of production; that the *raison d'etre* for economics is that a society must produce goods and services efficiently or it will cease to function. In the work of the classic economists, Adam Smith and David Ricardo, these laws were immutable; they were like laws of nature – fixed and predetermined. Distribution seemed to be inherently entwined with other economic ideas. As a consequence, throughout the 19th and 20th Centuries, economists seemed to accept that the way things are made and sold determines how society operates, and who gets the rewards was not such a critical question. Karl Marx's (1847: 49) captured this line of thought when he suggested that the economic base determines the social superstructure. As he explained more than 150 years ago:

> 'Social relations are closely bound up with productive forces. In acquiring new productive forces men change their mode of production; and in changing their mode of production, in changing the way of earning their living, they change all their social relations. The hand-mill gives you society with the feudal lord; the steam-mill society with the industrial capitalist'.

So this begs the question: what does today's digital age of the internet, the smart phone and social media give us?

As suggested in the section on human resources, the internet and related technology has seriously changed the nature of work. In some sectors, it is as if labour has been divided into two polar extremes: a small band of highly skilled – and highly paid – innovators that manage and adapt new technology, and a large number whose jobs have been replaced by machines and robots, or reduced to tasks that are far less demanding. This has seriously affected the reward structures, as has the explosion in executive and director remuneration, which is discussed in more detail in Chapter 4.

For example, one of the many statistics bandied about is the fact that the richest 1% in the world absorbed more than 60% of the increases made in real incomes between 1988 and 2008 (Milanovic, 2013). The only section that did better was the top tenth of that 1%; and the top 100th of that 1% did best of all. Specifically in the UK, there was some debate in 2015 about whether those on the lower and middle incomes had actually benefitted at all from the recovery from the great recession. In short, new economic thinking has always been concerned about distribution; as the data universally demonstrates that the benefits of economic growth are going to increasingly smaller numbers of people each year. The scale of the inequality was succinctly captured by an Oxfam advert in November 2014 which pointed out that the richest 85 billionaires had the same wealth between them as 3.5 billion poor people – i.e. half the entire global population.

Inequality on such a tremendous scale is the outcome of wealth tending to concentrate into the hands of fewer and fewer families. The rich get richer and the poor get poorer. As Piketty (2014) observed in his widely read treatise *Capital in the Twenty-First Century*, wealth accumulation is 'one of the great divisive forces at work today', and this is particularly worrying as the percentage return to capital (wealth) is higher each year than the percentage of economic growth. In short, the problem of inequality is getting steadily worse. This is a serious problem, as there is potential conflict between the 'haves' and the 'have nots'. The billionaires, whose income is from property and assets, and ordinary people involved in the production of goods and services, experience life and the opportunities it offers in totally different ways.

### Does an unequal distribution of income and wealth matter?

It is not only the empirical evidence on inequality that should concern us, as there is evidence to suggest that the rise in income disparities will eventually limit economic progress across society as a whole. In the context of the storyline explored in this text, the problem of escalating inequality has also been used as an explanation to account for the run-up to the financial crisis of 2008 and the subsequent recession. This theory was first put forward in 2005 by Professor Raguhuram Rajan, when he was still chief economist at the IMF (he is now governor of the Bank of India). As he saw it (and the implication is that he was one of the few economists who actually 'saw' the crisis coming), deregulation and securitisation encouraged bankers to take on more complex risks. At the root of these risks were the subprime borrowers – the poorer members of society seeking loans to purchase housing – whose stagnant incomes would not conventionally support sizable debts.

When this group of borrowers defaulted on their mortgage payments, banks were put into serious difficulties – and it was not just those directly granting mortgages, but anyone holding securities which included the subprime debt. In fact, the collapse of subprime mortgages in the USA quickly raised questions about the ability of banks to meet their worldwide commitments, and a good number of banks around the world had to be bailed out by governments. We examine this part of the story further in Part B of the text.

**Part A**

# Chapter 2
# The Language of Profit

The property world is full of stories where a newly qualified professional has managed to turn a few thousand pounds worth of investment into millions, seemingly more or less overnight – and many of these stories stem from the good years before 2008. Admittedly, investors and developers are now faced with a far more difficult market and fewer opportunities to act on 'gut instincts'. Thus, the premise of this chapter – and much of the book – is that those entering the world of property after the Great Recession will make far better decisions and give far more reliable advice if they can add to the professional approach an academic input based on the ideas and language of economics.

Graduating into the world of 'property' is an honourable position, which should not be taken for granted; in the broadest sense, it enables young people to participate in shaping the future. Remember, the built environment is made up of various types of property (residential, commercial, industrial etc.), linked by infrastructure (sewers, canals, roads, tunnels etc.) and separated by public spaces in between (parks, woods, playing fields, landscaped areas, squares etc.). The professions shaping and creating this environment – architects, engineers, planners and surveyors – have specialisms that can inform the overall pace and nature of development. It might seem that they are disjointed by culture and attitude, but they tend to speak the same language when it comes to money. It is this common denominator that allows them to share aspirations and visions with one another as, ultimately, it is financial returns – profit and yield – that incentivise and unite the professions of the built environment. It is important, therefore, that the signals are understood and can be monitored with some respect.

*New Economic Thinking and Real Estate*, First Edition. Danny Myers.
© 2016 John Wiley & Sons, Ltd. Published 2016 by John Wiley & Sons, Ltd.

**Part A**

## It's all about profit

**Profits** are sometimes called the 'bottom line', because they are the most important piece of information that a decision-maker needs to know, and that information includes the decision of the architect, the surveyor, the engineer, the occupier, the civil servant or the businessman. In fact, anyone making a business decision in the public or private sector is probably familiar with the question: how much is it worth?

We should avoid getting into a debate about 'filthy lucre', about the nasty face of capitalism or the utopian vision of some spiritual idealist. If you want to work in shaping the built environment, you need to appreciate that whoever is the boss, they will be concerned with identifying the bottom line and asking if this is a fair return for the time, effort and resources put in. Remember, the profit of a business, or any accounting unit involved with developing and maintaining property, infrastructure or green spaces, is the level of reward for taking on the risk of managing that resource effectively. Profit *per se* is not a bad thing – it is the way that profits are distributed that is controversial and might offend some political consciences. However, that debate is a topic for another book (although you will have seen some introductory remarks relating to the broader consequences of economic inequality at the close of Chapter 1, and we revisit how it is measured in Chapter 8).

In each sector, the level of acceptable profits vary according to the perceived nature of the risks and availability of resources at that point in time. If the level of profits fall in one area of activity, entrepreneurs may move their resources to another sector where the returns are higher. To take a simple example, six new office blocks were completed in Hong Kong (during a phase of rapid change), and before they were even occupied they were replaced with luxurious apartment blocks, because that way the property asset would generate far more profit. To illustrate this profit-maximising behaviour economists employ a concept of **normal profit**.

Normal profit is included in the cost of production, as it is regarded as the essential minimum reward necessary to attract the entrepreneur into that area of economic activity. The concept of normal profit also highlights that all resources can be employed in several ways (that is, all resources have alternative uses). Consequently, what is meant by 'profit' in economics differs from the general meaning it has acquired in everyday usage. To portray the general meaning of profit, the following formula could be used:

profits = total revenues – total costs

For economists, an alternative formula is required:

Economic profits = total revenues *minus* total opportunity cost of all inputs used

The process is complicated further by the fact that, for most developments, a price needs to be stated before the activity commences – when all the costs are not yet known. In the commercial sector, rents are often fixed for five years or more before review. In other words, the pricing of property-related assets contrasts sharply with manufacturing, where the producer does not have to determine a price until the activity is complete.

*The profits of property developers*

Profit is a factor input seen by the developer as their just reward for initiating and organising the scheme. Obviously, it will be dependent on the nature of the property, in terms of its size, type and funding. The degree of competition for the site and development is also a factor to bear in mind, as well as whether or not it is sold before construction – as a developer will be far more confident of a pre-let property than a speculative build. In short, the acceptable profit is determined by the level of risk and the scale of finance. In effect, it reflects the developers' opportunity costs of capital.

Unfortunately, from an academic perspective, 'actual' profits are not commonly discussed, except to qualify and complicate what they represent. In the business world, they are described as 'confidential' – *not* a topic for public debate. What we can assume, however, is that most developers calculate profit as a percentage of costs, as that is easier to estimate than future revenue in a changing market. In the early 1990s, Marshall and Kennedy (1993) suggested that such profits for residential and commercial development typically lie be between 15–17% which, expressed as a percentage of turnovers, would approximate to 12–14%, as the sales figure (the gross development value) are expected to be a larger amount.

Another academic study, published 20 years later in 2013, suggested that the profits for residential developers lie in the region of 15–25% on costs – equivalent to approximately 10–20% on value (Coleman *et al.*, 2013). The broader range probably provides a more realistic margin, but the latest figures should be qualified by the possibility that the profit margin obtainable from residential development is usually lower than from commercial property, because of the relatively competitive nature of the house building industry.

From the perspective of the valuer, this dilemma of profits being a movable feast is problematic. As Coleman *et al.* (2013: 150) perceptively remark:

> '*It is clear that estimating a required rate of return for development opportunities requires data that typically do not exist or assumptions that are difficult to verify but, whilst problematic, it is important to acknowledge that required rates of return are implicit in all conventional development appraisal techniques when applying simple profit on GDV (Gross Development Value) and profit-on-cost ratios*'.

Thus, levels of profit relating to development sector are difficult to benchmark or verify for appraisal purposes. You can also bet your bottom dollar that the precise level will vary – from project to project, from time to time, and between residential and commercial developments. In broad terms, however, anecdotal evidence would suggest that today's schemes typically expect a profit of between 15–25% on costs (i.e. 11–20% of GDV).

## The residential developer's dilemma

During the last decade, I have been involved in advising local authorities to set realistic targets for the amount of social housing that they can request private developers to provide in return for planning permission. The setting of such targets is a minefield. Housing developers continually appeal against unfair treatment, while local authorities continually highlight the need to create sufficient affordable housing provision to meet the growing waiting lists of those who cannot afford to occupy housing of their own. In other words, the likes of Taylor Wimpey, Persimmon, and Crest Nicholson, who construct thousands of residential units per year, alongside the smaller local firms who might not build more than five units per year, are all profit-driven private enterprise organisations. Challenging them on the other side of the equation are the local authority planning offices [1] (approximately 375 of them across England and Wales alone) who, faced with increasingly restrained budgets and lengthening waiting lists for homes, need to accept greater responsibility for the welfare of their communities.

Alongside this tightening of margins is a raft of complex and costly legislation designed to secure greater energy efficiency and improve sustainability generally. In the decade leading up to 2008, developers complained about this, but by and large accepted the government demands as market values at the time were rising. During the decade following the Great Recession, however, margins in the building sector became distinctly difficult.

In the language of this chapter, the dilemma between developers and planners all boils down to **viability**. What percentage can the private developer agree to contribute to the local community and still achieve a reasonable rate of return on their investment? The process brings into focus the challenging negotiations that local authorities face in securing a local stock of affordable housing to provide for the millions of families on their waiting lists (up to two million in 2014). The private developer must have enough capacity in the budget to construct private property at market price and still have a sufficient margin to contribute to the local stock of social housing. As *The Economist* (2014), reviewing housing developments in London, observed: 'Planning applications become a negotiation: politicians try to extract subsidised housing, schools, and parks for voters; developers vie for the right to build as many profitable luxury apartments as possible'.

As government advice acknowledges planning authorities need to *strike a balance* between the policy obligations to provide for affordable housing and the realities of economic viability. As the official literature expresses it: 'There should be both clear justification for local standards and policies, and reasonable returns for landowners and developers' (Harman, 2012: 10). This is easier said than done.

To sum up this scenario, the process obviously rotates around identifying what is an acceptable level of profit for taking on the risks of property development. Is it 15% or 25%? Interestingly, a group of developers, responding to questions about the so-called barriers to housing development in 2012, complained that local authorities negotiate from a completely unrealistic position: 'by only allowing' a 10% margin for the affordable housing and 15% for the private sale units. As the developers explained in their defence, 'this implies 10% for construction risk and an additional 5% for sales risk, which is ridiculous!' (GLA, 2012: 41).

The acceptable rate of profit, however, changes as economic circumstances change. For example, work completed on viability in 2014 assumed a target profit that was approximately 5% lower than the target employed in economic models used in 2007/8 (i.e. before the Great Recession). In terms of the storyline, profits are a function of the property cycle, and since 2008 they have been generally

**Table 2.1**  Developers' profits 1989 to 2008

| Year | Profits as a % of turnover | Profit as a % of costs (Equivalence) | Position in the property cycle |
|---|---|---|---|
| 1989/90 | 23% | 30% | Peak |
| 1992/93 | 10% | 11% | Falling market; point of inflection |
| 1994/95 | 13% | 15% | Slow recovering market |
| 2000/01 | 15% | 18% | A rising market |
| 2002/03 | 16% | 19% | A continuing rising market |
| 2007 | 19% | 25% | Nearing top of the market |

*Source*: Adapted from Barker (2003) and company accounts published in 2008.

squeezed in a falling market. A portrait of their volatility in the years leading up to the crash in 2008 is presented in Table 2.1. The data is drawn from the profits record of a number of house builders.

One concern in the post-recession years was the vulnerability of the residential development sector to the general downturn in economic activity. To paraphrase the Construction Industry Council (2009: 9): the housing market was the first to feel the cold chill winds of recession and will be the last to see the green shoots of recovery. There were certainly significant structural changes, as the number of small builders that survived the crash was greatly reduced and, through increased levels of consolidation, more power fell into the hands of a big five companies, namely: Barratt Developments, Taylor Wimpey, Persimmon, Berkeley Group Holdings and Bellway.

As this chapter has implied, these UK house builders are big business players and, as such, are primarily interested in 'lining their own pockets'; and an initial examination of the key financial information relating to these big five firms would suggest that they have managed to do just that, regardless of the recession. They adopted a strategy of 'prioritising margin over volume' (Taylor Wimpey, 2011) – or, as Barratt Developments (2011: 5) expressed it, 'maximising value rather than driving volumes'. In plain English: in the midst of the recession, big house builders focused on squeezing as much as possible from the most profitable sites, rather than maximising their overall housing output.

A further tactic that distorts the market are the land banks that the Big Five can afford. That is, they have the resources to buy up land when it is relatively cheap, obtain planning consent, and then do nothing with it until the market is ripe for development. As a result, supply suffers and new units increase in price despite a backdrop of declining average house prices nationally. By way of evidence, each of the 'Big Five's profits increased from 2010 onwards, so the financial results confirm that the big house builders were not 'on their knees' for long after the recession (Archer and Cole, 2014).

Ironically, however, the housing market is still in a mess – particularly the social housing market. There appears to be an ongoing political debate about how to achieve public policy objectives in housing supply using different planning instruments. However, putting politics to one side, it is illuminating to see how changing economic conditions also play havoc with the expected level of profit. In other words, the business case for residential or commercial development can go from black to red overnight as circumstances change. Regardless, the usual economic response from business is to put self-interest before the public good.

## It's all about yields

'Yield' is a term closely associated with property bought for investment purposes. It brings into focus the income stream that follows from a capital outlay. For example, if an investor purchases a tenanted office block, they are in effect buying the right to receive a stream of rental income in the future. Let us say an investor pays £1 million for a small office building (typically let on a full repairing and insuring lease, where the tenant bears the running and maintenance costs) at a rent of £57 500 a year. The investment yield is 5.75%. The simple calculation is as follows:

$$\frac{\text{Income}}{\text{Pricepaid}} \times 100, \text{ or in this case: } \frac{£57500}{£1000000} \times 100 = 5.75\%$$

The precise same principles apply when calculating the yield on an equity (share) or bond. This prompts the question, why would an investor accept a return of only 5.75% on property when he can get a perfectly safe return of, say, 10% on a fixed-interest government stock – a gilt-edged security? The answer, of course, is that the rental income from the property could grow as the general level of rents rises, whereas the interest income from the gilt-edged security will remain exactly the same throughout its life. In short, it might be worth accepting a lower yield today in return for the expectation of a rising income in the future.

Furthermore, the more facts that are known, the less the risk will be. Thus, a commercial property which is already occupied is more attractive than one which is unoccupied (there will be no risk of losing income because of failure to find a tenant). Similarly, a tenant who is financially sound is preferable to one who may go bankrupt. Development sites involve even greater risks, since they will take many months or years to be completed, by which time the demand may have evaporated.

Clearly, however, the income stream does not account for the whole picture. For instance, if the rents from the office block rise, not only does the owner get a higher income, but the capital value of the investment (the price somebody would be prepared to pay for it in the market) should also rise. The investor therefore has a potential capital gain to add to the rental income. These different levels of return are distinguished by precise terms. Surveyors tend to talk of 'yield' when referring to the return the investor receives in the form of income, and 'total return' or 'overall return' for the return achieved from the combination of income and appreciation in the capital value of the property.

Most forms of property investment ultimately come back to the question of income or, more precisely, producing a rent, inasmuch as the higher the yield, the higher the capital value. The buyer of a revenue-producing property investment – a tenanted office block – is effectively paying a capital sum today in return for the right to receive a stream of income in the future. In other words, the

**Table 2.2**  Prime yields

| | |
|---|---|
| **Shops** | 4.25% |
| **Offices (City of London)** | 4.25% |
| **Industrials** | 5.25% |

*Source*: CBRE Monthly investment yields, April 2015.

capital value of land or property (which is just another way of saying 'the price') is usually related to the income it produces or could produce. Hence, the yield on a property is generally defined as the initial return – in the form of income – that investors receive on the money they lay out to buy a property.

Another term you will come across in discussion of property as an investment is **prime yield**. This is slightly difficult to define, because the term tends to be used in different ways in different contexts. Its general purpose, however, is to set a benchmark of the very highest quality property in each of the main categories (shop, office and industrial). Prime properties, therefore, tend to be well-specified, well-located and let at current market rent to a financially strong tenant on a lease with a minimum of 15 years. In other words, these properties are low-risk and have high growth potential. Most investments would be better compared with average yields but, even then, individual properties will vary according to age, lease lengths, financial reputation of the tenants and time left before review.

As an example, in April 2015, CBRE (one of the largest commercial real estate agencies in the world) was stating the prime yields shown in Table 2.2:

To reiterate, prime property represents the very lowest yields that investors are prepared to accept for the lowest risk property. They are useful as a benchmark for valuing real-world properties, as only a small proportion of property in any of the categories would qualify as 'prime'. Most buildings held as investments by the insurance companies and pension funds, therefore, tend to be valued on higher yields.

Thus, in April 2015 terms, the £1 million office block producing a rent of £57,500 a year is clearly not prime, but secondary, and is therefore valued on a slightly higher yield. For example, it could represent a slightly older property located on the edge of the city centre.

## Timing is everything

As suggested above, the viability of a project can change overnight. To illustrate the significance of this tricky conundrum, we shall follow the timeline of one of London's most protracted skyscrapers – *22 Bishopsgate*. As its name (and its address) suggests, when completed it will occupy a site in the heart of the City of London – although, given its proposed height, it is destined to be seen, on a clear day, from 40 miles away in Reading, the South Downs, the Chilterns and Southend.

The initial idea for the development dates back to 2001, when the scheme was first proposed. In those early days it was known as the Pinnacle or Helter-Skelter project. An initial planning application for a 307 metre tower was submitted in June 2005. However, concerns about flight paths from the Civil Aviation

Authority, and restricted views, prompted a revised planning application with a 19 metre height reduction. Final consent for a 288 metre tower was granted in April 2006. In November 2006, the developers secured funding for the project, and construction began on site late in 2007. Some ground-works and foundations were put in place before the financial crisis began to raise its ugly head: no pre-lets were forthcoming, and finance dried up. In 2011, HSBC and HSH Nordbank agreed a £500 million debt facility with the scheme's Middle Eastern owners to allow above-ground construction to commence. By January 2012, only nine floors of concrete core had been completed and the project ground to a halt, having aptly acquired the nickname 'the Stump'.

Round two – 2013: The Pinnacle project morphs into *22 Bishopsgate*. The property agent CBRE was drafted in to search for new funding to revive the mothballed scheme. In these huge commercial projects, form tends to follow finance so, to make the project more attractive, it was agreed that the nine-floor Pinnacle 'stump' could be knocked down to allow for a modified design with changes to the floor plates to maximise office space. In fact, it now boasts of 1.4 million square feet of lettable space – 30% more than was planned for the Pinnacle. The redesigned building, at 278 metres tall and 62 storeys high, is still destined to be the tallest on the London skyline (as it is only 10 metres lower than the previous design). In July 2015, a fresh planning application was submitted and, during the following months, the 'Stump' was removed, so that *22 Bishopsgate* could commence construction early in 2016. Providing all goes to plan the building, should be complete by November 2018 – some 17 years after it was first started!

## The development pipeline

The above case study more than adequately demonstrates the lengthy time horizon between conception and completion of a real estate project. It certainly highlights the intricate web of relationships and negotiations that a completed building represents. For example, 22 Bishopsgate currently involves more than 20 separate agencies [2], such as the developer, architect, contractor, engineer, property agent, and so on. The underlying transactions are completely 'invisible', and unknown, to the passer-by. Therefore, although the visible construction phase can take up to four years, depending on size and complexity, the development of a commercial property will take far longer to complete.

Figure 2.1 identifies some of the main events in the property development process, and it can be thought of like any other form of economic production, as it involves the integration of land, capital and labour. The time dimension is emphasised by the distance from the beginning to the end of the pipeline, and managing the chain of events inevitably requires some creative vision for a successful venture.

The pipeline analogy tends to oversimplify the process, as effective property development depends on bringing together all the resources at the right time and place; the risks of a poorly managed project can be quite costly. In fact, it can be argued that the property development process, more than any other industry, demonstrates the importance of the entrepreneur. The essential ingredient to any

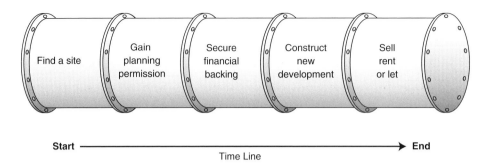

**Figure 2.1**   The development pipeline.

successful property project is timing. A developer with sufficient vision to take the risks necessary to bring resources together to create assets that will form a sufficient stream of future income to generate profit is a rare talent. Relatively few property developers will own land, capital and labour in their own right; they just bring all the factors of production together. Furthermore, it is only within the last 30 years or so that this process has stopped being initiated by the developer relying solely on 'gut' instincts. Nowadays, appraisals of property development decisions are increasingly supported by research data.

The development pipeline – the process of development – is unlike other forms of production. There is not a continuous chain of events producing one building after the other, dependent on employment of the same team of labour. Each development project, and its associated team, is different. Each unit of production needs to be negotiated, planned and designed before construction and occupation can commence. The analogy of a film set may be useful to illustrate how the various professions and trades are brought together to do their work (complete a development) and then leave for another location to do 'similar' work for another developer.

Finally, before completing this introduction to the development process, it is worth remembering that the majority of residential property is usually speculatively developed, in the sense that it is built ('on spec') without a specific purchaser (or tenant) being identified. However, commercial property is becoming increasingly developed for a named tenant (i.e. it is 'pre-let' or 'bespoke' for sale or rent). The sharpest contrast between these two sectors, however, is in the pattern of ownership; houses are mostly owner-occupied, whereas commercial property is usually rented by businesses on long-term contracts. The implications of this separation of interests between the ownership and use of commercial property are explored further in the sections below, which detail socially responsible investment and the circle of blame.

## Chasing the dragon

Do not be misled by the drug-related imagery used in the above section heading, as the message is more complicated than merely 'smoking opium' – and commercially a lot healthier. We still need to understand the frenzy surrounding the notion of profit, and the metaphor will prove useful in setting up the storyline that we are seeking to clarify. Imagine, if you will, a young property developer gaining their first taste of profit in a booming market, similar to that of 2005/6. Understandably, this can lead to an adrenalin rush – a high – the world is peaceful, and the young property developer appears to be a success.

However, a year or two afterwards, the rewards and associated feelings start to dwindle; the young property developer is no longer living in a dream world. They desperately need another hit – or, more simply, the boss expects them to seek out more profit-making opportunities. Prospect of the next project becomes more and more important, as the young property developer craves to achieve the same level of success – the same buzz – as they did in 2005/6. Unfortunately, they cannot go to the market and develop property similar to their first project, as this time the setting is not right and the profit, if any, is greatly reduced. The young property developer is stuck, it is now 2009 and the bottom has fallen out of the market. They don't know what to do. They want to go back to the time when the economy was booming – when they were riding on the crest of a wave – and stay at that level forever. But the economy has changed and the notion of normal profit has been reduced; diminishing returns have set in.

The young property developer now has two options: to invest more and more, like a hooked junkie; or to wait patiently until the market picks up. In short, their life becomes difficult, as they search opportunities to make a profit and become rich, all in search of a repeat of the first 'high' in 2005/6. That's kind of chasing the dragon. It also begs the question of how does one know when they are at the top of the market, when is the time to stop investing, and when should they start again? Unfortunately, no two cycles are identical, and opportunities will come and go. When should they go for it, and when should they show the wisdom to leave well alone?

This is why the expense and patience to run a financial appraisal is an essential habit to develop. It is immaterial if the building produced is for sale, investment or occupation; the decision to proceed is nearly always driven by a profit motive. The volatility of development appraisals demonstrates just how quickly a profitable property project can become loss-making. It is therefore important to consider these risks when considering the level of profit that can be generated.

## Socially responsible investment

Returning to the opening remarks made at the beginning of this chapter, there is plenty of scope for the truly rigorous investor in property to make a significant contribution to the future shape of society. For example, there is a growing interest in all things sustainable. Thus, developments that include energy saving measures, natural ventilation and other environmental features are increasingly attractive.

Indeed, economists have long drawn a distinction between direct and indirect costs and benefits. The former are associated with monetary rewards – those that directly affect the demand side (in revenue terms(and/or the supply side (in cost terms). In contrast, the latter – indirect costs and benefits – are more concerned with evaluating the broader – external – impacts on society. These are the third party or neighbourhood effects that inevitably arise from a project or activity, but which are rarely included as part of the appraisal. The indirect impacts are harder to identify and express in monetary terms, but this does not mean that they should be ignored.

Economists have always stressed that a fully efficient allocation of a society's resources is dependent on evaluating the *direct* and *indirect* costs and benefits. As Vilfredo Pareto rather clumsily expressed it in 1890, in a truly efficient competitive market, all the exchanges that members of the economy are willing to make have to be agreed at fair prices, and – here is the real important and famous bit – *no one should benefit at someone else's cost*. In Pareto's terms, an efficient allocation of resources is dependent on resource decisions that benefit some people without anyone else being made worse off. All members of the economy face the true opportunity costs of *all* their market-driven actions. Private resource decisions that impact on the welfare and neighbourhood of others must bear all costs. The time has arrived for surveyors – and economists, for that matter – to act on this advice!

In fairness, mainstream economists have always acknowledged these dilemmas, and the impacts of externalities play a part in most introductions. In fact, ever since the 1960s, welfare economics has had its place in the main curriculum, but profit-orientated business has taken little heed. Equally, at the turn of the Millennium, when welfare economics broadened to issues of sustainability, mainstream economists acknowledged it as worthy but, again, the profit constraint meant that it was taken up by relatively few in business. This is particularly the case in the world of property, where energy assessment criteria and environmental labelling have been available for more than 25 years – but have not been taken up by the majority. Questions of sustainability and the unethical market are raised again in Chapter 3.

## Costs and price

To understand the development of property, it is useful to distinguish between cost and price. When a producer sells or rents any good to a consumer, the cost and price should not be the same. Whenever a property – or anything – is sold, it is important that the cost and the asking price should not be identical. The usual assumption made by economists is that all producers (suppliers) developers – whatever their line of business – seek to maximise profit! Therefore, it is most important that the cost of providing any property is less than the selling price – and this applies equally to all goods and services. To take a simple example, it is usual in construction for the cost of a project to be estimated, and a mark-up for profits (risks) and overheads added before arriving at a price for the job. The contractor's mark-up is the difference between price and cost.

A similar principle is commonly used to identify the value of land. A property developer commences by estimating the optimum price – the Gross Development Value – that they will be able to charge once the project is complete, taking into consideration the prevailing market, future prospects, and other considerations. From this price, the builder deducts all the inherent costs in developing the site, plus an allowance for profit. What remains is the price which the developer can afford to pay for the site.

In other words, the value of the completed development *minus* the build costs *minus* the target profit *equals* the site value. This process is known as the **residual method** of valuation or, more specifically, the **residual land value**; it is often used to identify the maximum price that a developer can afford to pay for development land. The process is briefly outlined in the next section, but you can rest assured that your valuations lecturer will also go through it.

*Part A*

## Identifying the value of land

A basic framework for development appraisal involves conducting a residual (land) valuation. This is commonly expressed in the form of a formula:

$$GDV - (BC + P) = RLV \qquad \text{(Equation 1)}$$

Where the notation stands for the following:
GDV = Gross Development Value;
BC = Building Costs, including fees and interest;
P = Profits (normal profits);
RLV = Residual Land Value.

Gross Development Value *minus* Build Costs & Profits *equals* Residual Land Value.

For property investment purposes, this basic equation can be rearranged in two ways, as follows:

$$GDV - (BC + RLV) = P \qquad \text{(Equation 2)}$$

Here, the Land Value is known. The Profit is a residual in this equation.

$$(BC + P + RLV) = GDV \qquad \text{(Equation 3)}$$

Here, the GDV is made up of the three main 'cost' elements, which explicitly include the developer's profit.

From these different equations, we can identify critical values:

- Equation (1): for those who are seeking to sell or buy land;
- Equation (2): the amount of profit that might be achieved by the developer having bought the land; and
- Equation (3): this reveals the three basic 'costs' that make up the GDV.

## Diverse forces

This relatively short chapter has highlighted the importance of profits to those involved in business and property investment. It does not, however, profess to fully address the question of property valuation, as there is a subtle but important line of distinction between what is regarded as economics and what is regarded as valuation. Valuation is about assessing the 'level of returns' and 'usefulness' when transacting on a specific property in an open market. By definition, therefore, valuation is a narrower discipline that involves interpreting property markets. Economists are keen to emphasise the benefits of markets and the importance of maintaining a healthy level of competition between suppliers, whereas surveyors prefer to identify an absence of competition, as the best properties to value and develop are those that have no comparable. As Diane Coyle (2012) made patently clear in a lecture about the nature and responsibility of new thinking: 'Some economists take the corporate shilling and make pro-business *rather than* pro-market or pro-competition arguments.' Coyle has helped to highlight the subtle but important distinctions, between valuations and different types of economics.

There is no doubt in my mind that what happens in textbooks and what happens in reality is subject to some debate. To take a property-related example according to mainstream texts, developers of real estate maximise profits by comparing the extra rents – the marginal rents, as they call them – that they receive, in relation to the costs they incur to construct or acquire them. However, we rarely hear about the costs incurred for advertising, planning deals or contributions to political parties – and even the cost of financing is sometimes overlooked.

New economic thinking seeks to encourage a way of teaching that is based on real-world events; or, as the CORE (2013) [3] strapline captures it: 'teaching economics as if the last three decades had happened'. This sparked the initial enthusiasm to design this text and identify the economic ideas that will contribute to the process of valuing properties in the 21st Century. Valuation is a difficult skill to acquire at the best of times, but particularly whenever there is a diminished amount of trading activity taking place. Furthermore, a post-recession environment is characterised by increasingly difficult credit arrangements and relatively weak business confidence.

Taking each of these in turn, clearly the rate at which funds are borrowed is a key consideration to any appraisal, as it impacts heavily on the costs, and also the viability of projects. Secondly, whenever the level of market transactions are low, due to poor confidence, purchasers seek higher returns for higher risk and are prepared to wait for it. Furthermore, as the cost of debt rises, buyers face unrealistically high prices and are not willing to trade at that level. Consequently, markets can be sluggish for many years, as investors continue to be hesitant until attractive opportunities are presented. Hence, a change in property market temperament is often dependent on the valuation of a brave surveyor who has the courage and insight to buck the trend and break the downward spiral.

A similar set of tensions unfolds in the next chapter, where we make it clear that markets are amoral. This problem with markets pre-dates the financial crisis, as there have always been things that money just cannot buy; as the Beatles song reminds us: 'Money can't buy you love'. But this should not be regarded as flippant, as economists do seem to assume that all goods are commensurable – that is, they can all be translated into a single measure or unit of value. As a consequence, markets – and the values of markets – have acquired an all-pervasive nature, and we have unwittingly accepted the commodification of everything. This dilemma can be witnessed in the marketisation of health, education and even water.

Sandel (2012) – a renowned critic of the moral, political and economic merits of free markets – argues that economics is to blame for the extension of market-like thinking into wholly inappropriate spheres of life. His examples include: blood, nuclear waste, friends, carbon offsets, pollution permits, and even a fast-track place at the front of the queue. As he states at the beginning of his 200-page book (which expands on his Reith Lecture series of 2009): 'We live in a time when almost everything can be bought and sold' (Sandel, 2012: 5). His argument is that markets have led to a degradation of moral and civic goods, because they introduce an inappropriate mode of valuation. This is clearly evident in the market for what we referred to in this chapter as socially responsible investment, and what we refer to in Chapter 3 as sustainability. The worrying point is that sustainable development does not appear to influence capital or rental premiums, so the market valuation becomes questionable. This is despite there having been a government agenda and professional support from the RICS since 1990. In fact, it is a fine example of failure in the real estate market, and there is a neat circle of blame that summarises how markets are too selfish and too fragmented to consider the greater good.

## The circle of blame

In the UK, and elsewhere, there is a mind-set that tends to fragment the responsibility for change. Construction firms argue that they can only adopt holistic approaches if clients ask for them; developers imply that there is no demand for sustainability, and investors are hesitant to fund risky new ventures. There is a so-called 'circle of blame' that perpetuates the existing traditional approach to construction. This idea is captured in Figure 2.2, which characterises four typical views from the industry.

Since this idea was coined in August 2001, the 'circle of blame' – or 'cycle of blame', as some prefer to call it – has become a standard part of the academic literature dealing with sustainability. It effectively emphasises the conservative nature of the property and construction sectors, and serves as a good way to highlight the problematical nature of markets and valuations. The new thinkers have the same fear, and realise that without intervention, the vicious circle of blame is unlikely to be transformed into one that is a virtuous circle for the good of society.

This will become clearer as we examine how markets work and allocate resources in the next chapter.

## Food for thought: Is profit the measure of everything?

By the end of Chapter 2, you are probably still struggling with the question: what is the point of economics? Chapter 1 gave the impression that the objective is to make as much output as possible; to maximise production – so to speak – to make sure that global GDP continues to grow. Chapter 2 has been more about regarding profit as the be-all and end-all of each related activity; the motive behind each investment and unit of production. The tradition of economics has always placed great trust, and importance, on the freedom of people to maximise profit. In many ways, it is as if money is the measure of all things. When global GDP and profits are on the up, mainstream economists feel justified by their approach; when recessions, occur questions arise.

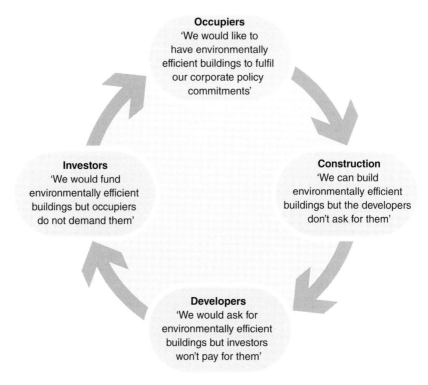

**Figure 2.2**   The circle of blame.

As a consequence, in the wake of the financial crisis, economists are revisiting a series of questions about the maximisation of output, income, and wealth. Central to these questions is the notion that there is more to economic life than increasing the size of the annual turnover and making a greater profit than last year. This section introduces the relatively new idea of measuring wellbeing and happiness.

The idea was formally floated by Richard Layard in 2003, as part of a series of lectures celebrating the work and times of Lionel Robbins. In broad terms, Layard's lecture theme introduced the notion of happiness as part of the modern economic curriculum. There was, however, a certain irony in the timing of the events. In his time, Professor Lionel Robbins had been an outstanding free market economist; indeed, the lecture series was conceived to commemorate his 50 year association with the London School of Economics, from 1929 to 1980. His book *An Essay on the Nature and Significance of Economic Science*, which had been penned during his LSE career, contains the famous all-encompassing classic definition of economics that was quoted in Chapter 1, (page 14).

Indeed, you may remember – or you can look it up – Robbins (1932) defined economics to be about 'the relationship between given ends and scarce means'. As such, he had made a clear distinction between economics and related disciplines. In his terms, how the 'ends' or preferences came to be formed were beyond the boundaries of economics. Yet, 70 years later, Professor Richard Layard is making the case that, to be good economists, students need to think beyond the narrow questions of 'means' and 'ends'. Eighty years later, new economic thinking is suggesting that the curriculum should broaden to encompass such ideas.

## Measuring the standard of living?

Up until the 21st Century, the standard reference point for economists was Gross Domestic Product (GDP), which measures the monetary value of goods and services produced in a country (some idea of how this is done is explained in Chapter 8). As such, the size and growth of a nation's GDP is seen to reflect its economic performance, and is often used as the headline indicator of a society's success, progress or standard of living – and, in some people's minds, even the wellbeing of society.

However, it has become increasingly apparent that GDP is not necessarily a good measure of personal happiness or national wellbeing. By focusing on the 'cold' numbers of production and *per capita* incomes, economists tend to overlook income inequalities and deprivations. For example, as discussed in Chapter 1, rising GDP does not necessarily mean that incomes of the worst off or the majority of citizens are increasing. There is no hard and fast rule, or research, to confirm that greater wellbeing is achieved from more consumption. In fact, there are those who argue that there is no link whatsoever between income and happiness (Easterlin, 2001) – and, by extension, it is presumably also argued that there is no moral case for tackling income inequality.

Furthermore, GDP includes economic activity that is not always productive or desirable, such as the buying and selling of financial derivatives (discussed in Section B), cleaning up oil spills, rebuilding after a tsunami or repairing a car after an accident. Finally, from the wellbeing perspective, it is also important to remember that GDP excludes all unpaid activities such as housework, craftwork, cooking, caring for older family members, DIY repairs and so on. In short, there is more to life than the things you pay for.

Obviously, much of the debate rotates around what is used to measure or monitor wellbeing and happiness. The current tendency is to gather a range of factors to form an index, or dashboard, of measures. The data includes economic, environmental and social variables, such as: education and skills; personal security; civic engagement and governance; social connections; health status; income and wealth; jobs and earnings; housing; environmental quality; subjective wellbeing; and work-life balance. The responses are used to form an index.

For example, Figure 2.3 presents the wellbeing index for the UK, in 2014, ranking it in relation to other rich countries in the Organisation for Economic Co-operation and Development (OECD), which ranks its 34 member countries across the 11 dimensions shown. For those who want to know more about the OECD wellbeing project [4], there is up-to-date information in eight languages and a three-minute video on their website.

Figure 2.3    UK wellbeing rankings.
*Source*: Adapted from OECD *'Better Life Initiative'*, 2014.

# Chapter 3
# Real Estate Markets

Students of real estate are expected to be able to make confident economic statements on all sorts of property transactions by the time that they graduate. Hence, this chapter, with its technical references to price signals, the Marshallian cross, inelasticity, equilibrium, price systems, market clearing, supply side problems and so on may, at first sight, seem rather daunting. But as Ha-Joon Chang (2014) the Cambridge professor, who conscientiously supports the new economic thinking initiative, has asserted: '95% of economics is common sense – made to look difficult with the use of jargons and mathematics.'

While not wishing to enter into a debate about the precise percentage that could be deemed technical, and what percentage is common sense, I totally endorse the sentiment that much of the economic advice that is given by surveyors is relatively straightforward and can be expressed in everyday language. For example, we have already touched on the idea (in Chapter 1) that many social and economic inequalities are spawned by the market mechanism, as those with the greatest wealth have most 'votes' about what is produced, while those with no incomes, if left to fend for themselves, get nothing. On the other hand, the market mechanism does provide a system of communication, relaying messages between producers and consumers about 'what' to produce and 'how'. Finally, in terms of jargon, it might be worth remembering that all highlighted terms in bold are defined in the glossary at the back of the book.

Recognition of the **market mechanism** dates back to the beginning of economics, when Adam Smith, a founding father of economics, presented the market-based economy as a product of natural order, since market prices were seen to deliver signals that guide human endeavour. He demonstrated how prices and wages continually adjust to keep the general levels of supply and demand in balance. In his terms, the management of an economy could simply follow a *laissez-faire* approach. In other words, the power of the market justifies a limited role for governments.

*New Economic Thinking and Real Estate*, First Edition. Danny Myers.
© 2016 John Wiley & Sons, Ltd. Published 2016 by John Wiley & Sons, Ltd.

Following this analysis, governments are only needed to provide a forum for determining the rules of the game, and to act as an umpire to ensure that the rules are enforced. Without government intervention, high prices encourage enterprise and factors of production to be channelled into particular economic activities. Conversely, falling prices suggest a decline in the interest of the product, or an increase in competition, and ultimately there will come a low point when factors of production begin to exit the activity. Consequently, price signals can be seen to serve the greater good.

As a consequence of this, a belief in free markets and personal freedoms has spread to all corners of the globe, and neoclassical ideology has grasped the imagination of more than just an academic community. Today, 'freedom of choice' is a common mantra used to suggest that people choose leisure over employment, ownership over renting and so on. So, like it or not, we need to fully understand the price signalling system, especially as most property markets respond to money votes, cast within local planning boundaries and fiscal rules set by governments.

## Common sense price signals

For a market economy to function effectively, it is important that every individual is free to pursue 'self-interest'. Consumers express their choice of goods or service, through the price they are prepared to pay for them, in their attempts to maximise satisfaction. Producers, and owners of resources (and for most people, this is their own labour power), seek to obtain as large a reward as possible in an attempt to maximise profit.

If consumers want more of a good than is being supplied at the current price, this is indicated by their willingness to pay more to acquire that good – the price is 'bid up'. This, in turn, increases the profits of those firms producing and supplying the good – and the incomes paid to the factors producing that good increase. As a result, resources are attracted into the industry, and supply expands.

On the other hand, if consumers do not want a particular product, its price will fall, producers will lose money and resources will leave the industry. This is precisely what happened in the 'new build' market during the recession that followed the financial crisis in 2007/8. The demand for new houses declined and prices fell, and producers either concentrated on other construction work or went bankrupt. As a result, between 2008 and 2010, the completion of new homes fell by more than 30%, reaching the lowest level since 1924.

In simple terms, the **price system** indicates the wishes of consumers and allocates the resources accordingly. Or, as economists like to suggest, the price mechanism determines *what* is produced, *how* it is produced and *for whom*. To take a specific example, there are more than three million private firms in the European construction industry; indeed, there are approximately 200,000 private firms in the UK construction sector alone. This makes the markets for construction relatively competitive and very distinct from manufacturing. In the manufacturing sector, there are usually a few large national firms producing a recognised product that can be examined before purchase and, to a some extent, the firms involved can determine the price that will be charged in the market. In construction, the opposite seems to apply, as a construction project usually involves many small local firms combining their skills on site to produce a 'unique' product that will not stand up to close scrutiny or examination until it is actually finished. In fact, the terms of the contract will probably cover the possibility of work being handed over late, over price, or failing to meet the specified performance standards.

One reason why individuals and businesses turn to markets to conduct economic activities is that markets tend to reduce the costs of trading. These costs are called **transaction costs**, because they are part of the process of making a sale or purchase. They include the cost of being informed about the qualities of a particular product, such as its availability, its durability, its servicing, its safety, and so on.

Consider, for example, the transaction costs in the property market. Buyers of property have to search the market for information about prices and availability. Indeed, in the commercial and residential property markets, both buyers and sellers employ agents to negotiate on their behalf. The agent is relied upon to know about comparable price and rents and the availability of certain types of property. For their expertise regarding sales value and advertising, a commission has to be paid, and this can range from 1% or 2% in Britain to 6% in the USA. The commission costs cover: arrangements to view the property; providing information about the local market; explaining contractual requirements and features relating to the property; and last but by no means least important, giving advice on price and value. Ultimately, the agent negotiates a sale or purchase on behalf of the client paying the commission.

In a purely theoretical or highly organised market, these costs do not exist, as it is assumed that everybody has access to the knowledge they need for exchange to take place. However, this is not the case in the property market, where transactions, in relative terms, are infrequent, and both buyers and sellers have to make significant financial commitments and meet associated legal costs. As an example, the main transaction costs incurred in buying a house are listed in Table 3.1, where we itemise the costs involved in buying a house in England in 2015. Presumably, if these costs did not exist, people would move far more frequently.

Some economists argue that the increased use of electronic communication reduces transaction costs both between businesses and between businesses and consumers, and there is a broad debate about the **new economy** and its implications

**Table 3.1**    The transaction costs of buying a £200,000 house

| ITEM | COST (£) |
| --- | --- |
| **Buying** | |
| Commission a survey of property – a valuation report | 300 |
| Instruct removal firm | 400 |
| Processing searches (local authority and land registry) | 430 |
| Solicitors' fees | 750 |
| Stamp duty @ 2% of £75 000 | 1,500 |
| **Transaction costs for purchaser before moving** | **3,380** |
| **Selling** | |
| Single Estate agency fee @ 2% (including VAT) | 4,800 |
| Energy Performance Certificate | 100 |
| Additional legal work | 700 |
| **Total transaction costs prior to moving** | **8,980** |

for B2B (business to business) and B2C (business to consumers) transactions. A relevant example is a service provided by the Land Registry [1] that enables users to find all the prices a specific house has traded at throughout its history (the significance of the new economy is examined further in Chapter 8).

## The Marshallian Cross

Analysis of the price (market) mechanism has played a significant role throughout the history of economics. As far back as 1776, Adam Smith wrote in *The Wealth of Nations* about the 'hidden hands' of supply and demand determining market prices. However, it was not until a hundred years later that Alfred Marshall – in his first edition of *Principles of Economics* (1890) – brought together the two concepts in one graph. Since then, a standard part of any introductory economics course has involved the study of supply and demand graphs. This is probably because it is easier to communicate an idea visually – as the saying goes, 'a picture is worth a thousand words'. A supply and demand graph enables the relationship between price and quantity to be explored from the consumers' (demand) perspective and the producers' (supply) perspective. The standard layout of each axis is shown in Figure 3.1.

Using the labelled axis in Figure 3.1, can you determine what the pattern of demand in relation to the price would look like? To put the question in more formal terms, can you plot a **demand schedule**? Clearly, as the price of a commodity rises, the quantity demanded will decrease and, as the price falls, the quantity demanded will increase – that is, from the demand side, there is an inverse relationship between the price per unit and the quantity purchased. This is because consumers seek to maximise their satisfaction and get best value for money.

Using the labelled axis in Figure 3.1, can you determine what the pattern of supply in relation to price would look like? To rephrase the question in more formal

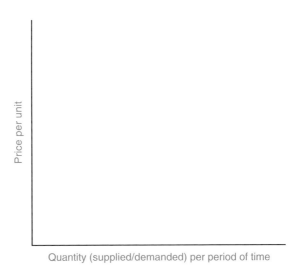

Figure 3.1    The axes of a supply and demand graph.

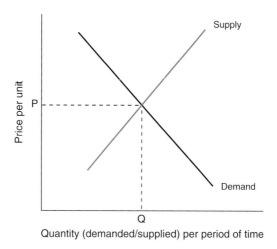

Figure 3.2   A simple supply and demand diagram.

terms, can you plot the **supply schedule**? Clearly, as the price of a commodity rises, the quantity supplied will increase and, as the price falls, the quantity supplied will decrease. That is, from the supply side, there is a **direct relationship** between the price per unit and quantity sold; an increase in price usually leads to an increase in the quantity supplied, and vice versa. This is because suppliers seek to maximise their profit and get the biggest possible return for their efforts.

As suggested, these basic principles seem easier to appreciate when plotted on a graph. See if you agree by considering Figure 3.2.

## Three methodological remarks

It is worth noting that economists have devised various procedures to add rigour and academic value to their analysis. Three of these small but important techniques need to be highlighted, especially as textbooks often fail to reiterate them.

1.  *Per period of time* On the horizontal axis of Figures 3.1 and 3.2, we ended the statement with the qualification *per period of time*. This is to highlight that supply or demand is a flow that takes place during a certain time period, and it is quite common to assume that the market period refers to a time when there can be no adjustments. Ideally, however, the time period should be specified as a month, year, week, or whatever. Without a time dimension, the statements relating to quantity lack accuracy.
2.  *Ceteris Paribus* The second qualifying remark relates to the Latin phrase ***ceteris paribus***, which means 'other things being equal' or constant. This is an important assumption to make when dealing with a graph showing two variables. For example, price is not the only factor that affects supply and demand. There are many other market conditions that also affect supply and demand, and we allude to these below. In the exercise above, constructing Figures 3.1 and 3.2, we assumed *ceteris paribus*. We did not complicate the analysis by allowing, for example, consumers' income to change when discussing changes to the

price of a good. If we did, we would never know whether the change in the quantity demanded or supplied was due to a change in the price or due to a change in income. Therefore, we employed the *ceteris paribus* technique and assumed that all the other factors that might affect the market were held constant. This assumption enables economists to be rigorous in their work, studying each significant variable in turn. The *ceteris paribus* assumption approximates to the scientific method of a controlled experiment, and it forms an important part of the neoclassical approach.

3.  *Supply and demand curves* When using supply and demand curves to illustrate economic analysis, they will frequently be drawn as straight lines. Although this is irritating from a linguistic point of view, it is easier for the artist constructing the illustrations, and is perfectly acceptable to economists, since the 'curves' rarely refer to the plotting of empirical data. It is worth noting, therefore, that so-called supply and demand 'curves' are usually illustrated as straight lines that highlight basic principles.

## The concept of equilibrium

Look again at Figure 3.2. Inevitably, there is a point at which the two curves must cross. This point represents the market price. In a standard textbook (such as Myers, 2012), it would be described as follows: the market price in Figure 3.2 is P, and this reflects the point where the quantity supplied and demanded is equal, namely point Q. At price P, the market clears. There is neither excess supply nor excess demand. Consumers are satisfied and producers make sufficient profit; both are happy. Price P is called the **equilibrium price**: the price at which the quantity demanded and the quantity supplied are equal.

To put it another way, adopting two favourite ideas from believers in market forces, the explanation can focus on weighing up 'costs' and 'benefits'. The supply curve measures the cost to producers; as output grows, costs increase, so the supply curve slopes upwards. In a similar way, the demand curve measures the benefit to consumers; as consumption grows, the benefit of extra consumption falls, so the demand curve slopes downward. At the point where the two curves cross, a price is set so that supply equals demand. At this price, output is efficient, as the benefit gained from consumption exactly match the costs of production.

All markets have this inherent balancing mechanism. When there is excess demand, price rises; and when there is excess supply, prices fall. Eventually, a price is found at which there is no tendency for change. Consumers are able to get all they want at that price, and suppliers are able to sell the amount that they produce at that price. This special market concept is illustrated in Figure 3.3. The concept of **equilibrium** is important in economics, as it provides a reference point when analysing different markets in different contexts.

The equilibrium price for each new house is £200 000 and the equilibrium quantity is 2000 units. At higher prices, there would be a surplus: houses would be in excess supply and may remain empty. For example, at £300 000, the market would not clear; there needs to be a movement along the demand curve from H to E and a movement along the supply curve from h to E. These movements necessitate

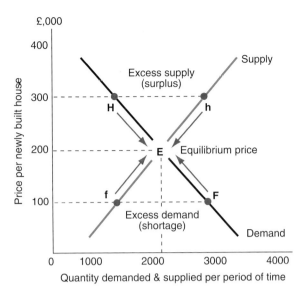

**Figure 3.3**   The equilibrium price.

the price to fall. At prices below the equilibrium, there would be a shortage; new houses would be in excess demand and there may be a waiting list. For example, at £100 000 the price would rise, reducing the demand from F to E and supply from f to E. The market will settle at a price of £200 000.

In other words, equilibrium prevails when opposing forces are in balance. If the price drifts away from the equilibrium point for whatever reason, forces come into play to find a new equilibrium price. If these forces tend to re-establish prices at the original equilibrium point, we say that the situation is one of **stable equilibrium**. An unstable equilibrium is one in which if there is a movement away from the equilibrium and there are forces that push price and/or quantity even further away from this equilibrium (or at least do not push price and quantity back towards the original equilibrium level).

In these terms, property markets can be characterised as unstable as, even in normal times, keeping demand and supply in balance is hard to achieve and the market often appears to be in a permanent state of flux. Some would claim the problems lie on the supply side, as we consistently fail to build enough new houses each year, while others would place the blame on the demand side, highlighting the problems of getting a mortgage and finding the deposit. As a consequence, whenever property markets take a jolt, they move away from equilibrium and tend to take a relatively long time to adjust to the new conditions of demand and supply.

The difference between a stable and an unstable equilibrium can be illustrated with two balls: one made of hard rubber, the other made of soft putty. If you squeeze the rubber ball out of shape, it bounces back to its original form. However, if you squeeze the ball made of putty, it remains out of shape. The former illustrates a stable equilibrium and the latter an unstable equilibrium.

Now consider a shock to the system. The shock can be shown either by a shift in the supply curve, or a shift in the demand curve, or a shift in both curves.

Any shock to the system will produce a new set of supply and demand relationships and a new equilibrium. Forces will come into play to move the system from the old price-quantity equilibrium to a new one. A perfect example is provided by the financial crisis that caused the property market to collapse in 2008 and 2009. House prices fell so far that those who became unemployed and were carrying 100% mortgages could not even sell their house to cover the debt – in the jargon, there were cases of **negative equity**. The house price bubble had popped, and the prices collapsed; across several countries, it took years for the market to recover, with various implications. Financial institutions became more wary of 100% mortgages, and deposits of 25% and 30% became a common requirement. As a consequence, there were more people struggling to get on the housing ladder, and more young people were reported to be still living at home with their parents.

This happened right across Europe as markets adjusted. In Sweden, they even coined a new word that combines *bo* (the Swedish for 'to live') and *sambo* (cohabit) into *mambo*, to live with your mum. In trying to avoid exacerbating these situations any further, the central banks tended to push down long-term interest rates to new lows. Keeping interest rates at ridiculously low levels for several years created the fear that, when they rise, there will be more – new – trouble ahead. Another outcome was that private rents increased, and fewer new properties were built, as developers were hesitant to build until they were confident that the market had recovered. These scenarios paint a picture of what can happen while markets adjust.

To assess whether house prices are sustainable, there are several ratios and benchmarks, such as the loan-to-value ratio monitored by the central banks (see Chapter 5), the ratio of house prices to rents monitored by businessmen seeking to compare returns in different markets and, of course, **affordability**, measured by the ratio of house prices to income per person after tax. Such ratios are monitored by the *Economist* house price indicators [2] that track the health of housing markets across all continents by making a regular assessment of 26 national markets. When the gauges are higher than their historical averages, property is deemed overvalued; if they are lower, it is undervalued.

According to the set of indicators produced in April 2015, houses were at least 25% overvalued in seven countries. Judged by rents, the most glaring examples were Hong Kong, Canada and Australia; judged by income, the most worrying were Japan, China and South Korea. The overshoot in these economies and others bears an unhappy resemblance to that prevailing in Britain at the height of its boom before the crisis. Furthermore, the 2015 data suggested that there were still eight countries where house prices remained below the 2008 peak – namely Ireland, Spain, Italy, Greece, France, Japan, United States and the Netherlands.

## Property markets

In the years leading up to the Great Recession, mainstream economists taught that markets 'clear' continuously. The logic behind this theory was that, providing wages, prices and rents were completely flexible, then resources (as defined in Chapter 1) will always be fully employed. Any shock to the system would result in a relatively quick adjustment of wages and prices to the new situation.

This notion of a stable equilibrium is now being challenged, but it certainly does not apply to markets dealing in property. That includes the housing market, the construction market, the market for rented commercial property, the market for student accommodation, the retail market, and so on.

In fact, it is essential that, before going any further, it is made abundantly clear that there is not just one market for property, but many. For example, the buyers and sellers of industrial buildings, office blocks, houses and retail units are brought together in totally separate markets to determine exchange details. Hence, each submarket operates differently, at different yields, and in different geographical areas. As John Lanchester (2014: 241) humorously pointed out: 'the property value in the sleepy Surrey suburb of Edenbridge is worth more than the whole of the Glasgow area added together'.

In short, there is no single market for commercial property or residential property. There are, in fact, several, determined by location, size, age, accessibility, design type, function and, ultimately, price! Property may be traded at auction or negotiated by estate agents and surveyors. The important point is that, at any one time, there will be a multitude of property transactions taking place at different locations and at different prices.

## Property characteristics

As suggested in Chapter 1, property has a unique set of characteristics that sets it apart from all other economic goods. First and foremost, each unit, or structure, tends to be different – in the jargon of market economists, units of property are rarely 'homogenous'. The most obvious distinction is that property always comprises two elements – the land itself and a man-made structure. This has several implications, not least the existence of a separate parcel of land (and hence location) for each property that comes to market. This means that each property will vary in quality – ranging crudely from urban land to rural land – but is always distinguished by accessibility, physical attributes and planning controls. In short, all developments are different.

Also, because of its durability, there is a big market for existing property and a much smaller market for new builds. We also know that, in the UK, about half of the total stock of commercial property is owned by investors who receive rent paid by occupiers in return for the use of property. The other half own the property that they occupy, but we can assume that the price or value of each property asset is the capitalised value of rent that would be paid if the property were owned as an investment. This means that we can focus our economic analysis of price determination in the property market on rental values, and assume that capital values bear a relation to these.

Next, we need to consider the complexity of the market. Property is only available for purchase in relatively large, indivisible and expensive units, so financing plays a significant role in market activity. For example, whereas a listed security can be purchased in a matter of seconds, acquiring property involves coordinating a wide range of range of activities that inevitably stretches over a number of months at best, and often a number of years. Indeed, the term 'appraisal' is often associated with the process of buying or renting a property, and this signals the wide number of considerations that each specific investor would need to review before the transaction in a property is complete. In other words, the complex amount of information that is required to close a property deal accounts for the long time they take to transact, and why they are rarely traded as quickly or as frequently as other goods and services.

In a nutshell, property assets can be described by two odd terms: 'lumpy' and 'illiquid'. Following a debt crisis, vendors of real estate will often reduce the asking price of their property several times in rapid succession, in an attempt to free up the market. For example, the fire sales that took place across 2007 to 2008 to reduce mortgage debts caused the house price bubble to deflate rapidly.

The characteristics of complexity, durability, and heterogeneity inevitably make real estate transactions difficult and costly. As a consequence, when property prices experience a crisis, it takes some time to re-establish stability in the market.

## Stock exchange analogy

The level of efficiency between one market and the next is largely determined by the standardisation of the product and the degree of formality in which it functions. The stock market in any Western economy, for example, provides instant information about the prices and quantities of shares being bought and sold during the current trading period. By contrast, property markets tend to be more informal, less structured, more diverse, and determined by geographical location; in many ways, each property market transaction can be regarded as unique. It is for this reason alone that much of a surveyor's work seems to focus on commercial property.

This is not because the housing market lacks activity – far from it – but the valuation of residential property is relatively easy, as often some kind of comparison is available between similar styles in the same area, whereas it is far more difficult to employ a comparative method for commercial property. To continue the analogy with the stock market: one ordinary share in a company is just like any other ordinary share in that company, but no two properties owned by that company could be treated as identical in terms of location, structure, and lease. In short, property– particularly commercial property – cannot be regarded as a standardised investment.

Secondly, property can never be regarded as a pre-packaged investment. If you buy shares, the management runs the company, produces the profits and pays the dividends. If you own a property, however, you will need to manage it yourself, or pay someone to do so on your behalf. Indeed, active management can add value by buying in leases, refurbishing or even redeveloping the structure itself.

Thirdly, the price at which property transactions take place is not always made public, as there is usually some confidentiality associated with rents paid and the final settlement price that is agreed after the property has come to market. Worse still, it is not unknown for a certain amount of disinformation to be fed to the press to improve confidence and overall market performance. In other words, the quantity and quality of property information is not as transparent or as freely available as that relating to stocks and shares.

To conclude, in comparison to other markets, property markets are relatively complex, in the sense that buyers and sellers rarely come together and simply strike a quick bargain, as they usually need to get agents with local knowledge to act on their behalf and provide independent valuations to verify the transactions. There is room for pricing errors, with price and value diverging by as much as 15%, particularly in the commercial markets. The reasons for the greater margins of error are the level of heterogeneity and infrequent rates of trading in a specific local market. The RICS debate relating to the subtle distinctions between 'market price', 'market value' and 'worth' are picked up in valuations texts such as Wyatt (2014). Finally, to compound the complexity, a wide variety of other factors also influence property transactions, such as finance, planning laws and fiscal considerations.

## Property is not like a sack of potatoes: a summary

The list of characteristics makes it abundantly clear that commercial and residential property are atypical products. For example, housing certainly does not respond like other economic goods and services. As Danny Dorling (2014), Oxford Professor in Geography, likes to provocatively point out: 'Homes are not like potatoes. You can't suddenly flood the market and watch the price come down.' Dorling believes the problem is distribution. Some people have too little, because others have too much. The solution, therefore, in his view, is not to increase housing supply but to redistribute the housing stock that is already there. To put it crudely: to kick the rich out of their houses, and put the poor into them.

This is not, however, how a market systems work – although Dorling's argument does support the Royal Institution of Chartered Surveyors' proposal to exempt people over 65 from stamp duty when they downsize from a large family property to a smaller one. This is a difficult problem, and only rehearsed here to highlight how, as people live longer and incomes become less equally distributed, markets struggle to resolve social issues and allocate resources efficiently without some scale of government intervention.

## The basic requirements of life

The introduction to the characteristics of property has highlighted some of the complexity of interpreting market signals and the problematic nature of achieving an efficient allocation of property resources. Markets, however, are all-embracing, as we need a system to allocate: homes for shelter; retail outlets for goods and services; office, factory and warehouse premises for commercial activities; and various forms of infrastructure (e.g. schools, hospitals, power stations and so on) to support the common good. As we have suggested above, each of these property market sectors are unique, and are largely atypical from markets for other economic goods and services. However, this does not preclude the notion of a market system from being a useful and relevant part of a surveyor's economic toolkit.

We have to start somewhere as a basis for understanding property markets, and it seems self-evident that changes in supply and demand do influence the overall value of land and property. In other words, the market concepts taught by mainstream economists provide an important starting-point, but they must be used selectively and shaped by the experience of the Great Recession. Although mainstream economics may no longer produce all the answers, it will become apparent that, from working through the consequences of the market processes, you will be better equipped to structure analysis and reach important conclusions.

The attraction of the neoclassical approach is that it breaks phenomena down to the individual level and provides a precise framework and logic that can be applied across a significant number of markets, but its theoretical strength is also its downfall. As Ha-Joon Chang (2011: 253), a critic of free market systems, expressed it: 'the market is an exceptionally effective mechanism … but it is no more than that – a mechanism, a machine. And like all machines it needs careful regulation and steering.' With these qualifying remarks in mind, demand and supply analysis can be used to provide a good introductory basis from which budding surveyors can mature. Therefore, in the broader interests of understanding property markets, demand and supply are basic building blocks and we dedicate a section to each of them – it will certainly do you no harm – but if you have been here before and cannot stand the pain of going through all this again, then jump to the section commencing with the heading *Know Your Markets* on page xx.

## The basics of demand

Whenever economists speak of demand, they refer to '*effective demand*'. Effective demand is money-backed desire; it does not refer to the demands of a crying baby, or of a spoilt child wanting and grabbing at everything it sees. Demand analysis focuses on how much is being spent on specific items, and how that demand may alter if its price changed. In other words, demand from an economist's point of view is real, 'genuine' demand, backed by the ability to make a purchase. It is distinct from need. For example, in 2015, the total number of households needing accommodation exceeded the total number of homes in the housing market. Only those who had sufficient means to 'demand' accommodation – that is, they could afford to buy or rent at market prices – were confident of securing somewhere to live.

This anomaly partly explains why more than 11 million homes lie empty across Europe – enough to provide a choice of house for all of the continent's homeless, estimated at 4.1 million. More than half of the empty properties were in Spain and France, often in holiday resorts built during the feverish housing boom that ran up to the 2008 financial crisis. On top of this bizarre allocation of resources is the fact that many of the properties were bought as investments – and never fully occupied!

In fact, there is currently a whole new market emerging in London, funded by investors from China, Malaysia, Singapore, Sweden and Russia, who are seeking to 'buy-to-leave' – or, as the press like to brand it '30 000 homes acting as safe deposit boxes'. This problem of allocation qualifies the meaning and significance of effective demand as, in many cases, housing is seen an asset rather than a place to live, while millions of poor people remain dependent on state housing benefits. Even more shocking is the report that thousands of half-built homes have been bulldozed during the Great Recession to shore up the prices of existing properties In short, free market dynamics are pricing those who need shelter out of the market (Neate, 2014)!

*The law of demand*

As established above, in Figure 3.2, a demand curve has a negative slope. It moves downward from left to right, and this shape is self-explanatory when one considers the basic **law of demand**. The law states that, at a high price, a lower quantity will be demanded than at a low price (and vice versa), other things being equal. In other words, the quantity demanded of a product is inversely related to that product's price (again, other things being equal).

To be able to use this law, however, we must consider the 'other things being equal' phrase carefully. Clearly, demand is not only affected by price, but by a host of other factors as well. Changes in the conditions of a market may change significantly, enough to cause consumers to change the quantity demanded regardless of price. For instance, focus on the demand curve in Figure 3.2 and imagine that it represents the demand for a specific type of property. What events may cause more or less demand for that product at every price?

As implied above the determination of demand for property is a complicated process, determined by size, cost, government policy, level of income, expectations, longevity and the investment quality of the building. Just how complex markets can get will become clearer as we consider more carefully the factors affecting demand for housing and commercial property.

## Demand for housing

There are more than 26 million households in the UK, and a significant majority of them can afford to demand a home. It is important to remember, however, that at any point in time there is always a minority that cannot afford a home. As the introductory point about **effective demand** emphasised, a distinction should be made between 'need' and 'demand'. Each household requires: a flat, a bungalow, a terraced house, a maisonette, a semi-detached house, or at the very least some kind of shelter. In most cases, the related resources are allocated through the market mechanism, the public sector, or through a mix of the two. As a consequence, it is difficult to envisage just one housing market, and professional surveyors tend to discuss the housing market using four sectors, as follows:

1.  *The owner-occupied sector* – made up of households that ultimately own their properties, once they have paid off a related mortgage.
2.  *The private rented sector* – comprising private property that is let at a market rent deemed 'fair' to tenants and landlords.
3.  *The registered social landlord sector* – made up of property that is managed by non-profit-making organisations that combine public and private funds to provide housing for those in need.
4.  *The local authority rented sector* – made up of housing stock made available by the local authority (council) at a subsidised rate from public funds.

These four sectors have been listed in order of size. In general terms, however, it is sufficient to understand that housing demand is either for owner occupation, or rent, or for some combination of the two, via shared equity organised by a housing association, or some similar arrangement to make the market 'affordable'. The next sections consider the main factors determining demand for housing within each of these sub-markets.

### Demand for owner-occupied housing

Most households in America, Australasia and much of Europe want homes to own and occupy, and around 65% of residential property in the UK reside in this form of tenure. The equivalent sizes of the owner-occupied sectors in Spain, Ireland and Finland are even larger. This form of ownership is often supported by government initiatives to encourage demand, by making the process of home buying as fast, transparent and as consumer-friendly as possible. For example, across much of Europe, America, and the Nordic states, there is a strong tradition of tax incentives for owner occupation, usually paid in the form of a subsidy on mortgage interest payments. In the UK, however, **Mortgage interest tax relief**, as it is generally referred to, has not been offered since 2000. Regardless of mortgage subsidies and the economic downturn in 2008 (which led to reduced mortgage availability and stricter lending criteria), there continues to be something of an obsession about home ownership on both sides of the Atlantic.

The logic behind governments providing incentives (such as allowing homeowners to deduct interest payments on mortgages from their taxable income) and benefits (such as the 'Help to Buy' scheme) to support owner occupation is that if people own the property they occupy, they will maintain it better. Furthermore, the feel-good factor derived from ownership makes the transaction costs of choosing and funding worthwhile, especially as a house provides an investment as well as a shelter.

As you can imagine, there are, in fact, several factors that determine the demand for privately owned housing, and in Table 3.2 the main ones are identified.

### Demand for privately rented housing

Since the economic downturn in 2008, there has been a marked increase in the number of households in the UK seeking to rent a property from a private landlord. The rise in demand in this sector is a direct result of the increased value of

**Table 3.2**  Demand factors for owner-occupied housing

The current price of housing
The price of other forms of housing
Income and expectations of change
Cost of borrowing money and expectations of change
Government measures, such as stamp duty
Demographic factors, such as the number of households
Price of associated goods and services, such as maintenance, furniture, council tax, insurance, etc.

the deposits that need to be paid to secure a mortgage. Gone are the days when one could get a 100% mortgage (loan) to buy a house. In 2009, for instance, first-time buyers had to find 28% of the house price as a deposit to secure a mortgage. Since that time, deposits to commence on the housing ladder have begun to decline slightly but, seven years after the downturn, the scale of expected deposits continues to be at historically high levels of more than 20%. As a consequence, home ownership among the younger age groups has declined considerably. Another contributing factor to the increase in demand for private rented property is the decrease in average household size (nowadays more than 30% of households in the UK consist of only one person), so renting is often a realistic option in a time of high house prices. As the press continually suggest, *Generation Rent* is here to stay.

At present, around 20% of UK households live in privately rented accommodation – double the number that were living in this market sector at the beginning of the millennium. However, this is still low by comparison to some European countries, where as many as 40% of households live in private rented accommodation. In general, therefore, the market for private rented accommodation varies greatly from country to country, and from time to time, for a number of cultural and economic reasons. The main economic factors affecting the demand in this sector are listed in Table 3.3.

## Demand for social housing

Housing rented from local authorities and registered social landlords, such as housing associations, is generally referred to as social housing, although there is a current trend to regard this whole sector as '**affordable housing**' – which implies that it is available at a subsidised rate. The origins of social housing lie in the idea that governments should provide rented accommodation at a rate that is below the market rate, to make up for the shortage of accommodation available to low-income families. However, in the UK during the 1980s and 1990s – with both Conservative and Labour governments favouring free-market policies – much of the local authority housing stock was transferred to housing associations to allocate, manage and maintain or sold to tenants, thereby transferring stock to the owner-occupied sector. Similar processes have been experienced in other countries such as Russia, China, Czechoslovakia and Poland, where privatisation of the housing stock has been a key feature of the transition process from a centralised command economy towards a free market.

Regardless, the local authority and registered social landlord sectors still represents 'home' for around five million households (i.e. slightly less than 20% of the total

**Table 3.3**   Demand factors for privately rented housing

Current rent levels and expectations of change
The price of owner occupation
Income distribution, which determines affordability
The cost of borrowing and expectations of change
The law on rents and security of tenure
Demographic factors, such as household formation

**Table 3.4**   Demand factors for social housing

The current rent (price of social housing)
The price level of other forms of tenure
Assessment of need
Availability of finance, such as benefits and mortgages
Levels of government subsidy

UK residential stock). The more significant problem, however, is the fact that the demands for property in this sector far exceed the supply, with a similar number (around 4–4.5 million) on waiting lists. As a result, much of the subsidy that flows to those on low income comes in the form of a housing benefit that helps tenants to pay rent to landlords wherever they find accommodation and, at times, it might become necessary to include bed and breakfast residences. The factors that determine the demand for social housing are markedly different from those driving demand for owner-occupied and privately rented housing. The main ones are listed in Table 3.4.

### Demand model for housing

The factors affecting demand in the various sectors of the housing market set out in Tables 3.2 to 3.4 suggest some general themes. For example, it seems that the recurring determinants of demand are the price (rent) of a property, the price of other forms of tenure, the level of income, and government policy. Economists can, therefore, state a generalised model for the analysis of housing markets. The model is set up in such a way that it can equally apply to any sector of the housing market. It is typically presented in the form of a general equation, as follows:

$$Qd = f\,(Pn, Pn-1, Y, G, Z)$$

This model is formally referred to as a **demand function**. It may look complicated, but it is only a form of shorthand notation. The demand function represents, in symbols, everything we have discussed above.

It states that Qd, the quantity demanded (in our example a specific type of housing) is equal to f, a function of all the things listed inside the bracket: Pn, the price, or rent, of a property; Pn-1, the price of other forms of tenure; Y, income; G, government policy; and Z, a host of other things. Remember, this type of equation may be adapted and extended as necessary to analyse the demand of any specific good, service or asset.

## Demand for commercial property

The first, and most important, point to note when thinking about the demand for buildings to support commercial ventures such as shops, offices, restaurants, pubs, warehouses, factories and so on, is that none of the buildings are required solely for their own sake, but for the services they provide. Consequently, demand

**Table 3.5**   Factors affecting demand for commercial property

The rent or price level
Location, nature and size of property
The state of the economy and government policy
Business expectations regarding profits and turnover
Level of technology

for commercial property is based on factors related to the specific sector in which the building will be used. Demand of this type is known as **derived demand**.

Derived demand emphasises that commercial property is rented or purchased not because it gives satisfaction, but because the property can be used to produce goods or services that can be sold at a profit. This is different from the factors affecting the demand to buy a house. For example, in the months following the September 2001 terrorist attack on the World Trade Centre in New York, global business confidence was dented and the demand for commercial property in the UK declined considerably (but during the same period, the demand for housing experienced a boom).

The factors affecting demand for commercial buildings are therefore dependent on the state of the economy and on business expectations concerning output and profit. In other words, because demand is derived, it is dependent on many things other than price. Some of the general factors of demand for commercial property are shown in Table 3.5.

## *Demand model for commercial property*

Adopting a similar approach to the analysis of the demand for housing, a model can be derived for commercial property. It would seem from the above analysis that the quantity demanded of commercial property can be generalised as follows. The quantity demanded, Qd, is a function of rent (price), R; the state of the economy, E; expectations regarding output, Eo; and the amount of space required per employee, shopper or service user, Sreq. Expressed in the form of an equation, the demand function for commercial property could be stated as follows:

$$Qd = f\,(R, E, Eo, Sreq)$$

# Demand for government property

The demand for community-oriented facilities, such as power stations, railways, roads, tunnels, bridges, hospitals, schools, prisons, museums, police and fire stations, can be judged on a similar basis to commercial buildings: price (or rent), state of public finance, political expectations, and space requirements, and so on. However, assessing the demand for these products is more complex, as the associated floor space may not generate a sufficient income flow to justify the investment; the value placed on public (collective) goods is largely subjective. The demand, therefore, is largely a political decision, dependent on an assessment

**Table 3.6**  Factors affecting demand for government property

Assessment of future and present need
Availability of public finance
Government policy
The age and condition of existing stock
Civic pride
Changes in technology

of need and the funds available. Some of the demand variables for the broad area of public goods that provide the essential physical and social fabric on which modern society relies are summarised in Table 3.6. In considering these factors, one can begin to sense the difficulties of choosing between society's competing needs and deciding which should be transferred into effective demand.

## The basics of supply

The number of property units supplied to any market at any one time, for rent or purchase, depends on existing and newly completed stock. As a very general rule of thumb, the latter represents approximately 1% of the total stock in any one year! For example, in 2008, the stock of housing increased by 0.7% and commercial property increased by 0.7%; in 2014, the respective figures were 0.5% and 0.8%. Even in a boom year with relatively high levels of completions, the total increase of supply of property rarely exceeds 2%.

As a result, at any one particular time period, the stock of property available for supply to the market, compared to other goods and services, is relatively fixed. We have already introduced the time-consuming process of bringing a large commercial development from the initial appraisal stage to completion in the market. You may well remember, from the case study in Chapter 2, that 22 Bishopsgate commenced in 2001 but is not expected to be ready for occupation until 2018. Seventeen years might seem like a long time for the development of a large commercial high rise building, but it is not that unusual. To increase the supply of new commercial property (offices, shops and warehouses) takes years; and in one locality, new additions would rarely exceed 50 units a year. The obvious – but important – point is that the majority of the property supplied in both residential and commercial markets already exists – it is second-hand.

To put this into context, you just need to compare the annual number of property transactions [3] to the number of completions [4]. During a buoyant economic period, such as the one before the Great Recession, up to two million properties could exchange hands in a year and, of these, approximately one-tenth (200 000) would be newly completed. In 2014, the ratio of old to new was similar, but there were fewer transactions – one and a quarter million to be precise. Also of note is the fact that in most years, more than 90% of the transactions relate to the residential market – although, in value terms, the relatively few commercial transactions that take place are far higher. In a typical year, they account for something in the region of 25% of the total market.

A further distinguishing characteristic of supply worth noting is that the majority of residential property is speculatively developed, in the sense that it is built (supplied 'on spec') without a specific purchaser (or tenant) being identified. In contrast, commercial property is increasingly being developed for a named tenant; it is 'pre-let' or 'bespoke' (for sale or rent). The sharpest contrast between these two sectors, however, is in the pattern of ownership; the majority of houses are owner-occupied, whereas commercial property is often rented by businesses on long-term contracts.

## The law of supply

The general idea of supply has already been introduced. In Figure 3.2, we explained that the **supply curve** slopes upwards from left to right, demonstrating that, in principle, as price rises, the quantity supplied rises and, conversely, as price falls, the quantity supplied falls. The law of supply, therefore, can be expressed as the opposite of the relationship stated for demand: namely that the higher the price, the greater the quantity offered for sale, and the lower the price, the smaller the quantity offered for sale, all other things being held constant. In other words, the **law of supply**, tells us that the quantity supplied of a product is positively (directly) related to that product's price, other things being equal.

The incentives – and the constraints – within a specific property market are roughly the same for all suppliers. Each individual developer seeks to maximise their profits, and each firm is subject to constraints imposed by its size, its land bank, its access to finance, and planning requirements.

# The stock of housing

To complete the portrait of the housing market, we need to continue the case study that we began in the demand section at the beginning of this chapter, and take a detailed look at the supply side of this specific sector (in theory, we need to get behind the market supply schedule – the curve introduced above and portrayed in Figure 3.2 – to understand how a specific market basically operates).

Much of the statistical information is provided by the National Home Building Council (NHBC) and the Office for National Statistics (ONS). Over the past 20 years, the number of active firms building houses has fallen from around 12 000 to 4000, mainly due to a substantial loss of small firms. For example, in the house building industry in 2014, there were eight large private companies in Britain – in descending order of size, Taylor Wimpey, Barratt, Persimmon, Bellway, Redrow, Bovis, Crest Nicholson and Berkeley – who, between them, supplied up to 50% of the annual output. At the other end of the spectrum there were around 3000 small house builders – defined as those building fewer than 100 homes a year – who supplied around 15% of the annual output. In between these two extremes were a small number (and the data suggests less than 40 in total) of medium-sized firms that had the capacity to build more than 500 homes per year, and they supplied something like 25% of the market. The remaining supply was made up of self-builds and one-offs that typically account for up to 10% of the completed units in the UK each year.

Fred Wellings, an historian of the UK house building sector, has made a detailed account of the transition from small localised housebuilders that dominated the 1930s to the large national housebuilders of today, and his work confirms that the number of builders supplying houses has declined markedly in the last 50 years. This decline has been through consolidations, closures, mergers and acquisitions, often following a period of recession. As a consequence, the number of houses that are built each year seems to have reduced. Interestingly, Wellings suggests that this predicament is entirely due to poor understanding of the market in terms of managing the stock and work in progress. As his research concluded: 'There has been not one suggestion that firms have declined or failed because they have been left behind technologically, that their product has been the cause of failure ... It was not a quality or technological issue; *house builders failed because they misjudged the market*' (Wellings, 2006: 245). In other words, they got the numbers wrong.

So, coming back to the idea of a market supply of housing, for decades after World War II, UK housebuilders supplied more than 300 000 new units a year. In stark contrast, the industry today seems hard pushed to supply half of that number. Figure 3.4 shows the precise long-term downward trend since 1970.

From the graph in Figure 3.4, it is clear that the number of new houses supplied across the UK, has steadily tumbled from 378 000 in 1970 to 141 000 in 2014. This decline was despite government policy targets of more than 200 000 units per year. For instance, in 2004, the *Barker Review of Housing Supply* noted that about 240 000 homes needed to be built in the UK every year to prevent spiralling house prices and a shortage of affordable homes. Subsequently, this figure became a benchmark for the number of homes to be built each year in the UK.

Unfortunately, however, all housing targets have been missed. The closest the industry has come in recent years was just before the start of the Great Recession

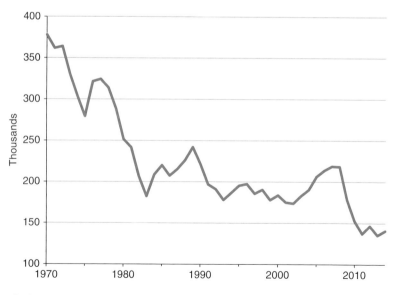

**Figure 3.4**   UK house building, 1970 to 2014.
*Source:* Department of Communities & Local Government.

in 2006 and 2007, when 214 000 and 219 000 units were produced in each respective year. In the wake of the financial crisis, however, from 2010 to 2014, output hit a post-war low with around 140 000 homes being built per year – little more than half the number required.

The shortfall was not only due to the financial crisis and the subsequent recession, but also due to the complex nature of the housing market. In economic terms, there is little the government can do to ease the mismatch between supply and demand. The supply side of the housing industry clearly has deep structural problems. As Mark Carney, governor of the Bank of England, cryptically observed in May 2014: 'We're not going to build a single house at the Bank of England and we can't influence that.' He went on to add that, surprisingly the UK, the annual rate of homebuilding was half that in his own country, Canada, despite the UK having a population twice the size (although Carney did not continue with the analogy by comparing the available land mass in each country, his remarks do reveal some of the tensions that exist between government targets and market outcomes). His comments certainly go some way in explaining what economists mean when they point out that the country is facing a supply-side crisis in house building, and why property prices are exceptionally high – particularly in London and the South East.

Furthermore, as we observed in Chapter 2, house builders are not in business to serve the public interest – except incidentally. Their primary concern is to deliver profits for their investors, both now and in the future – in short, to ensure that their business is a good investment. As a Government report, examining the delivery of housing, reminded us: 'Housebuilding executives are answerable to their investors, not to Ministers, the wider public or the central bank' (Callcutt, 2007: 4).

It follows, therefore, that Governments operating in market systems have limited options and are not in an easy position to place performance targets on housebuilders. Their only real choices relate to fiscal and monetary interventions, but these are more likely to put production at risk than to deliver the objective of growth.

In fear of stating the obvious, we need to conclude that residential property is supplied into various markets, for rent, ownership and investment purposes. Thus, while it may be theoretically possible to estimate construction supply by adding up what the firms in the market are willing to supply at various prices, the range of sub-markets in each geographical location significantly complicates the process. Also, as pointed out above, a further complication to add to the supply side mix is the large number of second-hand houses that are put on the market. It is probably best, therefore, to sum up by envisaging several discrete residential markets operating with distinct factors of supply within each specific geographical location.

To some extent, much of this mirrors the approach taken in the section on demand so, to complete the picture, we need to briefly overview two further sections detailing the supply – or, more precisely, the stock – of commercial and government property. Similar to housing, the supply in these two sectors is comprised of a significant number of existing properties (that might undergo refurbishment), set alongside a relatively small number of new developments. Remember, from our introduction to the basics of supply, as a general rule of thumb, additional (new) commercial-type property rarely exceeds one per cent of the stock per year.

In terms of evolution, this means it could take in the region of 100 years to replace the existing stock with modern equivalents.

This characteristic of longevity adds a further twist to the complexity of property markets. It also accounts for surveyors preferring the notion of 'stock' to 'supply', as 'stock' highlights that the lion's share of the market already exists, and is not necessarily determined solely by additional flows (or, in property parlance, newly completed developments). Such language encourages a focus on durability, adaptability and, most importantly, functionality. As they used to say in the design world, a building's credentials are based on 'form and function' or, as they prefer it nowadays, 'form and finance'. Either way, it is the available stock that shapes the market.

## Stock of commercial property

There are approximately two million existing commercial buildings in the UK, and the majority of these are rented. As an example, Table 3.7 shows the distribution of the stock of commercial property, derived from the Valuation Office Agency (VOA) rating list. As rates are collected on each commercial address in the country (in some cases, even when they are empty), the data provides a comprehensive picture of the stock of existing commercial property in England and Wales by use, size, and value (Scotland and Northern Ireland have slightly different systems).

Rateable value is based on a range of factors, including use, location and age, but the most important determinant is the size – the total floor space – of the property. It gets a bit complicated if a commercial property contains several units, such as on a business park or in a shopping mall, and the way the data is recorded is somewhat *ad hoc*. But the important objective is to recognise that every commercial property asset, regardless of its physical size or function, is categorised and included in the data shown in Table 3.7. In short, if it has a postcode, it is listed.

The data is divided into five broad categories and forms the basis of the **business rates** which are issued by local authorities. Thus, even units that lack physical presence, and are not buildings in the strictest sense, are included, as they are allocated a rateable value and form part of the commercial supply. The data

**Table 3.7**  Stock of commercial property in England and Wales

| Valuation office classifications | Floor space (000 s m²) | Number of units (hereditaments) | Rateable value (£ Million) |
|---|---|---|---|
| Retail | 118,151 | 560,000 | 17,488 |
| Offices | 92,720 | 356,000 | 14,092 |
| Industrial | 323,101 | 451,000 | 11,786 |
| Other | 41,798 | 146,000 | 2,804 |
| Excluded |  | 345,000 | 12,957 |
| **Total** | **575,770** | **1,858,000** | **59,126** |

*Source*: Adapted from *Business Floorspace (experimental Statistics)* VOA, 2012.

therefore includes unconventional premises that are not necessarily valued on floor space, such as buildings that serve the community – educational establishments (schools, colleges, and universities) hospitals, police stations and even odder commercial units, like advertising hoardings, ATMs, beach huts, car parks, war game courses and gypsy campsites. Rather confusingly, these are categorised as *excluded* in Table 3.7, but they are all subject to business rates. For a definitive list of the commercial property assets that make up the categories in Table 3.7, look at the release notes that accompanied the data (VOA, 2012).

For our immediate purposes, a closer look at Table 3.7 is worthwhile, as it broadly clarifies what is meant by the commercial stock of property, and it provides a snapshot picture of the scale involved. It distinguishes the total number of units (sometimes referred to as **hereditaments**), the total floor space and the total rateable value of commercial properties in England and Wales. Table 3.7 also reveals that industrial premises (factories and warehouses) account for most floor space, while retail units – which are subject to far higher business rates – are responsible for most of the rateable value. Finally, there is the bottom line that highlights that potentially £59 billion worth of additional business costs are associated with occupying commercial property.

The important point, which has already been raised in the respective section on demand, is that none of these buildings or structures are required for their own sake, but for the services they provide. Consequently, the demand and, in turn, the supply of commercial property is based on factors related to the specific sector in which the building will be used. The state of the economy will determine whether the risk is worth the cost of the rent, rates and so on. In other words, commercial properties are not worth developing unless they can be used to support a broad range of economic activities. This is different from the factors affecting the supply of residential property – unless, of course, it is part of a buy-to-let portfolio, in which case it will be subject to council rates and market assessment.

Investments in commercial property, therefore, depend on the expectation that the occupiers will make profits in the future. If business confidence is generally low, investment in new developments become difficult to arrange, as the factors affecting the supply of commercial buildings are largely dependent on the state of the economy, and business expectations. In short, supply is dependent on far more than price alone. For example, in the months and years following the bankruptcy of Lehman Brothers in September 2008, in New York in the United States, global business confidence was significantly dented and the demand for commercial property on all sides of the pond declined considerably.

Finally, as described in the opening pages of this chapter, the **new economy**, based on digital technology, has had a significant impact on the demand, and supply, of commercial space. The number of offices and warehouses supplied to the market has significantly increased, while high street stores have not. It was estimated that before the Great Recession, about 30% of the world's top companies employed 35% of their workforce outside the boundaries of the formal workspace. In other words, 'hot-desking', working from home, and 'click-and-collect' shopping via the internet had already begun to reduce the amount of desk space required per employee and the floor space needed per shopper. A decade later, the proportion of business and retail activities conducted over the internet has increased even further. In fact, we conclude the text by taking a specific look at the impact of technology on the High Street, and the economy generally, in the *Food for Thought* section of the final chapter.

## Stock of government buildings

In market-orientated economies (such as those of OECD countries), governments do not tend to develop properties for business ventures – commercial property development is largely a private sector activity. Government does, however, still own, manage and rent a significant amount of real estate to support its various functions. For instance, in the UK, there are more than 5000 buildings supporting the central government departments alone – the so-called civil estate – costing in the region of £3 billion per year. These facts exclude the military estate, the NHS estate, the rural estate and the Foreign and Commonwealth Office overseas estate which, when added together, dwarf the civil estate by a significant margin (for details, see State of the Estate [5]). As the commentary on Table 3.7 made explicit, the stock of commercial property includes that used by public sector agencies and departments. Therefore, government offices, community buildings, laboratories and museums and so on do make a significant call on a nation's property-based resources.

In this context, an interesting experiment began in Britain in January 2014, when the central government launched a web-based tool that mapped all its land and buildings, and set up a system inviting the general public (and that includes the developers of property) to suggest better uses of specific plots and buildings. Although each case would be arguable, it was hoped that this '*right to contest*' [6] would encourage a greater public debate about using property resources more efficiently and save the government funds. The government promised to release for sale any property where the current use could not be justified. Alongside this development, another website was also created the government property finder [7] to map and list assets available for sale or to let, as well as furthering the challenge of sites under the '*right to contest*' scheme. Obviously, historic assets like Downing Street or the Treasury were not going to be sold off, but the online tools do list everything from ambulance stations to vacant airfields. In fact, 13,911 different government property holdings are potentially up for grabs.

As observers of the British political scene will know, such schemes are part of an ongoing programme to cut back on government costs and get the most out of the resources they use. Similar government-led schemes are opening up across various states in America and Europe. Indeed it has been a clear UK Government intention since 2010 to sell off land and buildings, and get out of lease agreements on rentals where the property is no longer fully occupied. As a result, the stock of government buildings to date has decreased by 1250 buildings, the cost of running the government estate has reduced by £647 million, and £1.4 billion were received in capital receipts. Future plans, up until 2020, are targeted to save a further £6 billion through disposals, and reduce the amount of office space in the public sector down to an average of eight square metres per employee by 2018 (currently, public sector workers have around 16% more space per person than their private counterparts – i.e. a roomy 13 square metres per employee). Finally, the number of costly government buildings in central London is planned to fall from 143 in 2010 to 23 by 2020 (Cabinet Office, 2015).

*Development of a nation's building stock*

As we have seen, the supply of real estate is not as straightforward as the elementary textbook theory suggests. As the description of the UK building stock has implied, there are several complicating factors that delay change. Property is always fixed in location, expensive to demolish and long-lasting. This sluggish system is exacerbated by the institutional arrangements for funding via mortgages and loans alongside the conventions of long leases in the commercial sector. As a consequence, property markets are slower to adjust than most other market sectors. As a general rule, as property prices, or their rents, increase, the quantity supplied, in the short run, does not alter!

To put it another way, price movements in property markets do not affect the immediate available supply. The stock of property is slow to change, and supply can be described using the technical jargon as **perfectly inelastic**; that is, the quantity of property supplied is fixed, regardless of changes in price. In other words, in the short run, the same quantity of property exists regardless, of the level of rent or prices achieved. This should not imply that the stock of property is not allocated by a broadly competitive system; it is simply stated to make a clear distinction between short run and long run time horizons in the development of real estate. The short run is defined in economics as any period when at least one factor of production is fixed, so a change in price cannot lead to a change in the supply of real estate. In the long run, all factors are variable, so adjustments can be made to changing market conditions.

In the short run, however, rental values and property prices are demand determined. In fact, it is the inelastic supply relative to demand that causes property markets to be unstable and characterised by fluctuating prices. In technical terms, at any one specific time period, the supply of buildings is fixed and the supply curve is a vertical line. This scenario is demonstrated in Figure 3.5. This shows that the quantity supplied during a three-month period is the same, regardless of price. For any percentage change in price, the quantity supplied remains constant.

Hence, regardless what mainstream economics textbooks suggest, it is obvious that there is no unique precise price for property set by the market; there is only a range of possibilities. The ballpark figure that the surveyor estimates is usually as good as it gets. The value of each property will depend on timing, quality, location, its age, the client's requirements, and a confident recognition that the surveyor appreciates the monopolistic element pertaining to each unit of real estate.

## Supply and non-price determinants

So far, we have conducted the discussion of supply on the assumption that only price changes. We have not effectively considered any other determinants that might influence a developer's behaviour. We have employed the *ceteris paribus* qualification – a methodological convention that assumes that 'other things' are held constant. Some of the 'other things' in a developer's world are the costs of construction, technology, government policy, the weather, the price of related goods, expectations, developments that are in the pipeline, and so on. Indeed,

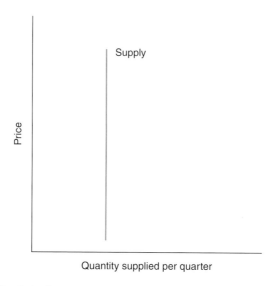

Figure 3.5    Perfectly inelastic supply.

there are many non-price determinants that affect supply. An interesting one that is not usually mentioned in mainstream texts, but is particularly relevant to real estate, are the institutional arrangements.

## Institutional arrangements

Property development involves integrating and managing a whole host of activities and processes before the final product can be delivered. A development pipeline, from finding a site and gaining planning permission, through to managing the sale or rent of the property, has already been presented in Chapter 2 (see Figure 2.1), but the purpose of this section is to highlight the significance of private property rights and the associated legal and financial frameworks that form an essential prerequisite for markets to work. As Professor Lee Alston (2008) has observed: 'it is the impact of institutions via property rights and transaction costs that ultimately affect the ability of individuals and societies to extract the gains from trade and enhance wellbeing'. In short, without contractual conventions, property development would be impossible in a market economy.

During the last decade, this **institutional model** has captured the imagination of property economists as an explanation of the supply side of property markets, by focusing on the customs, norms and regulations that prevail. As such, the model recognises the importance of the legislative, financial, political and cultural norms that influence the ways in which the property sector operates. Clearly, such institutional characteristics vary from one generation to the next, and can form the basis of an account for the changing nature of the supply of property.

For example, in the mid-1980s, banks, building societies and insurance companies began to compete in each other's markets, and the competition that ensued increased the flow of funds that were available for investment into property. Subsequently, this trend spread to the international financial network, and the flow of funds supporting commercial and residential development acquired an increasingly international character. To a large extent, these changes to the codes of practice of financial institutions increased the rate of transactions for homes and commercial property through the nineties and into the mid-noughties. In theoretical terms, this historical period could be represented by a supply curve shifting to the right, as more was supplied at each and every price. Then the sudden financial hiatus that brought about the current crisis arrived, and left markets generally struggling to find a new equilibrium.

Another example of changes to institutional arrangements that we should briefly overview is the standard commercial lease. For economic purposes (although it will be no doubt be raised by the valuation and law lecturers), we simply need to understand that, until quite recently, most commercial property was let for a fixed period of 25 years, with upward-only rent reviews every five years. This arrangement allows owners a surety of income and occupiers long-term commitment, but it is not particularly market-sensitive. At present, however, there is a marked shortening of the lease length. As a consequence of this change, the proportion of firms with leases coming to an end will increase, and the market will see more firms seeking to relocate.

For example, when the typical lease was 25 years, it could be assumed that every year, one in 25 companies was seeking to review the terms of their lease and possibly relocate. However, the typical lease is now nearer eight years in length, so in any year we should see one in eight companies seeking to review their contract. In short, there is in the region of three times more potential activity in the commercial property market today than there was ten years ago. The emerging field of new institutional economics emphasises that, in order to understand the supply of property, we need to consider many related markets.

## Know your markets

As we have made clear, market behaviour is all to do with interpreting supply and demand. Remember, however, that traditional microeconomics seeks to promote a unified theory to cover everything. But a surveyor working in a specific area should know the local property market better than an academic economist – even if they are based in the same town! The textbook model works from the premise of understanding a generalised, perfectly competitive national market, presented as an idealised picture where all is well and fair but, in reality, those people employed in business need to be able to interpret a specific imperfect local market, where the number of players is limited. The modern surveyor, therefore, needs to take the theories and laws with a pinch of salt, remembering that the new approach does not claim to offer hard and fast rules. The principles of economics need to be adapted to understand a specific market, and then they provide powerful insights. In the language of new economics: the notion of a competitive property market is a useful approximation of how markets actually behave (Stevens, 2015).

To take an odd, but interesting example: 'Airbnb', an American internet firm that specialises in linking 'hosts' (property owners wanting to let their home) and 'guests' (those looking for a place to stay) needed to achieve an equilibrium – to get supply and demand lined up. The initial problem facing the firm was that New

York and San Francisco were so popular with visitors that there was a shortage of supply of property owners wanting to let their home. In other words, the number of hosts on the books fell short of demand. Facebook adverts, targeted locally, were used to boost supply. Boston and Portland, on the other hand, had plenty of willing hosts but little demand. Google ads, targeted at people thought likely to visit these cities, lifted the demand.

Even with supply and demand theoretically in balance, though, the market still did not work. The hosts – who, to be fair, were homeowners rather than professional renters or hoteliers – found themselves playing an unfamiliar role. It took the employment of a new breed of economist to nudge the supply to meet the demand. Analysis of online behaviour showed that some hosts were better market players than others. Interrogating the data economists discovered that the quality of photos of a host's abode was a key factor in them renting it out to the guests searching on line. Therefore, 'Airbnb' decided to draw from its economic tool box and offer a free professional photography service to *all* those listing available accommodation, reasoning that better market information would make the business work better. The firm has gone from strength to strength; it began trading in 2008 in America, and it now offers it services globally, listing more than one million properties across more than 34,000 cities in 190 countries (a good business, as both hosts and guests pay service fees).

In adapting products to match supply and demand, this new breed of economists used data and economic ideas to understand the actual behaviour in the market place. While they are too busy to realise it, such firms are also providing the best defence of economics against its critics. Far from being unrealistic and out of touch, the behavioural economist input at 'Airbnb' has helped to improve the efficiency of the market, the way the firm works and the profits it reaps.

## Do markets work?

To complete our introductory overview of basic supply and demand concepts, we need to recognise the existence of **market failure**. The standard textbook approach emphasises that the market provides the best means of allocating resources and, at the introductory level, market distortions are often overlooked. For example, it is commonly assumed that labour moves freely to wherever work is most profitable, and consumers buy whatever they desire in freely determined markets. Yet, in reality, monopolies, oligopolies, upward-only rent reviews, irrational behaviours, immobility, subsidies, trades unions, externalities, high transaction costs and other market imperfections all distort the situation. In the following two sections, we examine three complicating issues that are pertinent to property and the ways their markets work, namely planning restrictions, fiscal charges and moral sentiment.

## Planning boundaries and fiscal rules

Fiscal matters and land use regulations are complications that distort free markets. This is particularly problematical, as fiscal and planning rules tend to restrict the supply of land and raise its cost, so the price of floor space increases and economic activity and welfare are affected. To state some quaint examples, there are strict rules in London that prevent new structures from blocking certain views of St Paul's Cathedral. As it is expressed in the legislation, eight separate 'view corridors' of St Paul's Cathedral (both foreground and background) are protected from building above 55 metres. Equally, there are 'Conservation Areas' that limit changes to the external appearance of buildings, and there are 'plot ratios' controlling the total size of buildings relative to the size of the site. There are even regulations affecting the design of buildings which limit height and space within them.

Inevitably, such regulations impose additional costs. In fact according to research by Cheshire and Hilber (2008), the build costs of office space can increase by as much as 800% in London's West End, where there are many conservation areas, height restrictions and individually listed buildings, to 70% in Belgium, which is well known to have a flexible land use regulation system. Obviously, if the various regulatory limits on building heights and density were relaxed, fewer plots of land would be needed to satisfy the current level of demand.

Similarly, it has become common practice to impose taxes and duties on the value of land and property. Several examples exist in each rich country. In the UK, for instance, there are business rates that are charged on all commercial property (as described above), and council tax (the residential equivalent of business rates) and stamp duty (which are discussed at length in Chapter 7). There are also indirect, or 'shadow' taxes on land development, such as the developer's contributions to social housing that were detailed in the previous chapter. The idea of taxing the windfall income that accrues from land ownership when it is developed can be traced back to the 19th Century, when David Ricardo discussed **economic rent**, and later (around 1880), when Henry George made the general case for a **land value tax**. His general argument was that that, from a government perspective, land taxes are efficient and are difficult to evade, as the supply of taxable units cannot be reduced – they cannot get up and move to Luxembourg. Regardless, land taxes still only account for a relatively small share of government revenue, and this is partly due to land owners claiming that it undermines the development of new supply.

Finally, it is interesting to note that, according to most indices (e.g. those produced by JLL [8] and CBRE [9]), office space in London is not just more expensive than anywhere else in the world, it is some three times as expensive as Paris, the next most expensive city in Europe. A significant proportion of the increased value of Europe's commercial real estate can be accounted for by planning laws that make building difficult, and fiscal rules that increase their cost.

## The unethical market?

Markets know few boundaries; if something is in demand and it can be produced at a profit, it will be supplied. A favourite example of those keen to peddle the value free nature of the subject is prostitution, although it applies equally well to drugs, tobacco, alcohol and fossil fuel energy. In short, there are markets for 'goods' and 'bads'. A large body of research dating back to the 1980s confirms that improving the environmental quality of buildings can seriously dent the bottom line. Bills relating to energy, lighting, air conditioning and 'sick building syndrome' can all be cut by good design but, so far, relatively few in the real estate professions have taken notice of this research. It appears that the old boys' network – more descriptively referred to as the 'old guard' – cannot accept that sustainable developments will influence capital and rental premiums. Therefore, many surveyors are still not interested in exploring the possibilities. As a favourite academic analogy explains it, the real estate profession is like a supertanker that will take years to turn around.

This is despite a substantial shift in general attitudes towards sustainability. Since the turn of the millennium, the issues of socially responsible investment and environmental accounting have become a key part of the corporate agenda (see for example, Myers, 2005). A stream of professional guidance from the RICS has encouraged surveyors to recognise these developments and to take a lead in this area. Commencing with a report prepared for the United Nations Conference on Environment and Development (the Earth Summit in Johannesburg) in 2002, it was suggested that ignoring the sustainability debate was a risky strategy for surveyors to adopt. As the report concluded: 'it seems much more cost effective to become involved sooner rather than later – taking the opportunity to set the agenda rather than being led by it' (RICS, 2002).

Seven years later, the RICS were still encouraging surveyors to come on board and take a lead in this area, although there still seemed to be some hesitancy to commit fully to the notion that the hallmarks of sustainability add rental value to a project. In fact, rather surprisingly, the 2009 guidance included the following qualifying remark: 'if, at the date of valuation, the market does not differentiate, in terms of either occupier or investor demand, between a building that displays strong sustainability and one that does not, there will be no impact on value' (RICS, 2009).

Alongside this so-called professional guidance has been a host of academic papers suggesting how real estate appraisals could incorporate sustainability – as examples, see Meins *et al.* (2010) or Lorenz and Lutzkendorf (2008, 2011). The point is that valuers can adapt their models by treating sustainability alongside other risks, so it is becoming increasingly important that surveyors reflect on this professional advice. They cannot simply become more experienced at doing the same thing, year in, year out. As academics are keen to suggest, professionals need to pause from time to time and reflect on developments, to find the time to adapt to change. It is all too easy to believe that current practices of real estate appraisal are sufficient, and that the young generation can simply carry on regardless, doing the same as their experienced colleagues. 'Business as usual' can not last forever.

## Be the change

In markets where information is not equal on all sides, it is incumbent on the younger members of a profession to make ethically correct decisions, and the Great Recession provided a real opportunity to reshape mindsets. It would seem plausible, as environmental awareness rises alongside increasing energy costs and legislation relating to climate change, that longer-term values will be affected. Indeed, there is a growing school of thought to suggest that, for buildings to be 'future-proofed', they need to comply with forthcoming performance legislation and corporate values.

In short, someone needs to get the ball rolling – but, be forewarned, once you become immersed in a working culture, it is all too easy to quickly forget your academic training and the ideals of your youth. To paraphrase George Monbiot (2015) from one of his more provocative columns in *The Guardian*: those who graduate from universities have more opportunity than most to seek enlightenment, intellectual spirit, creativity, and change. Yet many end up trapped in a rut maintaining the status quo. To simply take the highest paying job offered at graduation means that you might lose your bearings, your attachments to the world you inhabited before, and become immersed in the culture that surrounds you.

## To sum up

The frame of mind fostered by new economic thinking complements new methods of real estate appraisal. As Hill and Lorenz (2011: 214) argue, becoming a professional surveyor carries a certain ethical responsibility. As they positively express it: 'property professionals have a stewardship or guardian role for society and the built environment … this means the right and a duty to challenge what "the client" or "the market" may seek'. In other words, those who graduate into real estate need to be competent in current practice, and yet carry a commitment to genuinely reflect 'changes' in the market that respect the broader values of society – or, to coin a phrase, 'to be prepared to champion the future'.

It is not surprising that the shock of the Great Recession has undermined some elements of mainstream textbook theory. The so-called **efficient market hypothesis** had been called into question, as problems in the finance, investment and property markets led to further problems in the wider economy. To paraphrase Bishop and Green's (2010) argument: it was an unbelievable level of trust in the efficiency of the market mechanism that was largely responsible for the crisis. Neoclassical theory is dependent on agents having perfect information in perfectly formed free competitive markets; but, when crises occur, no one knows what will happen next. The alarm bells are still ringing in the distance, and we find ourselves in interesting times.

Acknowledging the complexity and irrationality of the market mechanism, and not blindly accepting conventional theory from the past, are some of the first steps towards new economic thinking. As already pointed out several times in this text, market prices do not necessarily convey *all* information accurately, completely or transparently … economics cannot be learnt by rote or by following hard and fast rules … hence the art of interpretation and intuition is imperative. Following the discussions in the first three chapters, this should now begin to make sense. The next important steps involve unravelling the financial networks. This is the objective of Part B, and it will take another three chapters to complete.

## Food for thought: Behavioural real estate economics

In reviewing this chapter, it should be clear that the idea of the free market is central to the thinking of economics and, even though the real world does not operate in a perfectly free market, it is evident that the principles of supply and demand and

**Table 3.8**  Thought processes to explain behavioural economics

| **Automatic system** | **Deliberative system** |
| --- | --- |
| Considers what comes to mind. | Considers a broad set of factors |
| Narrow frame | Wide frame |
| Effortless | Effortful |
| Associative | Based on reasoning |
| Intuitive | Reflective |

an equilibrium price do provide a reference point from which we can broadly judge the performance of the imperfect world. The Great Recession, however, has raised some recurring questions. For example, how come people buy houses even when they cannot afford the repayments on the mortgage? How can people respond to increasing house prices without selling? To some extent, these types of question are answered by a new approach to economic analysis, namely behavioural economics. This was introduced in Chapter 1 in the section on methodology, where we drew a distinction between two modes of thought, and these are reiterated in Table 3.8.

The starting premise for this new approach is based on ideas of how people think and behave; as such, it is based on psychology and experiments. It looks at how people think, drawing a distinction between the automatic and the deliberative thought process.

To demonstrate how the automatic system is dominant and leads us into making irrational responses, behaviourists like to use a classic example, derived from Daniel Kahneman's Nobel Prize lecture, of the cost of a bat and a ball. The example – and you will have to concentrate to avoid being tricked – goes as follows: a bat and ball cost a total of £1.10. The bat costs £1.00 more than the ball; so how much does the ball cost? Most people answer '10 pence', since £1.10 can be easily broken into £1 and 10 pence. The automatic thought system provides a plausible response, based on what comes quickly to mind, before the deliberative system has time to intervene and regulate our judgment. The correct answer is 5 pence (since $£0.05 + £1.05 = £1.10$).

When individuals are under 'cognitive strain' – due to time pressure or financial stress – it is maybe difficult for them to activate the 'deliberative' thought process. In plain English, when people are in hurry or do not concentrate, they have an excuse for not thinking too clearly. This is evidenced by the amount of times you may have bought things that you do not need or want, such as the two-for-one deal, or buy-two-get-a-third-one-for-free, and so on. Once we start looking carefully at everyday behaviour, it is also apparent that we sometimes buy what our friends or neighbour buy. We copy one another in our purchases, and also it is not always clear that we compete, as often, for an easy life, we might simply cooperate. In other words, people do not always act rationally in their own self-interest and they do not necessarily always weigh up all the costs and benefits before taking a decision. Hence, we make more mistakes than the neoclassical thinkers care to admit.

This new behavioural approach is a useful addition to the tools that you are acquiring. When a client is paying you to consult on a property deal, you should feel obliged to offer careful and deliberative advice. This may be counter-intuitive, and against what they are thinking, but it does not necessarily mean that you are wrong. The psychology of economic decisions should also be of some use in an auction room.

The point is that the right price or correct value has a lot to do with supply and demand, but it is so easy to try and employ the principles too rigidly. Markets are made up of many cultural and social influences, as well as economic. With care, the deliberative system can be used to regulate the automatic system to secure the best decision. The message is 'do not be fooled by narrow, closed-ended thinking'.

*Rational or irrational: the case of a cut in a stamp duty*

An example of how the deliberative thought process can reveal how a market actually works can be demonstrated by a cut in stamp duty, like the one that was announced in December, 2014. The characteristics of stamp duty are described further in Chapter 7 – but the important point here is that a reduction in its rate was presented as an incentive to boost the housing market. With a little economic thought, it is quite easy to see that this is not precisely correct.

As we have seen in this chapter, housing supply is not very responsive to price, as it proves to be difficult for a house builder to respond quickly to take advantage of a price rise – residential property in the jargon, presents a classic case of 'price inelasticity'. Economic logic would suggest, therefore, that a cut in stamp duty should lead to house price rises, but what is not so obvious is that buyers end up absolutely worse off.

The key to solving the mystery lies in estimating the behavioural response of taxpayers. Most buyers are what economists call 'credit-constrained'. In straight-forward English, what they can splash out on a new house is limited to what they can borrow, and the amount they can borrow depends on how much cash they have to put down as a deposit in the first place.

Stamp duty represents a bill that must be paid immediately on buying a property – it is a type of sales tax that happens at the point of transaction – so, when stamp duty is cut, buyers can afford to put down higher deposits and meet the criteria to borrow more. As a result, demand increases and prices rise by more than enough to offset the initial benefit of the tax cut. In fact, the OBR (2014: 126) estimated that for every one percentage point reduction in stamp duty, house prices could be expected to rise by 1.4%. In this scenario, buyers of a property costing £300 000 benefit from a £4000 reduction in stamp duty, but face higher costs of £5600, due to higher house prices. Therefore, buyers are faced with a bigger overall bill and homeowners are the ones that gain.

Do not get hung up on whether people respond rationally or irrationally to tax and price incentives. The aim is that you are being trained to think like a modern economist, and that involves accounting carefully for market behaviour, by whatever means are available – statistical, psychological, historical, sociological and so on – and not blindly accepting each variable solely at face value. Remember, the overall aim is to be able to understand, as far as possible, the behavioural responses in real estate markets.

# Part B
# Financial Systems

# Chapter 4
# The Macroeconomy and Financial Flows

The world of macroeconomics has changed in many ways, and the traditional introductory model used by mainstream texts is no longer appropriate. The idea that banks and similar financial institutions can be treated like any other firm as a place where labour, capital and land are combined to produce a good or service has become outmoded. The modern monetary system – comprising commercial banks, central banks, international monetary organisations, merchant banks, investment banks, hedge funds, pension funds and building societies, providing bonds, certificates of deposits, derivatives, mortgage-backed securities and other credit and loan instruments – has become incredibly complex, to the extent that it is hard to capture everything that has recently evolved under the heading of financial flows.

If we are to understand the financial crisis, however, financial flows are a central part of the storyline. This was a crisis, incidentally, that most economists and bankers were not able to predict, even though there were warning signs and research commentary going on worldwide that pointed worryingly at the alarming increase in the scale of debt in relation to GDP. This admission, however, is not particularly surprising when we note that, up until the onset of the crisis, conventional economics had failed to regard 'debt' and 'credit' as important key macroeconomic variables.

To defuse this minefield, we commence with the standard textbook introduction of economic activity in a two-sector model economy, where macroeconomic relationships between households and businesses are the main focus.

*New Economic Thinking and Real Estate*, First Edition. Danny Myers.
© 2016 John Wiley & Sons, Ltd. Published 2016 by John Wiley & Sons, Ltd.

## The circular flow model

As implied above, economists usually begin explanations of the macroeconomy by ignoring the government sector, the financial sector and the overseas sector – that is, the simple introductory circular flow model represents a scaled-down economy, in which relationships are assumed to exist only between households and businesses.

To make the model effective, it is assumed that households sell factors of production to businesses and, in return, receive income in the form of wages, interest, rents and profits. This is shown in the bottom loop in Figure 4.1. The businesses sell finished goods and services to households in exchange for household expenditure. This is shown in the top loop in Figure 4.1. These assumptions are reasonably realistic. Businesses will only make what they can sell. Production will necessitate buying in land, labour, capital and enterprise, and the monies paid for these factors of production will generate respective income payments.

Already, without building in any of the complications of the real world, we begin to sense several insights into the macroeconomy. For example, there is a close relationship between the income of a nation, its output and the level of expenditure. In turn, these will obviously influence the prevailing levels of employment and prices. More importantly for our current purposes, the model highlights the importance of 'real flows' within an economy; that is, how the factors of production owned by households are converted into goods and services by business units. In short, the emphasis is all about output – or, as economists like to call it, **Gross Domestic Product** – GDP.

The slightly more advanced textbooks introduce governments and financial institutions as intermediate sectors, respectively, linking taxpayers and the spending of government departments, and savers and those borrowing funds to invest in fixed and working capital. The emphasis, however, continues to be about explaining the flow of goods and services within an economy – identifying the ways that 'real' transactions fluctuate due to changes in interest rates and/or government budgets. These respective relationships are indicated in Figure 4.2, where we outline the traditional flows of funds model.

It is only the most up-to-date authors that have begun to challenge these neoclassical conventions. As a result, some of the more modern textbooks, published during the crisis years, began to acknowledge that banks and financial institutions have become increasingly involved in the development of financial instruments, to the extent that nowadays, this side of the business greatly outstrips the traditional

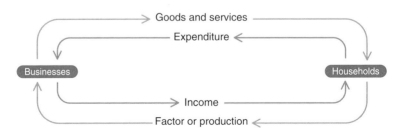

Figure 4.1   Circular flow model.

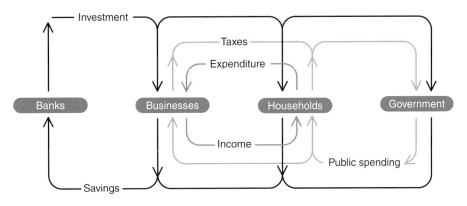

**Figure 4.2**   Traditional flow of funds model.

transactions that banks used to rely on. To use the jargon that has developed to explain the cause of the Great Recession, the 'investment' and 'retail' arms of the banking industry have become blurred; the 'casino and gaming' element have become disproportionate and riskier, relative to the 'bread and butter' work that banks traditionally undertook. At the peak of the problem, in 2008, the market in speculative transactions totalled more than a trillion dollars a day – 50 times greater than the value of all real commercial trade exchanges. The problem, there-fore, was that bankers seemed to have become more concerned with moving money to transact *financial speculative instruments*, rather than supporting con-ventional *real trade transactions*.

Although this dual role of banks supporting output and credit arrangements might seem obvious to younger students, it had, to a large extent, been overlooked by conventional mainstream approaches. Indeed, banks and related financial inter-mediaries have been mostly absent from economic theory for many decades. This is evidenced by the fact that, for many years, the major central banks employed models of the macroeconomy in which private banks played no real part in deter-mining the level of economic activity (see, for example, the models of the Bank of England [1], the European Central Bank [2] and the Federal Reserve [3]).

In effect, the new emphasis acknowledges that the world is driven not only by output, but also by credit arrangements. Banks and financial institutions are cen-tral to making both sets of activities possible. The distinction between these approaches will become clearer after the next two sections.

## The traditional flow of funds model

As outlined above, the traditional model used over the last 60 years to explain the performance of the macroeconomy is based on the circular flow of funds model. In these crude and simple introductions, banks and governments are regarded as being much the same as any other business organisation – that is, primarily concerned with supporting the output of goods and services within an economy. Furthermore, there is a tradition, at the introductory level, that the economy is closed – insulated from all external forces such as international trade and international exchange. For our purposes, this exclusion is a blessing, as the overseas sector merely adds a further layer of complication to an already complex set of relationships.

The important point of distinction between the traditional model and its modern counterpart is the role played by the financial sector. In the traditional model, banks are regarded as financial intermediaries that link the savers with those who need funds for investment purposes. In other words, the financial sector is presented as no more than a sideshow to the main economy. The quantity of debt, wealth and credit appear to add little relevance to the jobs, factories and shops that make up the real economy. These traditional relationships are outlined in Figure 4.2.

## The modern flow of funds model

The more recent model that has gained credence since 2007 explicitly focuses on the financial sector, analysing the growth and contraction effects caused by levels of credit in an economy. Banks are no longer seen as just facilitators of economic exchange, they are recognised as inherently different from all other firms. As Keen (2011: 362) explains in his attempt to *debunk neo classical economics*: 'Banks generate and honour promises to pay that are used by third parties to facilitate the sale of goods (and they incur essentially no cost in doing so – the cost of 'producing' a dollar is much less than a dollar). Therefore businesses and banks must be clearly distinguished in any model.' In short, the post-crisis world requires a clear line of distinction to be drawn between 'real assets' and 'financial assets'. The modern flows of finance through an economy are highlighted in Figure 4.3.

The modern approach emphasises the *monetary* aspects of an economy. That is, each economic transaction has a corresponding payment (such as income, expenditure, taxation, government spending, fees, interest and dividends), and those transactions that cannot be funded through one of these channels will access some form of credit from a financial institution. Household and businesses often draw on the capital value of their real estate to support (securitise) these debts.

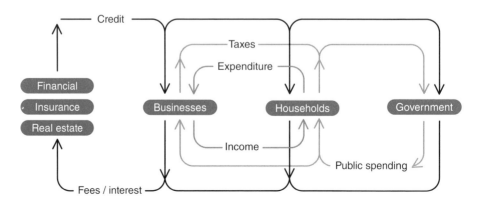

**Figure 4.3**    Modern flow of funds model.

In effect, each flow comes from somewhere and goes somewhere. In the traditional model, money flows are made in return for a good or service. As economists say, for every factor payment there is a factor service. In the modern version, each transaction is represented by a payment or loan. As the jargon has it, every credit or debit creates a related financial instrument (financial instruments are discussed further in Chapter 5 – but for quick clarification, see Table 5.1, where typical examples are listed).

Distinctively, in the modern account, funds clearly originate in the banking sector, and either circulate in the real economy or return to the finance sector as investments, savings, interest payments and fees. As a result, total credit flows (in nominal currency units) tend to increase year on year, reflecting positive profit and rates of interest. It is possible to broadly represent these flows in a balance sheet manner, where liabilities and assets balance by definition; hence, this macroeconomic model is sometimes referred to as the accounting – or flow-of-funds – model. This new approach is detailed further in the food for thought section at the end of this chapter.

As Figure 4.3 highlights, a distinguishing feature of the flow of funds model is the importance attributed to the finance, insurance and real estate sectors. This includes all sorts of businesses that generate credit and manage wealth, ranging from the obvious deposit-taking high street banks to the more obscure fund managers (described as 'shadow banks' in Chapter 5). The modern model places the focus on financial flows from commercial high street banks, pension funds and insurance corporations, through to brokers, asset managers, financial advisers and real estate agents and so on. In turn, these institutions provide credit to firms, households and the government as they borrow funds (in various forms) to fulfil their economic wishes.

For example, in business, government, and household sectors, investment in fixed capital (such as machinery, roads, and houses) is facilitated by loans from banks, the value of which – by accounting necessity – is jointly equal to real-sector incomes and assets in the form of profit, taxes, property and interest payments. As Wynne Godley, one of the pioneers of the accounting approach, explained: 'evolving finance in the form of bank loans is required if production is to be financed in advance of sales being made and if profit is to be extracted from firms and paid over to households'. Another element that he stressed is the importance of including interest payments in return for the supply of credit, 'as they are an inevitable cost given that production takes time' (Godley, 1999:405).

Modelling the flow of funds in this way makes a clear distinction between real sector assets and those assets created in the financial sector but, all the while, an accounting relationship between the financial and real economy is retained. For example, there is a close relationship – even a trade-off – between the financing of production (out of retained earnings and fresh lending) and the repayment of debts. Providing credit flows return to the financial sector, new debts can continue. When times are good, asset values are rising and loan defaults are rare, and it is all too easy to forget the trade-off between debt payments and credit provisions. Indeed, the trade-off is absent from the mainstream model and debate, but it is crucial to understanding the crisis that caused the Great Recession. As Friedman (2009) pointed out: 'An important question – which no one seems interested in addressing – is what fraction of the economy's total returns … is absorbed up front by the financial industry.'

The modern flow of funds model casts an interesting light, not only on the adequacy of our knowledge of financial institutions and practices, but also on the property world of the future. It plays up the importance of understanding how investment is financed and debts managed, in determining the state of the macroeconomy. To the layman, it might seem that everyone gets what they want from the financial system. The home owner, the businessman and the credit card holder certainly get loans and, as we explain in the next chapter, the banks seem to find ways to package up these increasingly risky debts and sell them for a fee to someone else.

However, it is obvious that spending more than you earn is unsustainable in the long run, and this rule applies equally to governments, consumers, businessmen and even banks. In short, every sector identified in Figure 4.3 faces the problem of growing debt. To illustrate the scale of the problem, economists like to use the analogy of a lily in a pond that doubles in size every day. The analogy originates from a magazine interview with Professor Steve Keen carried out in 2006 [4].

### The lily and the pond

The interview commenced with the following riddle. A lily in a pond is doubling in size every day. If it takes 31 days to grow to cover half the pond, how many more days will it be before it covers the whole pond? The answer, of course, is just one more day.

The object of the riddle is to point out the insidious nature of exponential growth. A sustained growth process – like a cancer – is almost imperceptible when it starts. If you ignore it, however, it will 'suddenly' overwhelm the organism. The lily, for example, goes from covering 0.75% of the pond on its 25th day to 1.5% on its 26th, and the average gardener would not even notice it. Yet, a few days later, when it grows from 12.5% to 25%, it starts to become a notable problem – and then, by the next day, when the lily covers 50% of the pond, the gardener may well be at his wit's end about how to manage the pond in the future.

The lily scenario – with its rapidly increasing size – goes some way towards explaining how the crisis happened. House prices went up and up, and debt levels increased exponentially until, eventually, the bubble burst. The outcome was a record level of mortgage debt in a declining housing market, and rising debt-service payments that diverted income from consumer spending. Taken together, these factors are compounded, and inevitably the 'real' economy shrinks and pushes a debt-ridden economy into a recession, or worse.

The power of compounding is in fact phenomenal, as the increased debt each year is added to the existing debt. So, when debt is already £100 billion and the interest is growing at 10% over a term of say, ten years, the debt *does not* increase by £10 billion each year, and the size of the debt *does not* increase to £200 billion after 10 years. Ten per cent growth in the first year increases the debt to £110 billion, and in the second year a further 10% interest will bring the total debt to 121 billion. By continuing like this for the next ten years, the debt will be £259 billion in total after ten years – not £200 billion. It will actually reach £200 billion after just seven years.

Economists have devised a simple rule of thumb – the so-called 'rule of seventy' – to calculate exponential rates of future change on the basis of today's rates. For example, if you have an interest rate of 10% and want to know how long the debt will take to double, simply divide seventy by the interest rate. Similarly, if a country grows at 1% per year, it will take 70 years to double in size, while it will take somewhere between 23 years and 24 years for the size of an economy growing consistently at 3% to actually double in size.

## The perils of debt

The flow of funds model suggests that there is always the potential for a financial explosion waiting to happen; a kind of ticking time bomb, where credit builds up and needs to be continually repaid to avoid a financial explosion.

Many businesses and households (and government departments, for that matter) have become 'debt-loaded' – that is, their repayments on credit cards, loans and overdrafts form a significant proportion of their gross income. For example, the *Resolution Foundation* [5], a high-profile think-tank that researches the economic impact on lives of those on low to middle incomes, has warned that, as interest rates raise from the historic low rates of the recession, literally millions of households (3.5 million, according to their calculations) will find themselves spending more than half of their pay on servicing mortgage debt.

As the Resolution Foundation (2013, 2014) explained: it is quite easy to foresee the base rate rising back to around 3% over the next few years, and this will lead to many households being dangerously overstretched. Within this large group of financial victims, a sub-group of 'mortgage prisoners' – some 770 000 households – will, because of their self-employment or small amount of equity in the mortgage on their homes, find it more or less impossible to find a way out with another mortgage. In short, the Resolution Foundation predict the coming of a second credit crunch.

An analogy that many economists draw is that finance is like the circulatory system of the economic body. If the blood stops flowing, the body goes into cardiac arrest; when the financial system crumbles, the economy collapses. Once a financial system has become global, its bad blood will poison all the related networks.

### The message

Whenever large debts accumulate, there is always a risk that they will not be honoured; the credit so readily accepted when times are good rapidly turns bad, into debts that cannot and will not be paid. Therefore, to discover what is actually happening in an economy, we need to look beyond GDP data. As outlined above, the period leading up to the Great Recession was driven by exceptional increases in borrowing. In fact, the UK entered the crisis with the highest level of debt of any large developed economy. By some measures, its total debt was nearly five times the size of its annual output or, as officially stated, the ratio of debt was 480% of GDP (Roxburgh *et al.*, 2011) – the first of three McKinsey Global Institute reports on international debt and deleveraging [6]. Subsequently, households (individuals), companies and government departments reined in their spending to try and pay off, or at least stabilise, this enormous burden. While it makes sense for individual households and businesses to cut their expenditures and the government to attempt saving through austerity measures, the economy as a whole suffers as fewer transactions take place.

This message was neatly captured by Tim Geithner (2014), reflecting on his American experiences as President of the Federal Reserve Bank of New York from 2003 to 2009, and Treasury Secretary from 2009 to 2013. To paraphrase his observations: when a financial system collapses, credit freezes, savings evaporate and the demand for goods and services reduce significantly, which leads to higher levels of unemployment and a decline in personal income.

As a consequence, to fully understand the nature of the economy (and its recovery), we need to look at financial data. These are usually made available through publications from a nation's central bank. In the case of the Bank of England, regular publications of the *Financial Stability Report*, *Credit Survey* and the *Inflation Report* provide a rich source of data and commentary. It is good practice to access each preferred series on a regular basis from the Bank of England statistical interactive database [7].

## Beginning to see the wood from the trees

As we move towards a close to this chapter, it should become clear that the monetary backdrop to the economy is in transition. In the wake of the Great Recession, the world economy is still recovering from the collapse of the financial system in 2008. This had initially been attributed to a regulatory system that had become too lax, and is now being micro managed with various new instruments and policy – but it is still far from stable. In fact, at the time of writing, pressure is mounting on the European Central Bank to agree a deal to keep Greece's bank system alive and within the Eurozone. Whatever happens, the ramifications will be experienced across Spain, Italy and beyond. As will be suggested in Chapter 6, it is slowly becoming apparent that financial recessions are here to stay – although from here on in, they will look and feel different.

Precisely how vulnerable the financial sector is at any one point in time is hard to discern, but some fresh research from the Bank of England has begun mapping out the UK financial system. The related paper pointed out that in 2014, when the UK economy had a GDP of £1.8 trillion, the balance sheets of the various banks and financial intermediaries totalled £20 trillion – more than ten times the size. Such balance sheets have grown rapidly in recent decades all around the world, but the UK financial system is notably bigger, relative to the size of the economy, than that of most other countries (Burrows *et al.*, 2015) [8].

Understanding the nature of the financial system in relation to the real economy, and its links to borrowers and savers in the nation's households and businesses, is a starting point for a wide range of important economic questions. For example, in the future, policymakers will want to know how much debt a nation's household and corporate sectors have. Which financial sectors hold that debt? How vulnerable are the most highly indebted households and corporates – and who has lent the funds? Addressing these questions requires comprehensive data from the balance sheets of the various institutions that make up the financial system, as well as understanding the connections between them. The related research and data has begun to emerge, and some of the basic principles and relationships are drawn out in Chapter 5, where we introduce the new products traded by financial institutions, and the expanding armoury of policy instruments used by Central Banks that have evolved in the last decade. This should help to clarify what is going on in the new world of finance, and to know where to look to see the next recession coming.

So, there are still some treats to unpack. As the Chief Economist at the Bank of England admitted to the great and the good in the profession, gathered at a meeting to review new thinking in economics, we are 'still in the intellectual foothills in terms of dealing with potential financial risks' (Haldane, 2014). This admission, made to a learned community, is cited to put in perspective why, at times, students may find the study of the macroeconomy and financial networks baffling. It should also help to put into context why surveyors, economists and businessmen alike need to prepare themselves to understand an economy that is different and more volatile than those experienced by their fathers and grandfathers.

## Food for thought: Flow of funds – what goes around comes around

As implied in this chapter, mainstream economists proceed from a principle of sectoral balancing. Sections of the real economy lend and borrow to and from each other, so – theoretically, at least – the surpluses and debts between each sector balance out, because every credit has a corresponding debit. This so-called flow of funds approach dates back to the early 1950s, but it is only relatively recently that it has become an integral part of the annual National Accounting process. As we shall see in Chapter 8, *National Accounts* measure the annual flow of economic activity through an economy and take stock of a nation's assets. In other words, they are a means of presenting national data on transactions, identifying economic flows, and stocks of assets and liabilities for the sectors and subsectors of an economy and the rest of the world.

The flow of funds approach provides a useful way of thinking about the imbalances that can occur in an economy, as it breaks down the various sectors according to inflows and outflows. If one sector takes more money out of an economy than it puts back in (saving), and is not compensated for by other sectors putting more money in than they take out (dissaving), then the overall flow of money will decrease.

Analytically, it is useful to divide the economy into four sectors, namely:

1. The domestic private sector (comprising consumers and businesses – or, as they are referred to in the official accounts, households and non-financial corporations). In this sector, savings should equal investments.
2. The government sector (commonly referred to as the public sector), where the target of a balanced budget between taxes and public expenditure is often regarded as an important reference point for economic stability.
3. The overseas sector (official transactions abroad are typically referred to as 'the rest of the world' in statistical tables). To balance the books, the monies

flowing into the country should equal the outflowing funds, so the value of imports and exports and foreign investments are important to economic stability.

4.  The financial sector (banks and other types of financial intermediaries often referred to in the statistical literature as 'financial corporations' to distinguish them from other business organisations). These organisations act as intermediaries between all the other sectors, and play a crucial role in managing the economy.

Dividing the economy into four or five sectors (as the private sector is sometimes identified as two separate entities, comprising households and businesses), and analysing the principal flows between each of them is becoming a standard part of economics. These commonly recognised ideas were broadly endorsed by a group of economists from orthodox and heterodox schools of thought when they petitioned the UK government to rethink its proposed policy of legislating to make governments run a budget surplus – to bear down on debt. The significance of a budget surplus was proposed by George Osborne (the UK Chancellor of the Exchequer) in his Mansion House Speech in June 2015, and formalised later that year as part of a Fiscal Charter. The signatories [9] pointed out that: 'Permanent budget surpluses … have no basis in economics…. If one sector of the economy lends to another, it must be in debt by the same amount as the borrower is in credit…. (A) government's budget position is not independent of the rest of the economy, and if it chooses to try to inflexibly run surpluses, and therefore no longer borrow, the knock-on effect to the rest of the economy will be significant. Households, consumers and businesses may have to borrow more overall, and the risk of a personal debt crisis to rival 2008 could be very real indeed.'

In other words, managing a modern complex economy is far more complicated than simply balancing the books. It demands a great deal of flexibility, and committing a government to a single positive yearly target means it will not be able to respond appropriately to constantly evolving circumstances. Annual government budget surpluses run the risk of causing a liquidity crisis, a bank failure, a fall in GDP, a crash, or all four.

As the 77 petitioners concluded: 'The plan actually takes away one of the central purposes of modern government: to deliver a stable economy in which all can prosper. It is irresponsible for the Chancellor to take such risky experiments with the economy to score political points. This policy requires an urgent rethink.'

This seemingly straightforward piece of economic advice challenged mainstream economics – an economics based on equilibrium. For examples, see a textbook explanation of the general equilibrium framework of Arrow and Debreu; Hicks IS-LM (investment and savings – liquidity and money) model, or the more recent development of AS-AD (Aggregate Supply – Aggregate Demand) analysis. It is worth bearing in mind, however, that these are all examples of what Professor Ronald Coase famously referred to in his Nobel Prize lecture in 1991 (and elsewhere) as 'blackboard economics'. By implication, this is a system, or model, that can be written down on a blackboard – or nowadays a whiteboard – using terms such as leakages, injections, interest rates, exchange rates, balanced budgets and so on. While such an approach is arguable, it certainly trivialises the complexity of the actual system. To paraphrase ideas that Professor Coase began to pursue more than 25 years ago: what economists study often lives in the minds of economists – but not on Earth. In short, equations, theories and analysis of equilibrium can quickly become figments of the economist's imagination.

## The real economy versus the financial economy

As suggested in Figure 4.3 and its related commentary, there is a pressing need to merge the real economy and the financial economy; to reassess the relationship of finance and real growth in modern economic systems. Fortunately, research is currently being done on this theme at the Bank for International Settlements (or, as it is sometimes comically dubbed, 'the central bankers' central bank'), the International Monetary Fund and the European Commission. For several good examples, see the proceedings of the Jackson Hole economic policy symposiums of 2011, 2012 and 2013 [10], published by the Federal Reserve Bank of Kansas. There is also the emergence of standardised data, made available from central banks [11] and international organisations [12].

These papers, and the related data, tend to confirm two basic economic notions. Firstly, that finance is good for growth, providing it is kept within certain limits; and secondly, there is a sensitive give and take relationship between the sectors that trade directly or indirectly with one another. As Cecchetti and Kharroubi (2012: 1), from the Bank for International Settlements, clearly state at the beginning of their paper: 'The idea that an economy needs intermediation to match borrowers and lenders, channelling resources to their most efficient uses, is fundamental....'

Financial intermediaries enable businesses to get the capital they need to expand, and savers to have a secure place to deposit their money – and on this basis, financial deepening and rising debt can (but not necessarily) go hand in hand with improvements in economic wellbeing. Without private sector debt, economies cannot grow, and without public sector debt, macroeconomic volatility would be far greater. However, there is nothing inherent to keep it all in check. As Professor Coase reminded his students: 'There is no single entity within the government which regulates economic activity in detail, carefully adjusting what is done in one place to accord with what is done elsewhere' (Coase, 1988: 19).

## Too much of a good thing

Inevitably, an economic system can quite quickly become out of kilter. Empirical-based studies, using a range of data from 1980 to 2010 monitoring debt levels across a total of 24 OECD countries (an Organisation for Economic Co-operation and Development – or as The Economist like to call it, a club of rich countries), suggests that, beyond a certain level, debt is bad for growth and makes an economy vulnerable. The trigger – or tipping point – varies from country to country and from sector to sector but, in general terms, problems appear to set in when debt in any one sector exceeds about 85% of GDP (Cecchetti *et al.*, 2011). Very similar findings were confirmed by Stephanie Lo and Kenneth Rogoff's research of 2015.

When debts are not honoured, a whole economy can spiral out of control very quickly. It does not matter if the initial spark is from a government 'defaulting' on its loans, or a business declaring itself 'bankrupt', or a household 'foreclosing' on its mortgage – they all represent a 'discontinuity' with debt repayment and they all cause negative flows. It does not matter what you call it, whenever sizeable loans are approved, there is always a risk that debts will not be paid and that the economy will be thrown into imbalance.

Another interesting observation relating to equilibrium and disequilibrium has to do with the actual proportion of workers employed by the finance sector. According to some detailed research on the broader impacts of finance on economic growth, once the proportion of the labour force passes 3.9%, the effect on productivity growth turns negative (Cecchetti and Kharroubi, 2012). To put it bluntly, there are simply too many bankers in relation to the value added to output – or, as Adair Turner expressed it, when he was Chair of the Financial Services Authority in 2009, much of the employment in the financial sectors appears to be 'socially useless'. Ireland, Spain, Switzerland, America and the UK have all suffered from employing too many in the financial sector. A further complication is the unbelievable levels of remuneration that some of the workers in the financial sector earn each year.

Even the august researchers at the OECD and IMF have found that the larger a country's banking sector, the more slowly an economy grows and the worse inequality becomes. Furthermore, while both organisations accept that enlarging the financial sector is critically important for a developing country, they also agree that, beyond a certain point, too much **financialisation** (as its been increasingly called since the 1990s) is counterproductive. This shift in gravity of economic activity towards the financial sector is one of the hallmarks of the 21st century, as the associated institutions and its culture have become a force in their own right.

An interesting explanation was captured at an international conference of central bankers and executives from the financial sector: 'The financial industry competes for resources with the rest of the economy. It requires not only physical capital, in the form of buildings, computers and the like, but highly skilled workers as well. Finance literally bids rocket scientists away from the satellite industry. The result is that people who might have become scientists, who in another age dreamt of curing cancer or flying to Mars, today dream of becoming hedge fund managers' (Cecchetti and Kharroubi, 2012: 1–2).

In other words, the financial sector has drawn in resources at a phenomenal rate – in the jargon, they have become 'skilled-labour-intensive'. It was only when they crashed that the extent of the overinvestment was realised. However, by then it was too late; the significance of the financial system relative to the real economy had grown out of proportion. Too many corporations, institutions, finance houses, brokerages, trusts and exchanges, etc. had been formed, with too much capital invested and too many people employed. Importantly, after the event, we can see that many of these resources should have gone elsewhere. For example, following the financial crisis in 2008, computers were scrapped, office buildings vacated and highly trained people laid off.

*More food for thought*

It is not just how much debt a government (or household or business) has, but what the borrowed money is spent on. Borrowing to buy a house is very different from borrowing for productive investment. Therefore, an economy's overall debt level and composition matter, and there can be amplification mechanisms across sectors that exacerbate the negative effect of debt on growth. For example, if households are suffering debt problems, this can lower demand and can lead to strains on corporate and government debt. It appears that there is something of a vicious circle at work. Too much debt reduces the demand for goods and services, which breeds instability in the corporate sector and leads to recession. Recession damages the public finances, which leads to government spending cuts, which in turn leads to slower growth and a greater reliance on debt.

Some of this presumably accounts for the extensive period of sluggish economic growth across many advanced economies in the post-crisis years. However, the scale of debt overhang is certainly not the only explanation that has been offered. Other possibilities include: an ageing population; a slowing rate of innovation; unchartered political waters, insufficient fiscal stimulus; and excessive financial regulation. In the final analysis, it is probably a mix of all of them.

There is currently a challenging set of research initiatives trying to identify the precise relationship between the rate of economic growth and the growth of debt. There is also a plethora of new data, such as the flow of funds data that, since 2008, has formed an integral part of the System of National Accounts, plus a whole new attitude to solving these questions – including those influenced by the behavioural approach. For example, in June 2015, the Bank of England introduced *Bank Underground* [13] – a blog where Central Bank staff (and academics) are encouraged to enter into a free and open debate about research output. This is all part of the new trend to make the thinking of those who influence policy at the Old Lady of Threadneedle Street (as the Bank of England is sometimes fondly referred) to be more transparent and more accountable to the man in the street.

Similarly, authors of contributions to the *Quarterly Bulletin* (the Bank's academic house journal) are encouraged to provide video clips to support their research output. In short, it is all part of a drive to modernise and open up an institution that, in the wake of the Great Recession, has become far less secretive, stuffy and closed. The trend of increased transparency of the Bank's view should help to make policy more comprehensible, more predictable and, in terms of macro-management, more effective. It certainly represents a step in the right direction – moving away for the 'whiteboard' and closer to reality.

To close this section, we need to raise the question: What happens when the flow of credit stops; when no one will risk lending to you anymore? In the summer of 2015, Greece provided a prime example, as its government could no longer meet its debt obligations to the IMF and ECB. The banks could no longer fill all their ATMs, or even risk opening their doors. Businesses could no longer afford to pay their employees' wages, and the government could not fund the benefits due to its 2.9 million pensioners. Fuel reserves were running low, and boats, buses and trains had few passengers. The daily newspaper *Ta Nea* had to apologise for being relatively 'thin', due to a shortage of paper. The whole economy was grinding to a halt.

The country was in a terminal state; it had already received two bail-outs and a debt haircut, and the economy was 25% smaller that it had been in 2008. In sum, the economy had a classic imbalance of debt hanging over it. Furthermore, the potential issues were not confined to just this one country, as it shared a common currency with 18 other Eurozone countries. Overall, the Euro-based flow of fund figures indicated that high leverage was still a major concern, seven years after the default of Lehman Brothers in September 2008. In fact, it would seem fair to conclude that most 'real', 'modern', 'dynamic', economies were rarely found in a textbook equilibrium situation.

# Chapter 5
# Central Banks and Monetary Policy

As outlined in Chapter 4, traditional textbooks of economics authored before 2008 made little mention of money, debt and banks. In the traditional approach, when finance was dealt with, it was as a direct relationship between a lending institution and a borrower. To paraphrase the words of Ha-Joon Chang (2014: 291): in the past, when someone borrowed money from a bank and used the funds to buy something, the lending bank owned the resulting debt and that was that. Nowadays, finance is not so straightforward, and it is slowly becoming recognised that banks actually create their own funds by offering loans – although this process might, at first glance, seem tautological, it is outlined in some detail below. Most importantly, since 1980, the number of lending institutions and the types of loans supplied has mushroomed and, as a result, a new network of inter-related financial organisations with different types of credit contract and agendas has emerged.

This new financial network of organisations and products is vast, international and highly speculative – in fact, in some quarters, the level of complexity is hard to follow, and this is not made any easier by the size of the markets involved. A conservative estimate of the value of the financial economy worldwide is certainly north of £500 trillion. It is only the exceptionally bright city trader, working in the system with the support of massive computer programs, who could possibly give a full account of what is going on – but most of them are too busy and too focused on next month's bonus to stop and reflect.

To put this in context, consider the story of a trader – an insider– with a conscience. Greg Smith (2012), a former executive director at Goldman Sachs (in charge of the firm's US equity derivatives business in Europe, the Middle East and Africa), publicly announced his resignation in a letter that was published in the New York Times: 'I attend derivatives sales meetings where not one single minute is spent asking questions about how we can help clients. It's purely about how we can make the most possible money off of them. If you were an alien from Mars and sat in on one of these meetings, you would believe that a client's success or progress was not part of the thought process at all....'

Understandably, this press announcement created quite a stir in the financial sector, as not only was this type of whistleblowing incredibly unusual, it also raised some challenging questions about Goldman Sachs – the company and their equivalents – and highlighted how few of those involved (regulators, economists, politicians, or journalists) had managed to grasp the complete picture for what it was. A major part of the problem lay in the fact that a large and growing share of the loan market was not held by banks at all, but rather by non-bank lenders (such as insurers, hedge funds, private equity, pension and investment funds), who became appropriately known as the **'shadow banking system'**.

Alongside these shadow institutions stood the huge established conventional banks, such as HSBC, Deutsche Bank, BNP Paribas and Citigroup – traditional high street banks, operating across several countries, doing everything from bond-trading to car loans. They were prepared to sell wherever, and to whoever needs their financial services. This complex maze of interconnected financial markets was heavily involved in various forms of borrowing and lending (and some examples of these are briefly outlined in the section below titled *Alphabet Soup*).

In providing any form of credit, an element of risk is always involved. However, it is arguable that by organising each transaction responsibly, the financial system can enable an economy to operate with both efficiency and stability. The post-2008 recession, unfortunately, showed this to be an illusion as, in many ways, it seemed that an incestuous community of 'bankers' were involved in a sub-plot in which the primary motive was to create personal wealth.

The Great Recession simply confirmed just how inefficient and unstable the financial system had become; in fact, it appeared that the banking system had gone completely haywire. As the distinguished economist Robert Solow (2009, p. 8) pointed out, when trying to explain the descent into recession after the 2008 financial crisis: 'I find it hard to believe ... that our overgrown, largely unregulated financial sector was actually fully engaged in improving the allocation of real economic resources. It was using modern financial technology to create fresh risks, to borrow more money, and to gamble it away'.

Much of the blame for this slide into the abyss was placed on the bankers and city workers that made up the financial sector. But it wasn't really them that were corrupt – it was the large, faceless, global, institutions that employed them. In some ways, the root of the problem lay in the neoclassical belief that markets are driven by rational competing individuals. The crisis, however, highlighted another version of that belief – namely that some markets are driven by impersonal, competing institutions. As the new saying goes, 'a buck that does not stop with an individual often stops nowhere'. Hence, a willingness to take risks – particularly excessive risks – became a norm in the financial sector that ultimately was underpinned by government assurance. In other words, finance became a world where the players assumed that their institutional employer, or the central bank, would always come to the rescue if the going got tough. This led to a decline in ethical conduct in the financial system – a dilemma that economists sometimes refer to as **moral hazard**.

# Ideology: In whose interests?

Whenever an economic decision is reached you need to ask 'who benefits?' For example, when introducing a new tax, the government needs to make sure that the payments are in the interest of the taxpayer. Similarly, a young surveyor going out to meet a client for the first time needs to bear in mind who is the beneficiary of the meeting – it should certainly not just be the surveyor or his boss. Efficient economic decisions should reap mutual benefits to all the parties involved. Looking back at the credit crunch, it is plain to see that many of the financial transactions leading up to it benefited the bankers far more than anyone else. It was as if they had stupefied those in business and those in government, leading them to believe that investments and credit depended upon an ability to spread risks as widely as possible. Actually, though, this was just a ruse, as the transactions were mainly in the bankers' interests – helping them to become fabulously wealthy and bewilderingly powerful, at the public's expense.

New economic thinking discusses transactions in which some of the parties involved know more than the others, under the heading of **asymmetric information**. Whenever there is a general problem of one-sided information – in which one party holds most of the cards – the market concerned can fail. Those who criticise the neoclassical stranglehold on market analysis like to focus on the contractual agreements between the parties involved. This focus on the **principal-agent** relationship questions the balance of power between the less informed client and the knowledgeable agent. The debate is around the extent to which the agent acts in the best interests of the client. This analysis of the principal-agent relationship demonstrates how the skills and experience of the agent can lead to a situation in which a trusting client may be misinformed. In fact, this criticism of market efficiency is not so 'new', as it has been around for more than 40 years. It originated from an academic paper that examined the second-hand car market – where the car dealer knows considerably more about the product than the purchaser (see Akerlof, 1970).

The idea of asymmetry highlights that whenever information is incomplete, the efficiency of the respective market is called into question. If some people know something that others do not, as in the recent financial debacle, there is a far greater need for government intervention. The banking community had clearly managed to hoodwink the world, with those inside the industry benefiting at the expense of the public. As a consequence, central banks have begun to clean up the market in an attempt to make it more efficient and transparent. There are now more regulations on money laundering, tax evasion, capital reserves, high-frequency trading and so on – and significant fines have been introduced for breaking the rules. In the world of finance, the cost of compliance has more than doubled since 2008.

This chapter examines these developments, and outlines what has been put in place to prevent such a crisis happening again. As such, we broadly review: the role of financial institutions in the creation of funds; the development of various new market instruments; the functions of central banks; and the main policy tools used to control the financial sector and the broader macroeconomy.

## What goes on in the traditional banking sector?

Simply put, banks are intermediaries that obtain funds from savers in the form of deposits, and provide funds to borrowers in the form of loans and overdrafts. It is instructive to think of each of these flows happening in separate markets, as savers are expected to supply funds at a lower rate of interest than the rate paid by those demanding them as loans. The difference in interest rates between the two markets is the institutional reward for taking the risk of originating a long loan from a stock of short-term deposits. The value added – in fees and spreads – is jokingly referred to in the parlance of the finance sector as the 3-6-3 principle (i.e. borrow at 3%, lend at 6%, and be home by 3 pm).

The system is largely built on trust in financial institutions – after all, the word *credit* stems from the Latin for *believe*. Savers (depositors) trust banks with their money, confident that they can repay them – with interest in some cases – at any time. On this basis, banks subsequently lend out money at a higher rate of interest, to businesses, government or households, for periods of up to 30 years or more.

However, this does not mean that the process is without risk, as confidence in the system can be called into question and banks can become vulnerable – or, as the textbooks like to call it, 'fragile'. The fragility comes from the possibility that those holding deposit accounts could demand their funds back simultaneously, in which case the bank would have to liquidate all its assets (even those that are not liquid) to fulfil depositors' demands. In short, even a seemingly healthy bank can become the victim of a *bank run*. Since almost no bank can liquidate all its assets within a short period without suffering a loss in value, a problem of illiquidity can essentially turn into a problem of insolvency, and the collapse of the whole banking system can happen overnight. Indeed, in today's digitised world, a bank run no longer involves much physical running – just the click of a mouse, or a swipe on a smart phone – and things can spiral out of control very quickly, as evidenced in 2007/8.

An obvious question is whether the credit crunch of 2008 would have occurred if politicians had had the foresight to maintain confidence in the system by not letting Lehman fail. In fact, three days after Lehman's bankruptcy the Fed – the Central bank of America – had to intervene to stop an electronic bank run on US accounts. It is widely acknowledged that within 24 hours, the world economy would have collapsed. As Professor Paul Krugman, Nobel Prize winner in economics, commented in an interview in *Newsweek* in December 2008: 'Letting Lehman fail – letting the market work, as some people said – basically brought the entire world capital market down'.

A revealing explanation put forward by the chief economist at the Bank of England was that policymakers at the central banks were navigating in the dark, as they assessed the risks in the financial system on a bank-by-bank basis – they did not look at the non-bank financial intermediaries, or make an analysis of the linkages between the various regulated institutions. As he put it: 'At present, risk measurement in financial systems is atomistic. Risks are evaluated node by node...' (Haldane, 2009: 12). In short, he was recommending that central banks should acknowledge and monitor the systemic nature of the financial network. This is not simply a case of being wise after the event, as Haldane is one of the new breed of thinkers who has the courage to recognise some of the pitfalls of orthodox economic thinking. He is quite prepared to draw lessons from other network disciplines, such as ecology, epidemiology, biology and engineering, to make sense of the financial sphere. To paraphrase his explanation: peering through the network lens provides a rather different account of the structural vulnerabilities that can build up in a financial system.

Given their inherent fragility, banks typically require credit enhancements in the form of insurance of deposits, or emergency access to funds from the central bank, or both. In most countries, public funds are the source of such provisions of emergency funding. Indeed, the financial history of the United Kingdom is replete with stories about bank runs and bank failures, dating back to the 19th century, and these are alluded to in the next chapter.

Our immediate concern, however, is the cause, duration and scale of the 2008 financial crisis, especially as policymakers have not only grasped the importance of a healthy banking system for the real economy, but they also recognise that bankers will not learn from their mistakes. The end of one bank run does not imply the end of bank failures. The very fact that banks seem to be able to create money out of thin air (discussed below) inevitably creates a significant hazard for the banking system, and raises a moral dilemma for anyone who advises clients on using borrowed funds, or forecasting investment opportunities. To add a final twist to this dilemma, it is worth also noting that, by providing the economy with the necessary purchasing power, banks can enable higher levels of output to be achieved. In short, not all credit creation necessarily has to end in tears.

To reiterate the traditional model detailed above, before moving on to the more modern model, bank loans are made possible by intermediation between savers and borrowers. In simpler terms, lending proceeds once a bank has collected deposits – or savings – from one agent, and ends when those deposits (or savings) are borrowed by another agent. In the jargon, banks intermediate savings. The idea is captured in textbook formulas variously called **credit creation**, the **bank deposit (or money) multiplier**. In the modern model, however, the emphasis is subtly but importantly different, as loans come *before* deposits. The key function of a bank is to provide finance – or create new monetary purchasing power – through loans, to a single agent who is both the borrower and depositor. Thus, rather than banks' lending out deposits, or savings, that have been placed with them, the very act of lending via, say, a MasterCard or Visa account creates deposits. A further distinction is that, in the modern version, the multiplier effect on loans is infinite. This seemingly complex system is the topic of the next section.

## The fairytale story of banking

The central part of the modern explanation of how a financial system functions lies in the idea of '*finance through money creation*'. There are several academic papers presenting this modern model, and notable examples have been authored by Adrian and Shin (2010), Borio and Disyatat (2011) and McLeay *et al.* (2014). The essence of the latter has been distilled by the Bank of England into an interesting five-minute video clip [1] that, given the opportunity, is worth watching. The following, however, is a simplified factual account that draws from the work of Jakab and Kumof (2015), but presented in a style partly inspired by Lewis Carroll, who wrote *Alice in Wonderland*.

There are several ways of describing the process, from simply keying in a pin number to authorise the electronic transfer of funds, to negotiating a loan from a bank (as the Mad Hatter said, 'it is very easy to take more than nothing'). The crucial part of the scenario is that it starts with a borrower – who, for convenience we shall call Mr B. He approaches a bank for a loan. If the bank considers the credit risk of Mr B acceptable, it will enter into a contract. The magical part of the tale is that when the loan is entered into the bank's books as a new asset, a matching deposit is simultaneously entered as a new liability. The bank has created new purchasing power – money – through lending. Both the loan and the deposit are in the name of Mr B, which means that this transaction involves no intermediation of loanable funds whatsoever. The bank has created money out of thin air – or, to be more precise, with the stroke of a keyboard.

Round two: Mr B now uses this new deposit to acquire a car from Mr C, by transferring the new money in his account to the account of Mr C, in exchange for the car. For the sake of simplicity – and to keep the story short – we will assume that Mr C leaves these funds in the company bank account. All of a sudden, Mr C has become a saver. However, the important moral to the story is that Mr C's saving is a result of the loan and of the car purchase. Mr C goes about his transaction with Mr B without any intention of becoming a saver. His only intention is to sell cars, and to accept payment for them. In a modern economy, MR C would not remain in business for long if he did not accept cheques, the electronic transfer of funds, or money orders drawn on bank accounts, as these represent the dominant means of making payments in today's society.

In a modern banking system, loans to finance cars form a relatively small part of overall bank lending, with a far greater amount being used to finance business investments, government activities and house purchases. In other words, credit or loans are used to finance the exchange of existing real or financial assets between different agents.

Of course, the flip side to the creation of money is that with every new loan comes a new debt. This is the source of the personal debt that countries face. As *Positive Money* [2], a pressure group formed to democratise money and banking, make clear, the mountain of debts that society faces is not money that had been prudently saved, but money that was created out of nothing by banks and then lent to people who could not repay. Eventually, the debt burden can become too high, and results in a wave of defaults such as those that triggered the start of the financial crisis.

To make this fiction a reality, whenever I introduce this concept, I like to set the scene by suggesting that the whole class might like to organise their families and friends to withdraw their entire bank-based funds in cash at the precise same time on one agreed date. This scenario quickly highlights just how vulnerable the banking system is, as it raises awareness that most of a bank's credit is recorded as electronic items, and that only a very small percentage is actually kept in the tills as cash (rarely greater than 3%). Hence, there is always the possibility that too many of the bank's customers will withdraw their funds at the same time, resulting in a bank needing help from another institution to continue operating. As was evidenced in several countries at different times during the period 2007–2009, these so-called 'bank runs' happen spontaneously – they do not need to be orchestrated by some lecturer having a wheeze!

The point is that once debt starts to become problematic, the whole process can switch with a vengeance, and this is precisely what happened, commencing in the USA, from the middle of 2007. From there, it spread globally in a contagious way – or, as the press prefer to call it through 'contagion' – to the rest of the world in 2008. It was a particularly dramatic collapse, whether measured by the ratio of total bank assets to GDP, or by the absolute sheer scale of loans that had been made and, once the debts were called into question, the whole edifice on which they were built began to crumble.

The problems began in the US sub-prime mortgage sector, where huge volumes of mortgages had been sold to persons who previously would not have been deemed credit-worthy. Alongside these loans ran other complicated financial instruments (such as derivatives and collaterised debt obligations – described below), which compounded the problems of bad debts. It rapidly became apparent that money creation has crept into almost every aspect of our lives. It is directly connected to public and private debt levels and the price of real estate, but it seemed to be very poorly understood. Indeed, a debate on the topic in November 2014 at the House of Commons found that seven out of ten MPs believed that only the government can create money!

## To sum up the story of money creation

There are clearly several ways of describing how banks create credit. The simplest versions can be seen in a traditional economics textbook where, usually, some fictional event describes how banks use the money deposited by savers to allow multiples of that money to be lent out to borrowers. However, as already stated, this is not a precise way of outlining how the process works in a modern economy. The important, and worrying, point is that banks do not need to wait for a customer to physically deposit money before they can make a new loan to someone else.

As a consequence of the money creation process, banks were responsible for creating 98.75% of the money that was in circulation at the start of the financial crisis. This astronomical percentage is based on the fact that, for every £1.25 held in reserves in 2008, £100 had been issued as credit! The amount that is created is largely a determinant of financial institutions' attitude to risk, not savings.

The data for the United States and the Eurozone, presented in Figure 5.1, confirms that the quantity of savings and the size of bank balances do not appear to be closely connected. The rate of savings appears to be relatively stable over the periods shown, whereas the scale of bank debt shows that there have been large and rapid fluctuations. For example, it is clear that, across both the United States and the Eurozone, there was a massive contraction in bank balance sheets at the onset of the Great Recession, while movements in net private saving were barely noticeable in the Eurozone, and only small in the United States (Jakab and Kumhof, 2015).

The power of commercial banks to create new money has many important implications for understanding the broader economy and its financial stability, as well as the markets for real estate. For example, credit and how it is allocated is rationed by banks, not governments, as is widely believed. Furthermore, the primary determinant of how much they lend does not seem to be related

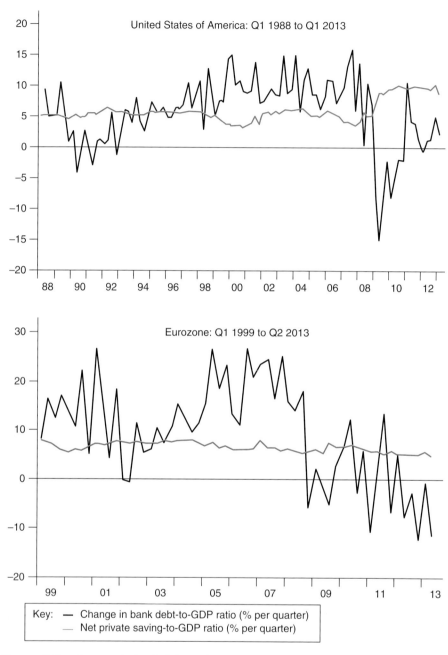

**Figure 5.1**   Changes in bank debt and savings.
*Source*: Adapted from Jakab and Kumhof, (2015: 56).

to the interest rates set by the central bank, but to confidence that the loan will be repaid, and confidence in the liquidity and solvency of other banks and the system as a whole. This basic analysis is neither radical nor new. Central banks around the world support the same description of where new money comes from. At the current time, the real challenge lies in managing and supervising the scale and allocation of the distributed funds.

## The market for derivatives: Weapons of mass destruction

As detailed in the previous section, the power of banks to create money resides in their ability to transfer funds electronically and to devise instruments of credit. Over the last four decades, both mechanisms have increased markedly, to the extent that, nowadays, something like £1 billion a day is transferred via internet banking alone, and trillions – literally thousands of billions – have been traded as commercial paper and IOU instruments. In fact, the range of new financial products that have been created by City institutions across Europe and America since the late 1980s beggars belief. By 2001, these debt-based instruments – derivatives of various types – had an estimated total notional value of $69 trillion (according to the ISDA – the International Swaps and Derivatives Association). By 2011, the equivalent global market had mushroomed to an estimated value of $707 trillion (according to the Bank for International Settlements [3]). For purposes of scale, it is worth noting that the respective figures for World GDP (which estimates the annual total output) were around $45 trillion in 2001, and $70 trillion in 2011. Within a decade, therefore, while the value of financial instruments had increased more than tenfold, actual output had barely doubled.

It should be emphasized that the above figures are based on world data, and it is not always easy to distinguish between data that estimates annual issuance and data stating total aggregate debt. In the case of the shadow banking sector, a further distinction needs to be made between market and notional values, the latter being based on the value of the debt-based product, whereas the market value approximates to the underlying debt upon which the new instrument is based (by definition, a smaller amount). In short, the granularity of financial data is not always sufficiently refined.

Therefore, be forewarned when researching for data – it is not always sufficiently robust. In fact, before the financial crisis of 2008, macroeconomic data on debt was relatively sparse, as the assumption was that, largely speaking, borrowers and lenders cancelled each other out, as a pound borrowed by a household or corporation had been lent by a supervised financial institution. However, the crisis highlighted just how wrong this assumption had become. Debt was no longer represented by just a few financial products and supervised institutions – it had become a major significance in the 21st century, and its unwinding had proved that it was no longer a simple zero-sum game.

Everything seemed more straightforward in the past, when financial institutions worked from the maxim that they only lent to people whom they could trust to pay back. There was certainly a direct relationship between the lender and borrower, and an understanding of what was expected of each party. However, the financial world has changed in so many ways that it is hard to know who to trust anymore. The number of financial innovations has grown at a phenomenal rate over the last few decades. Whereas traditional debts were unforgiving and had to be paid in full and on time, modern debt has become more varied, and is often designed to allow for transfer to third parties, trading and default.

In other words, the risks of lending have been extended across institutions – and national boundaries – and, in effect, institutions are lending in many instances to borrowers about whom they know nothing. In Professor Stiglitz's (2010) meta-phorical terms: banks have changed from the 'storage business' (of originating debt and holding on to it) to the 'removal business' (taking debt from the origina-tor, repackaging it, and moving it on to another investor).

As a general principle, the new debt-based products allow the same debt to be passed around from one financial institution to the next – in the jargon, the traded debt (the commercial paper) is '*derived*' from a loan. Thus, a mortgage initiated by a family in America could easily cross financial counters in other shores and be moved onto the books of a pension fund or investment bank, as some kind of derivative. This gives further insight to the notion of contagion as, once the debt turns bad, problems spread like wild fire across national boundaries and institu-tional organisations. It is little wonder that Warren Buffet (the billionaire Chairman of the American investment company Berkshire Hathaway) captured imaginations when he concluded the Company's Annual report for 2002, with the immortal words: 'Derivatives are financial weapons of mass destruction, carrying dangers that, while now latent, are potentially lethal'. Six years later, the financial crisis confirmed just how destructive they could be!

## Alphabet soup

These new assets form a significant part of modern finance so, although at first glance they might appear rather bewildering and complex, we do need to get some measure of them to proceed in the modern world of property, especially as real estate often forms the collateral that secures them to the real world. The media has tried to unravel the general mayhem that ensued across the financial markets but, for educational purposes, I often suggest that it is worthwhile to follow up at least one of the new debt instruments in detail in order to get the basic idea. As a guide, the more common ones are outlined below – but, be forewarned, you will need to concentrate, as it is like sifting through an alphabet soup of possibilities.

There are many derivatives and related new acronyms currently on offer (often in combinations) floating around the world's financial centres from Wall Street to Threadneedle Street and beyond. To name just a few obvious examples: Residential Mortgage Backed Securities (RMBS), Commercial Mortgage Backed Securities (CMBS), asset-backed securities (ABS) and Collateralised Debt Obligation (CDO). Collectively, these are often referred to as derivatives, securitisation, or structured financial assets.

Let us begin with the group of derivatives that was largest at the time of the crash – **mortgage backed securities** (MBS). These are bonds formed by mortgage loans that have been pooled together into a parcel, and sold as a collection of mortgage loans in blocks of 1000 to 5000 to investors. MBS come in two forms: residential (RMBS) and commercial (CMBS). The residential mortgage backed security was the most common form of derivative, and normally parcelled up in tranches of greater than a thousand mortgages per unit. At the peak of the market, in 2008, speculative transactions totalled more than a trillion dollars a day – 50 times greater than the value of all real commercial trade exchanges. The problem, therefore, was that banks had become increasingly concerned with moving money to transact financial speculative instruments, rather than conventional real trade transactions. The presumed solution was to separate the two functions and impose greater regulation, and one of the results is that the values of RMBS issued and held today are far smaller.

The commercial mortgage-backed security (CMBS) is, in principle, a very similar debt instrument, consisting of commercial mortgage loans on retail properties, office properties, industrial properties and hotels. As these mortgage debts represent properties that are income-producing, they are unlike residential mortgage loans and offer stronger protection. Another difference is that CMBS are normally shorter-dated, as they tend to represent ten-year, fixed-rate loans. CMBS are typically issued in smaller tranches, with blocks of 30–100 loans in each parcel; they represented about one-tenth of the total MBS market in 2008, and they are slowly coming back into favour. Total issuance of £1 billion worth during 2011 was seen as a positive revival. A recent development that forms part of the CMBS are bonds secured on sale and lease back transactions (detailed further below).

Asset-backed securities represent a similar pooling of debts, such as car loans, student loans, credit card loans and, quite commonly, commercial mortgage-backed securities as well. To appreciate these products, you need to recognise that the underlying loans from which they are made up are regarded as assets from the perspective of the originating bank. Whether they are quite as secure when they are a derived product is questionable.

Collateralised Debt Obligations (CDOs) are structured asset-backed securities (it is important not to lose the plot now, as these supposedly safer instruments are the most opaque and complex of the lot and, as a result, are potentially the most dangerous). A Collateralised Debt Obligation combines a number of other securities (such as those referred to above – RMBS, CMBS, ABS) into tranches with different levels of risk. A typical CDO can contain as many as 150 other packages of securities, structured into seven or eight tranches ranging from 'super senior', which has the least risk of default, to 'toxic waste', which carries far greater risks and has a higher chance of default.

Sometimes the tranches are subsequently repacked into bigger groupings. These provide second and third lines of defence – or, as those in the industry like to refer to it, squaring and cubing. Thus, the lowest tranche of the repacked CDO – the CDO of CDOs – would be dubbed a $CDO^2$, and so on. By combining the derivatives into packages, varying by type and level of risk, investors were being encouraged not to put all their eggs into one basket. The culinary references to what was being cooked up are interesting, as those who created this dizzying array of financial products typically described them as being diced, sliced, squared and cubed. There has never been a better analogy for cooking the books!

The classic example of the uncertainty around these derivatives, and the extents of the contagion they can cause, were brought into sharp focus when Lehman Brothers announced, in mid-September 2008, that they were bankrupt. They had debts of $613 billion. They were counterparty to around $5 trillion worth of Credit Default Swaps (a type of hybrid insurance between institutions, created to protect CDOs from default), and over-exposed by around eight times the size of their balance sheet. These admissions totally fazed the financial markets, including those in the insurance industry, who had to pick up the bill for the related credit risk protection, which had turned more or less overnight from a source of income into a variety of claims. This unwinding of the tangled web of credit default swaps between literally hundreds of counterparties was sufficiently complex to create a catastrophe on its own. AIG (the American insurance giant), for instance, also had to be bailed out by the government. For several days, related institutions across the globe were dumbstruck and froze to a complete standstill.

As introduced in Chapter 4, the banking sector (broadly defined by shadow and traditional institutions) allows everyone to get what they want from a financial system. The home owner and credit card holder get loans, and the banks have a way to package up their risky debts and sell them for a fee as they unload them onto someone else. As indicated, banks are no longer places that simply 'originate and hold' debt, as the newly designed derivatives provide a channel for them to sell off loans and pocket a tidy profit, rather than hold the loans until maturity and run the risk of having them go bad along the way. Ironically, as the crisis built, more and more loans were distributed to pension funds, insurance companies and institutional investors, to lessen the risk of a banking crisis. In principle, such a transfer of funds widened the pool of available capital and took the debt off the regulated books. To use Roubini and Mihm's (2011) phrases, '*originate and distribute*' had replaced '*originate and hold*'. As a consequence, banks no longer have to be as diligent in monitoring the underlying risk of loans and mortgages. In the new world of securitization, bad debts could quickly be passed down the line like a hot potato.

As pointed out in previous chapters, the absence of money, debt and banks from the overwhelming majority of 'mainstream' economic models has become a major criticism of the profession since the financial crisis exploded in 2008. The root of the problem lies in the fact that the debt-based derivatives create a string of claims between financial institutions and, as the debt pool widens and deepens, it becomes impossible to know who owns the actual debts (in conceptual terms, it might help to think of a final thread of discussion arising from a long series of email correspondence in an attempt to try and identify where it had all started).

To conclude this section, it will be useful to briefly consider the broad range of institutions (and instruments) that make up a modern financial system, and to begin to consider how best they could be controlled, supervised and managed. For convenience, the recognised institutional framework and the general nature of the respective forms of debt that they trade in are drawn together in Table 5.1, which identifies the broad range of institutions and instruments that modern monetary policy should ideally embrace.

As we move from the left to the right of Table 5.1, we progress from the traditional regulated financial intermediaries to the new shadow institutions (more commonly referred to in official data as the *non-bank financial sector*, or *other financial intermediaries* – OFIs). Although the ideal is to control them all equally, it is still proving difficult to capture and monitor all forms of money-lending effectively. The underlying dilemma is that, as new regulations are introduced to constrain official bank lending, the non-bank financial sector tends to expand and innovate to plug the gap. For instance, following the financial crash, greater restrictions were imposed on the use of complex, opaque, financial instruments. As a result, the loans from non-bank intermediaries, corporate bonds and online lending platforms (such as peer-to-peer lending, crowd funding and payday loans) have markedly increased.

**Table 5.1**   The financial system for monetary policy purposes

| Monetary financial institutions | | | Insurance corporations and pension funds | | Other financial institutions | |
|---|---|---|---|---|---|---|
| Central bank | Deposit-taking corporations | Money market | Insurance corporations | Pension funds | Investment funds | Captive money lenders |
| | Retail banks (international and domestic) and building societies | Investment banks and discount houses | Life and general insurance companies | Various schemes | Unit trusts Hedge funds REITS | Credit brokers, crowd funders, payday loans |
| **Associated debt instruments** | | | | | | |
| Types | Loans | Repos | Equities | Derivatives | Bonds | Agreements |
| Examples | Overdrafts, mortgages | Treasury bills and gilts | Shares | RMBS CMBS | Fixed rate bonds, etc. | Online |

*Source*: Adapted from United Nations (2014: 40) and Burrows and Low (2015: 114).

## Specialised real estate funding options

Table 5.1 also provides an interesting template of the possible avenues for funding real estate developments. According to different needs, there exists a range of options, from the most common source of development funding – banks – to the more specialised and less common – hedge funds. The table, however, does not list the specialised ways that investors in property can raise business funds, as this is not a recognised part of the analysis. As indicated above, some data is available on REITS and related equity based instruments, but funding schemes, such as **Sale and Leaseback** agreements and **selling off-plan** and pre-lets, are rarely detailed in texts, although they are proving to be increasingly popular ways around cash flow problems in the real estate sector. Indeed, the different devices for gaining credit in any sector of the economy are hard to monitor and control.

### Sale and leaseback

This involves a company selling its freehold property, but remaining in occupation by way of a lease. The sale redistributes assets and reduces risks. In effect, a sale and leaseback agreement enables the property and operational aspects of the business to be split up. The classic examples date back to the late 1990s and early 2000s, when Shell sold the freehold of 180 of its petrol stations but continued to sell petrol from the same forecourts by leasing back exactly the same sites, and Debenhams sold (in 2005) the freehold of its 23 department stores to British Land for £500 million and then leased them back to continue trading. The process releases capital tied up in property, and generates cash flow to the trading company.

The system offers a way to fund business operations through a difficult period. For example, the troubled bank HSBC completed one of the largest sale-and-leaseback deals by agreeing to become tenants to the National Pension Service of Korea, who had arranged a sale and leaseback for its headquarters at Canary Wharf in 2009. The deal raised £772.5 million for the troubled bank. At around the same time, the Whitbread group raised £90 million by arranging a sale and leaseback agreement on 12 of its Premier Inns.

Presumably, if finance continues to be difficult to come by, more organisations will consider sale and leaseback as a means of raising capital. Such schemes are clearly a legitimate alternative to other sources of finance or debt. For example, a business facing a choice between issuing a bond, or disposing of real estate assets in return for a known rent liability for a number of years, may well choose a sale and leaseback agreement. In a nutshell, the choice boils down to raising capital that has to be repaid at some stage, versus one that does not. The property agents, such as CBRE, consider this market with some excitement, which is not surprising when you think of the arrangement fees that could be made on the back of the £2 trillion worth of commercial property currently owned by European businesses.

## Off-plan sales and pre-lets

As you are probably beginning to realise, the real estate business is a costly and risky exercise at the best of times. Not only do the significant costs of construction and development need to be met, but there is always a risk – at the start of the pipeline – of the property remaining empty on completion. Off-plan sales and pre-lets help to reassure the developer and support the financial viability of a scheme. Off-plan sales are more closely associated with residential developments, and pre-lets with commercial contracts. Both greatly support the issue of finance, because commitments are made ahead of schedule.

For example, Maine Tower [4], a development in Docklands London, due to be completed in 2019, sold its first tranche of units in July 2015 – four years ahead of schedule. Interestingly, half of the units were sold to overseas buyers such as the Chinese (whose investors were facing a stock market slump at the time) and the Greeks (who faced stringent debt bailout conditions on investments in their homeland, due to the Euro crisis).

Thus, at the risk of stating the obvious, property does not simply provide a market for residents but can be offered overseas as well – it has an international element. Another noteworthy observation from this case study is the speed and scale of the sales – 208 apartments with a combined value of £140 million were sold in four hours. This is equivalent to £35 million per hour, which indicates the confidence that buyers from both the UK and overseas had in the London property market in 2015. It also reinforces how quickly residential developers can get their hands on cash, particularly as sales made ahead of completion can only be secured by people who do not need a mortgage, as a mortgage offer only has a six-month shelf life.

Equally, pre-lets are an important part of the office market and, according to research produced by the agents Cushman and Wakefield, there were126 pre-lets across Central London between 2000 and 2013 (i.e. 23.7 million square feet). Furthermore, it is reported that the number has been steadily increasing since 2009, and this could be due to a number of factors: existing leases due to expire; improved business confidence; and a limited number of speculative commercial developments in the pipeline. These are all key determinants in real estate decisions, but first and foremost; the finance needs to be in place to proceed.

## Central banks

All nations have some form of **central bank** to coordinate the various monetary functions of a state. Examples are the Bundesbank in Germany, the Federal Reserve (or the 'Fed', as it is fondly referred to) in the USA, The Riksbank in Sweden, The People's Bank of China and the Bank of England (the Bank for International Settlements provides a definitive alphabetical list by country [5]).

An interesting exception to this general rule is the European Central Bank (ECB), which provides support and supervision to those countries whose banks operate across the Eurozone. The ECB manages assets, currency exchange, emergency liquidity and interest rates across the 19 countries that share the single currency. In short, a one-size-fits-all approach. This means that the ECB cannot run separate policies for each individual country – there is one set of monetary policy for all nineteen countries of the Eurozone, and that is that. This structural weakness was highlighted by the debt problems that Greece and, to a lesser extent, Spain, Portugal and Italy faced from 2010 onwards; although they had the constraints imposed by monetary union, they did not have to listen to a finance minister in Brussels to control their tax and spending. The tension of being supervised by a common central bank, but not a common government, was particularly problematic in these economies.

In general terms, a central bank plays an important role in the plumbing of the financial system. It is responsible – and usually with a good degree of independence – for: maintaining an appropriate supply of currency; reviewing the purchasing power of a nation's currency in terms of the rates of inflation; managing rates of interest and foreign exchange; supervising financial institutions; and manipulating the availability of credit. This broad range of responsibilities is captured in the term **monetary policy**.

In the days before the Great Recession, when there was not too much regulation and banks were left to decide their own fate in markets, monetary policy was relatively liberal. It boiled down to little more than raising or lowering the rate of interest in an attempt to manage consumer and corporate – aggregate – demand. Since 2008, however, there has been far more regulation and experimentation, to the extent that monetary policy can be divided into two historic camps – before and after the financial crisis – the old and the new. Or, as central bankers like to call it, conventional and unconventional monetary policy.

## Monetary policy before 2008: The conventional approach

In the decades before the Great Recession, there was principally one monetary tool that a central bank controlled – namely, the interest rate. The accepted wisdom was (and, to a large extent, still is) that the prevailing rate of interest significantly influences spending decisions and, in particular, the decisions of both businesses and households on whether to borrow (i.e. to incur debts) to pay for consumption and investment goods. The theory is that, as interest rates become higher and more volatile, businesses and consumers generally feel less confident about making new investments and negotiating future contracts. In short, higher rates of interest are expected to encourage saving and discourage investment and consumer spending.

In other words, if central bankers want to spur economic activity, they cut interest rates. If they wanted to dampen it, they raise them. To follow one sequence, higher interest rates tend to increase the cost of financing house purchases, and so reduce demand and lower (or at least slow the rate of increase of) house prices. In previous decades, therefore, a change in the rate of interest charged by banks and associated financial institutions has had a strong influence on the level of spending in an economy and on price stability.

## How interest rate manoeuvres are signalled

In the UK, the monetary policy committee (MPC) has full responsibility for determining the rate of interest used by the Bank of England when dealing with other financial institutions trying to raise funds in the money market. The official rate of the transaction is known as the **base rate**, which is sometimes referred to in monetary circles as the **repo rate**, as it represents the rate that a central bank is willing to lend (or transact) funds to other banks. The Eurozone equivalent set by the European Central Bank is called the **refinancing rate**, and the interest rate used by the Federal Reserve in America is called the **discount rate**.

At the introductory level you do not need to worry too much about the difference between the American, British or European terminology, or the precise open market system used to signal the changes (i.e. the gilt repo rate or the bill rediscount rate). The important point is that, in each case, the central bank sets a carefully considered unique rate of interest that determines the rate at which it will lend in the short term to the banking sector. Subsequently, this determines the rate that banks charge each other for overnight loans, formally referred to as LIBOR, which is an acronym for the London Inter-Bank Offered Rate. The rate of exchange used for these interbank transactions forms the basis of all other rates of interest, from which millions of financial contracts are agreed. The precise sequence is neatly captured in Figure 5.2.

The dealings in the interbank market affect the interest rates adopted in the wider economy by all other credit agencies and financial institutions, such as the high street banks. No bank would dream of lending to customers at a lower rate than the one at which it borrows, as it is in business to make a profit, not a loss. Thus, when the central bank announces a change to its Bank Rate (i.e. the repo rate), it is usual for banks to change their rates for mortgages, overdrafts savings and so on, by the precise same margin. However, when banks find themselves facing particularly difficult economic times, they tend to increase the rates charged on their loans, and they might even decide to ration the quantity of credit they are willing to extend. In effect, both these actions are captured in the term **credit crunch**.

Following the financial crisis, there was a collapse in demand, and central bank interest rates drifted downwards to stimulate a response. They ended up, in fact, sitting with repo rates close to zero for a significant period. For instance, the Bank of England offered a base rate of 0.5% for more than six years from March 2009

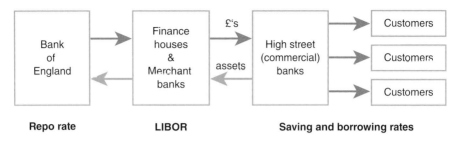

**Figure 5.2**   The money market.

onwards. Even lower rates were offered by the ECB and Fed, where 0.15% and 0.25% were the respective low points. Regardless, this low base rate did not guarantee that other rates stayed as low, or that funds were actually lent out. The credit crunch had led to an abrupt change, financial stability was replaced by instability, and markets went into 'crisis' mode. There was a distinct loss of trust between banks and lending between them, to the extent that general bank credit dried up and a downward spiral ensued that had severe consequences for the wider economy. Lenders would no longer lend, and borrowers could not borrow; hence, builders could not build and buyers could not buy. In effect, the credit crunch had starved the economy of its productive capacity.

## Things can only get better

In the conventional old world, a change in repo rates was mirrored by an immediate and proportionate change in other financial rates, insofar as the spreads between the official (repo) rate and all other rates were adjusted more or less in tandem, and more or less on the same day. However, the years following the financial crisis were starkly different, as commercial banks began to revise their margins and increase the costs of borrowing. For example, when the base rate fell to 0.5% in March 2009, the banks were slow to respond and did not adjust their rate by the same old margins. Where the conventional spread between the base and mortgage rate had traditionally been around 2%, it had now widened to at least 3.5% – 350 **basis points** – above bank rate.

This widening of interest rate spreads is one of the more worrying features of the financial crisis, and it was global. As Professor Alan Blinder (2013: 237) remarked, based on his experience at the Fed: 'Aficionados used spreads as a handy market measure of the severity of the crisis'. In fact, many of the emergency actions adopted by central banks in recent years have been designed in one way or another to reduce the spreads and get the financial system working again. In a nutshell, the financial crisis had robbed the financial markets of their dependability, and the conventional approach had begun to look relatively weak.

There is also the added problem of having nowhere to go if another hiccup or crisis developed. As pointed out above, the central banks' benchmark interest rates are currently historically low, only hovering slightly above zero – in fact, the average for rich countries in 2015 was around 0.3%. In the jargon, economies became 'zero lower bound'. In other words, if central banks were to face another recession, they have almost no room to boost their economies; they have nowhere to turn. This is a very new world, as records dating back to the 17th century show that, before 2009, central bank's rates had never fallen below 2%. The logical answer to this dilemma is to get back to normal rates of interest as fast as possible. As *The Economist* (2015a) remarked in one of its leader columns: 'The sooner interest rates rise, the sooner central banks will regain the room to cut rates again when trouble comes along'. Obviously, this is easier said than done, as raising rates too quickly can push economies back towards deflation and recession.

As we have already seen in Chapter 4, there is a whole body of research produced by the Resolution Foundation to suggest that when base rates hit around 3% (possibly in 2018), a significant number of mortgaged households will find themselves dangerously overstretched. What is being predicted here amounts to a second credit crunch, although next time round it would primarily affect households, rather than banks and businesses.

Finally, there are those – such as Kothari *et al.* (2014) and Sharpe and Suarez (2014) – who use empirical evidence to point out that the investment decline following the financial crisis of 2008 represented a fairly typical response to changes in profits and GDP, rather than an unusual reaction to problems in the credit markets. In other words, the accepted wisdom that market interest rates are a key determinant of corporate investment has been broadly called into question. To support the argument, there is American and global data, relating to corporate investment from 1952–2010, that strongly suggest that investment is largely unrelated to changes in interest rates or the spread on corporate bonds. In fact, the research has demonstrated that investment is more related to profits, share returns, demand and expectations, and always has been. However, this analysis is complicated by the widely recognised understanding that interest rate changes take time to work through the economic system. According to the Bank of England, the macroeconomic model – the **transmission mechanism** – can take up to two years before the full effects of an interest rate change is played out (MPC, 1999: 3 [6]).

Such views have important implications for those interested in understanding commercial real estate. Clearly, investments in property are not determined by a simple knee-jerk reaction to changes made to interest rates, but by a far broader reflection on the economy as a whole. Other variables, such as demand, technology, expectations and profits, come into play. Establishing precisely what drives investment into commercial property is particularly difficult, as it tends to expand and contract far more dramatically (in the sense that property investment is more volatile) than the economy as a whole. The answer, if there is one, is that the more specialised you become in one sector of the market, the more likely you are able to judge what is going on within that sector and be able to assess changes to interest rates in a specific context. Waiting for the time when you see the cranes on the horizon means you have left it too late; reading ahead and between the economic data is the goal to aim for.

## Times are changing

Since the onset of the Great Recession, central banks have been dogged by particularly difficult circumstances. To state the obvious examples: bank failures; rigged markets; sovereign debt; weak economic growth; and a general climate of financial instability. As a consequence, the conventional paradigm of orchestrating interest rates to target credit facilities and secure price stability has undergone a transition towards a new world, where the broader macroeconomic environment relating to financial stability has become a key objective.

In some quarters, these largely unforeseen and, it seemed, inexplicable events led to increased debates about the level of accountability that could be trusted to central banks and the policies they enforced. To take just one example from the UK: in 2011, the House of Commons Treasury Committee published a report entitled *Accountability of the Bank of England*, which called for a radical overhaul of the Bank's governance. According to one commentator of life inside the Bank of England, during the decade of independence prior to the onset of the Great Recession, the Bank had lost its way and the confidence of parliament, and acquired a distinct arrogance and a disregard for process (Conaghan, 2012:289).

This loss of confidence was captured by the cynical attitudes that accompanied the first attempts at something relatively different, namely *quantitative easing* or, more simply, **QE**. As this confusing process to expand the money supply has been deployed since 2008 in several different countries, and on several separate occasions, we need to at least acknowledge the process.

## Quantitative easing

As described above, when official interest rates got closer to zero, the effect they had on regulating the economy became muted. Consequently, governments looked for other ways of affecting the price of money and stimulating the economy. One approach that was adopted was to increase the supply of money circulating in the economy. This was done through a process known as **quantitative easing** – a system where, essentially, central banks print money to buy bonds. It has now been tried by all the big financial centres of the world – Japan, the United States, the UK and the European Community (through the ECB). By some definitions, China also joined in when they tried to stabilise their stock market in July 2015. By engaging in QE, the rich countries expanded their balance sheets by trillions of dollars, creating new money potentially for use in the 'real' economy.

The monetary impact of quantitative easing spills out of asset trading in the repo market, and again Figure 5.2 is useful as a teaching aid. If a central bank such as the Bank of England wishes to inject money into the economy, it can purchase assets (such as government bonds or high-quality debt issued by private companies) from insurance companies, pension funds, banks or non-financial firms. The outcome – regardless of the particular assets purchased – is that the seller's bank account is credited, and the system finds itself with more funds. In sum, the idea is to push more reserves into the banks, at a near zero price, in the hope that the new funds will induce the banks to make use of them – by financing more lending!

Although it is regarded as 'new', it was experimented with in Japan in the 1990s so, to be precise, it straddles the divide between conventional and unconventional approaches. The complication is that, to date, it has only ever been used in a crisis. Nobody knows how much is required, or how long it takes to have the desired effect. At the time of writing, the Bank of England is working with the Treasury to launch a new emergency measure – the 'funding for lending scheme' – which is designed to boost lending to businesses by allowing banks to borrow from the Government. While this makes sense in theory, it remains to be seen if it promotes some growth in the economy. But it does act as some kind of acknowledgment that quantitative easing may not work.

## Monetary policy since 2008: The unconventional approach

According to an influential report that collated and analysed data from the IMF and BIS – the **International Monetary Fund** and the **Bank for International Settlements** – global debt grew by $57 trillion in the seven years after the crisis began in 2008. The global total had reached $199 trillion, representing a 40% rise in the post-crisis years (McKinsey, 2015). This is not as much as the 60% increase in the seven years before the crisis, but it was enough to raise fresh concerns. The perceptive reader may sense some contradiction between these figures and the data used to broadly assess the size of the shadow economy (see above). The McKinsey (2015) research, however, focused primarily on debt relating to the 'real economy' of households, non-financial corporations and governments. Data relating to credit securitisation were not included. Where financial-sector type debt was referred to, it was only in the form of traditional loans.

Table 5.2 provides a more detailed breakdown of this debt and its distribution. For example, one can see that government debt alone had increased by $25 trillion from the end of 2007 to midway through 2014, and a significant proportion of that amount related to bailouts to assist troubled institutions when the financial crisis commenced. Many of the household debts, which had more than doubled in size since the year 2000, were linked to real estate, and the report painted a general gloomy picture from this trend. In particular, eight countries were identified as having unsustainable household debt: the Netherlands, South Korea, Canada, Sweden, Australia, Malaysia, China and Thailand. It seemed possible that another property related debt crisis was in the making in these countries.

**Table 5.2**  Global stock of debt

|           | $ Trillion, constant 2013 exchange rates | | |
|-----------|:-------:|:-------:|:-------:|
|           | **Q4 2000** | **Q4 2007** | **Q2 2014** |
| Household | 19 | 33 | 40 |
| Corporate | 26 | 38 | 56 |
| Government | 22 | 33 | 58 |
| Financial | 20 | 37 | 45 |
| Total debt | **87** | **142** | **199** |

*Note*: numbers may not sum due to rounding
*Source*: *Debt and (not much) deleveraging.* McKinsey Global Institute, 2015

The data suggests that the central banks had spent years looking in the wrong place. The conventional interest rate approach and its younger associate QE would no longer suffice to avoid systemic risks and financial instability. Therefore, a new range of instruments evolved. Stress tests and macroprudential tools are two examples of the current state of the art. They are detailed further below.

## Stress tests

Since the crisis of 2008, central banks have begun to examine the major financial institutions in their national system to ensure they have enough available capital to withstand a global downturn – to ensure that a nation's financial system is sufficiently resilient to weather a storm or a crisis without calling on the taxpayer for support. Obviously, the extent of the test varies from one national financial system to another. Thus, in the Eurozone, with its nineteen member states, the examination is a mammoth task, involving 6000 people auditing the books of more than 130 big banks, whereas in America the tests involve less than twenty-five major financial institutions. In the UK, the representative institutions are HSBC, Barclays, Royal Bank of Scotland, Lloyds, Santander UK, Standard Chartered and the building society Nationwide. In general terms, the tests are designed specifically to assess the resilience of the financial network to deterioration in global economic conditions.

Inevitably, the actual tests and format will take different forms from one country to another, and from one year to the next. For instance, there was a marked difference between the 2014 and 2015 tests for UK financial stability drawn up by the Bank of England. The 2015 scenario focused on exploring vulnerabilities stemming from the rest of the world (as UK banks have large international exposures), whereas the 2014 stress test had emphasised domestic risks, especially those stemming from the UK housing market. Similarly, the 2015 scenario explored the effects of a deflationary macroeconomic environment, which – in turn – was associated with a reduction in Bank Rate, whilst the 2014 equivalent stress test had rehearsed an inflationary shock in the United Kingdom and an associated tightening of monetary policy. The 2015 scenario placed more emphasis on exploring risks stemming from corporate exposures, in contrast to the 2014 version of the test, which considered the effects of adverse shocks to household sector (Bank of England, 2015).

It should be patently obvious by now that the stress tests are not a forecast of macroeconomic and financial conditions. They are simply a set of events that could, with a little imagination and academic licence, be expected to materialise. The official literature likes to refer to them as a coherent 'tail-risk' scenario – one that has been designed specifically to assess the resilience of banks and other major financial institutions to deterioration in global economic conditions. In short, a 'tail-risk' event could happen, but the probability is exceedingly low. Then again, no-one predicted the severity of the financial crisis. Primarily, the objective is to judge whether there is enough capital in each bank to tide it over a period of adversity.

To close this section, it is important to be clear that a stress test does nothing to restructure the financial system or the way it is regulated; it can do no more than 'what it states on the tin'. It will not remove or reduce risks that threaten the resilience of the system as a whole; it will merely indicate whether the current system has sufficient flexibility to accommodate shocks and change.

## Macroprudential policy

Since the days of the Great Recession, central bank regulators have begun to monitor the financial system and impose a significant number of rules, such as reserve requirements, limits on credit growth, capital requirements, limits on loan to value ratios and so on. Similar tools had been employed before 2008 but, at that time, their use was motivated by monetary policy and microprudential objectives. A distinction therefore needs to be made between the new macroprudential policies and the traditional microprudential policies. The traditional approach focused on risks and the solidity of individual institutions, whereas macroprudential policies are primarily aimed at financial stability and countercyclical management. In the official language of the international (Basle) committee on banking supervision (CGFS, 2012): supervisory agencies are tasked not only to ensure the safety and soundness of individual institutions, but also to contribute to the stability of the system as a whole. This is fraught with difficulties because systemic threats are hard to discern, since they tend to fly beneath the financial radar, emerging from a setting of seeming economic tranquillity.

Macroprudential policy, therefore, offers a system-wide perspective focusing on the linkages and interconnections – the nodes and flows – between the financial and domestic real sectors (households, corporations and government), and between each sector and the rest of the world, and the structure of the financial sector linkages between financial intermediaries. Figure 5.3 attempts to map out this infrastructure. Panel (a) focuses on the flows between the sectors of an economy across time, and Panel (b) represents the linkages between the key financial intermediaries. Presented together, the two panels of Figure 5.3 should give greater meaning to assessed by sector, financial market and time.

Inevitably, assessment of the robustness of this structure relies largely on statistical data. However, in keeping with the new thinking that has emerged since 2008, it is emphasised that central banks should not ignore market intelligence or qualitative information on trends and financial market developments. The goal of the work is to identify the drivers of macroeconomic imbalance through a detailed monitoring of total credit flows between sectors and institutions.

## The classic macroprudential policy

Although macroprudential policy can take many guises, the most common relates to mortgage markets. There are two basic possibilities: introducing regulations that force borrowers to find bigger deposits (which can be achieved by increasing the amount of capital that banks must hold against mortgage debts); or imposing limits on the amount that people can borrow. Borrowing limits have been experimented with across Europe. They are usually stated as a ratio relative to the purchase price or household income or, as the respective jargon expresses it:

Panel A: Sectoral dimension

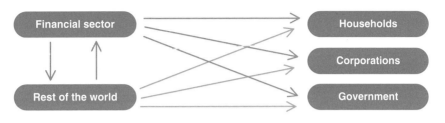

Panel B: Financial dimension

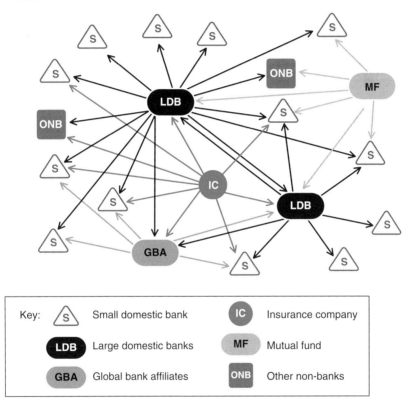

**Figure 5.3**   Systemic risks across the financial system.
*Source*: Adapted from *Brockmeijer et al.* (2013: 16).

'loan-to-value' (LTV) or 'loan-to-income' (LTI). As implied, several examples could be cited. For instance, in June 2014, the Bank of England announced that lenders (banks) could not extend more than 15% of their mortgages to customers needing to borrow more than four-and-a-half times their income.

The International Monetary Fund (IMF, 2013) assessed the impact of macroprudential policies across 46 countries, and they confirmed that by far the most common measure was a cap on the amount that people could borrow as a multiple of the value of the home. Half the countries had imposed LTV ratios, compared with one-third where central banks adopted a loan-to-income (LTI) cap. This preference for LTV controls is a shame as, by definition, LTV ratios tend to 'self-destruct'. From the moment they are imposed, the price of a house can still go up, which would allow somebody to borrow more money via a mortgage on the basis of the increased value. In short, LTV ratios can be a bit circular. By contrast, an LTI target is far more effective, as the ratio is defined in terms of the debt size in relation to a household's income.

It is certainly not simple or easy to rein in mortgage lending, especially as it effects people's dreams and aspirations. Economics influences decision-makers, but they often have broader political concerns. A country needs a housing policy that works alongside a stable and fair financial system. If a change in regulations raises the problem that some people can no longer get a mortgage who were previously able to get one, then the economic decision has been politicised. As Andy Haldane (2013), the Bank of England's chief economist, amusingly quipped: 'Macroprudential policy is roughly where monetary policy was in the '40s' ... (and).... 'If I were being charitable, that would be the 1940s, rather than the 1840s.'

In sum, macroprudential policy is designed to prevent a future financial crisis. As a consequence, much new institutional architecture has been put in place since 2008, across a number of countries. The first examples included the Fed, with the setting up of the Financial Stability Oversight Council (FSOC) in 2009. The equivalent European Systemic Risk Board (ESRB) that was set up by the ECB followed in 2011. Then, the Financial Policy Committee (FPC) was established at the Bank of England in 2013. These institutional arrangements were put in place to assure the regulation and monitoring of systemic risks.

Meanwhile, other central bank agencies were created to concentrate specifically on supervision and conventional monetary policy. Taking the relatively straight-forward case of the United Kingdom as an example (avoiding the complex labyrinth of supervision and rule enforcement across 50 states in America or the 19 countries of the Eurozone), there are currently three committees charged with the responsibility of regulating and managing the United Kingdom's financial system, which alone has around 1700 banks, building societies, credit unions, insurers and major investment firms. Although each committee has its specific duties, they have direct insight into one another's activities. An outline of their structure and overlaps are indicated in Figure 5.4.

Between them, the three committees are charged with the overall responsibility of maintaining a strong and resilient financial network and, consequently, they are represented by executives from the Bank, the Treasury and beyond. The Venn diagram is included to highlight the complexity of the tasks that a central bank has to deal with. Although they like to think of themselves as independent from political power, it is interesting to note the presence of the Treasury on the two policy making committees. Managing the macroeconomy and its interaction with the financial system is certainly fraught with difficulty. As pointed out by *The Economist* (2015b), both financiers and economists picked up much of the blame for the 2008 financial crisis: 'The first group for causing it and the second for not predicting it. As it turns out, the two issues are connected. The economists failed to understand the importance of finance and financiers put too much faith in the models produced by economists'.

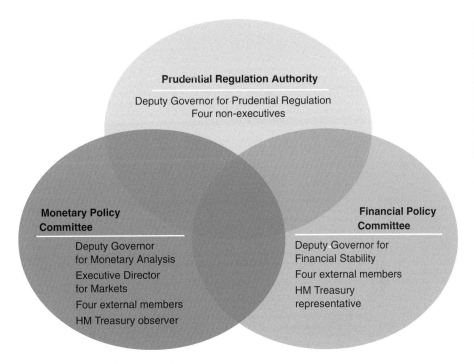

**Figure 5.4**   Membership of Bank of England policy committees.
*Source*: Adapted from Tucker *et al.* (2013: 197).

## The devil's in the detail

In theory, central bank policy sounds all well and good but, in practice, effective execution is dogged by problems of expectations, business confidence, forecasting and timing. Decision-making from the centre is undeniably complex. To quote a telling remark made by Mervyn King (Deputy and Governor of the Bank of England from 1998 (2003) to 2013), in defence of his monetary policy committee. 'First, the only certainty is that there is no certainty. Second, every decision is a matter of weighing probabilities, or the balance of risks, as we say. Third, despite uncertainty we have to decide and act' (King, 1999: 12).

In effect, monetary and financial policy boils down to being an art of judgment. Although it is possible to understand the principles and theories underpinning each policy instrument, it is well-nigh impossible to know confidently when, and by how much, to apply them. There is always some debate about the precise size and the exact timing of any new measure that is introduced. Furthermore, it can be argued that policy decisions should not only be judged on their results, but also on how they were executed. For example, in 2015, when interest rates looked set to increase, the Governor of the Bank of England announced his intentions in some forward guidance. His words alone were sufficient to prompt mortgage providers to re-price their products almost immediately, but certainly before any actual changes were made. As we have argued several times in this text, treating economics like a prescriptive rule book will get you nowhere. Good economists need to learn to deal with the world as it is, and fight shy of deferring to idealised academic models that can be lifted verbatim from a text book.

## Food for thought: Cosmetic accounting

This chapter has looked at the characteristics of the financial system and the nature of policies used by a central bank in its quest to secure macroeconomic stability. An underlying theme has been the importance of balancing the books, to maintain confidence that banks and other financial intermediaries are not over-exposed. As you may recall, the books (accounts) of major financial intermediaries are monitored by the central bank to assure that they can function effectively even under 'stress' conditions.

Balancing the books – bringing the credits and debits sides into agreement – is an important exercise used to account for all private sector transactions. The financial sector is no exception – it is just the terminology that is different. As the stylised approach adopted in most texts highlight, economists commence from an understanding that the total assets and total liabilities (the credits and debits, so to speak) of financial institutions should always be equal. For example, as detailed in this chapter, every loan will be counterbalanced by a deposit. In other words, a business balance sheet shows the financial condition of a company at a given point in time, as it identifies where the money has come from (the liabilities) and where it has gone (the assets). It should not, however, be confused with a company's income statement – its profit and loss account – which shows the financial position over a given period.

Figure 5.5 shows the traditional balance sheet approach, with a bank's 'source of funds' – its liabilities – on one side, and its 'use of funds' – its assets – on the other side. Similar to other private sector organisations, banks need to finance their activities, and this is achieved by a mixture of borrowing and share capital. In other words, liabilities represent what banks owe to others (identifying where the funds have come from), and the lion's share of these are the current and savings accounts from households and firms. Further funds can be borrowed from other banks and institutional investors, such as pension funds, typically by selling bonds (as IOUs) into the wholesale markets.

A bank's assets, on the other hand, include income-generating resources of all kinds that are expected to pay out at some point in the future – in short, they represent how the funds are used. The most obvious, and by far the biggest, group of assets is represented by various types of loan made to households and businesses. Other income-generating resources include loans made to other financial institutions and governments, although these tend to be for shorter periods of time than typical everyday loans, and often in the form of commercial paper. A small amount of assets are kept in reserve at the central bank (which are effectively a bank's current account, but they do earn a minimal rate of return). Finally, it should be noted that the stylised balance sheet in Figure 5.5 *does include* 'cash in the tills' as, although strictly speaking these funds do not generate income, they are critically important to running and maintaining the everyday business. If a bank does not have sufficient assets in cash to make payments to its counterparties and customers, it has failed.

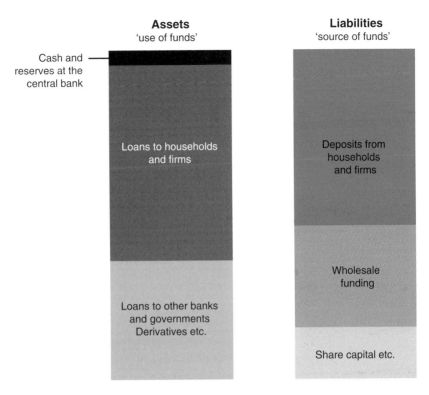

**Figure 5.5**   A simplified bank balance sheet.
*Source*: Adapted from Farag, *et al.* (2013: 202).

## Some unsettling thoughts

Three interrelated factors – 'time', 'price stability' and 'unpaid debts' – can play havoc with a bank's financial balance and, at the extremes, can contribute to financial crisis. To highlight the dilemma – or trilemma, as it initially appears, we focus on the aspect that is least dealt with by traditional texts – namely, 'time'. As students of real estate will already appreciate from their valuation exercises (e.g. to appraise whether or not to proceed with an investment), a clear distinction needs to be drawn between money today and a flow of related income in the future. To some extent, 'time' is usually accounted for, as loans are recorded on an 'amortised cost' basis – in plain English, as the value of a loans plus interest. In direct contrast, there is also a snapshot view, which involves measuring assets on a current market value. This is known as the 'trading book' treatment, and its relevance is detailed further in the following case study.

It has been made transparently clear that debts represent obligations to make future payments. Unpaid debts, therefore, have the potential to create circumstances that can make creditors – financial institutions – vulnerable to solvency and liquidity problems. Due to the interconnectedness of the financial networks, these problems can quickly escalate across an economy and extend to other countries, as evidenced by the contagion that virulently spread across the international markets in 2007/8.

A further twist that compounds this analysis is the period of time between the debt creation and debt maturity. To take an apt example, during their undergraduate years, the average student might rack up £40,000 in student loans, and the Government is prepared to advance these funds, although there is a risk that they will never be paid back. In official statistics, the loan will be granted – or paid out – but will not need to be repaid up until 30 years later. Thereafter, the debt is cancelled.

All the student loans paid out in 2015, therefore, are expected to be repaid by 2045; if not, the debt will be written off. In the interim, the Government has the licence – like any other creditor – to parcel up the debts and sell them on. In other words, the loan book – or part of it – can be sold to a third party. For example, a portfolio of loans, with a maturity value of £1.1 billion, was bought for £122.9 million in 2013, and the parcel comprised largely of student debts. At first glance, such figures seem highly unlikely, as it would appear that the Government is shooting itself in the foot and getting a return of less than 10% of its original funds. However, the underlying rationale is that the opportunity to get *some* of the funds is a better option than getting back nothing at a later date. Moreover, the funds of £122.9 million are available today!

Another way of thinking about this is that creditors will accept loss, as long as they do not lose everything. As suggested, this should make immediate sense to real estate students, as much of the intrigue lies in understanding **net present value** (NPV) – the value of money today in relation to a stream of costs and payments expected in the future. In this instance, we have a parcel of loans (and for simplicity's sake, we will assume they are all students loans) with a potential value of £1.1 billion. On the basis of past experience, the Government only expects 25% of the debts actually to be fully paid back. In other words, at some time in the future (and that could be up to 30 years away), the Government could expect £275 million (25% of the £1.1 billion) to be repaid. This is money that the Government in the interim has to borrow, administer and, presumably, see erode through inflation. Therefore, assuming a current cost of 3% per annum over 30 years, a government should be willing to accept anything greater than £113,300,000 today (use an online table [7] to check the net present value of £275 million at 3% annual interest over a 30 year period). In this example, the Government has actually exceeded the current acceptable minimum by £9.6 million. Or, to put it another way, they have saved £9.6 million of their funding costs.

The reason this should resonate with students thinking about real estate development is they get used to appraising various outlays (adjusted for inflation, prevailing rates of return (interest rates) and time) in order to identify the present value of a project that stretches over a number of years. The obvious example is a property investment that produces a rental stream over 25 years. Precisely the same calculation informs the trading of debt detailed above.

Finally, the inquisitive reader may be wondering what happened to the £825 million that has not been mentioned since we commenced with the assumption that 75% of the respective outstanding student loan book could be written off. An economist would regard this as the taxpayer's opportunity cost of education which, in this instance, appears to be £275 million cheaper than running a system without fees and with a maintenance grant.

# Chapter 6
# The Financial Recession

The Great Recession stemming from the financial crash of 2007/8 may well be the first recessionary phase that readers of this text have studied, but it will certainly not be the last. It is a well-recognised fact that recessions come and go in various shapes and sizes. Some even like to suggest that they are a regular occurrence – or, to be precise, are cyclical in nature. In principle, economists draw a distinction between two types of recession: the normal, run-of-the-mill recession and the more severe financial recession, such as the Great Recession that this text has as part of its story line. To date, financial recessions have not been as common: of the 200 episodes of recession identified (across 17 advanced economies) in the last 140 years, only 25% of them were regarded as financial in nature (Jorda *et al.*, 2014: 3).

A traditional recession is characterised by a gap between actual and potential output, which usually takes no more than a year or two to play out. However, a financial recession – often referred to as a 'balance sheet recession' –tends to be a far longer and more problematic event, as it takes a considerable time to adjust the massive overhangs of private and public debt. For instance, eight years after the problems experienced with subprime mortgage debt in the USA in 2007, the effects of the Great Recession still rumble on. In Spain and other parts of Southern Europe, a double dip recession – two separate episodes of prolonged negative GDP – contracted the economy between 2008 and 2013. Equally, there is still some debate about Greece, who might yet witness a third extended dip within a decade. In fact, the Euro area as a whole – all nineteen countries – have hardly recovered from the financial debacle, with more than 10% having been cut from global production since it started, and serious doubts being raised about the future of a single currency!

*New Economic Thinking and Real Estate*, First Edition. Danny Myers.
© 2016 John Wiley & Sons, Ltd. Published 2016 by John Wiley & Sons, Ltd.

## The language of recessions and recovery

A recession is broadly defined as a period of diminishing economic activity. For example, the National Bureau of Economic Research in the United States has moved to an interesting position, where it identifies and selects a month when the economy reaches a peak of activity, and a later month when the economy reaches a trough (the time in between is referred to as the recessionary phase), and all this is discussed by the oddly titled '*dating committee*'.

For instance, in NBER's terms, the Great Recession began in the United States in December 2007, at the peak of the previous economic cycle in the US economy, and ended in June 2009, at the bottom of the trough, when the recessionary cycle was formally declared complete (NBER, 2010 [1]). In terms of Figure 6.1, a new upward trend had commenced, although it was far below the longer-term growth path. In plain English, the recovery phase started in mid-2009, but the subsequent growth was slow and fragile. At the beginning of 2014, for example, employment in America had still not managed to return to its pre-recession level. We examine the problems of identifying the precise turning points of an economy further in Chapter 8.

### The recession

In Europe, however, a recession is more black and white, as it is classified as two or more consecutive quarters of negative GDP. In short, it is a period of time when the economy has gone backwards. This is not a short blip, but a slide into a pattern that has continued for six months or more.

Again, we need not be over-concerned with the differing definitions from one nation to the next, as long as we appreciate that a business cycle is characterised

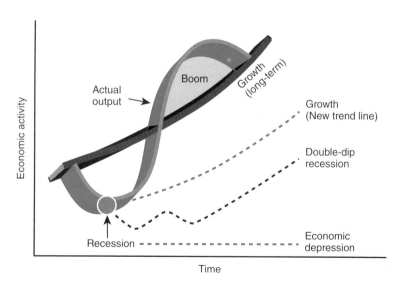

**Figure 6.1**  Economic fluctuations.

by peaks and troughs in economic activity. The period between a peak and a trough is described as a contraction or a recession, and the period between the trough and the peak as an expansion. The NBER does not separately define depressions, nor does it define a double-dip recession. Two periods of contraction will be either two separate recessions, or parts of the same recession. Time will tell whether the NBER's interpretation will become more widely accepted, or if there will be some other code of practice. The important point is that, regardless of language or national conventions, we need to be able to recognise a recession when we see one.

### The recovery

Economists tend to discuss three types of recovery, distinguished by their speed of travel – quick, slow and intermittent. To make matters appear more confusing, each of these is characterised by the shape of a letter, namely V, U or W. The 'V-shaped' recovery is quick; a 'U-shaped' recovery is slow; and a 'W-shaped' recovery is intermittent, as the economy experiences a swift recovery before plunging back down again. As described above, the 'W-shaped' recovery represents a 'double-dip' recession.

Much of the language relating to economic recessions and recovery is brought together in Figure 6.1. An important reference point is the long-term growth trend around which economic activity fluctuates. In reality, the variance is not as regular, or necessarily as steep, as the stylised artwork implies. This is captured in two other terms used to describe current economic cycles – 'flat-lining' and 'deceleration' – both of which are used to infer that the economy is progressing, but only at a slow and gradual rate. More recently, it has even been suggested that the business cycle has entered a new phase – a new 'norm'. Characterised by slow growth, higher levels of unemployment and fewer investment opportunities, this is referred to as 'secular stagnation' (and it is put in context in Chapter 7). Interestingly, this term was first used to shed light on the persistence of a financial recession during the closing phases of the Great Depression in 1938.

## A new world

Without doubt, the financial recession that stemmed from the credit crunch of 2007/08 heralded a new era, as it represented the longest and deepest global recession since the Second World War. In the jargon introduced above, it was indisputably U-shaped, as there was a weak below-trend growth for a number of years. Many jobs had been lost, such as those in real estate, construction and the financial sector. Those who had managed to keep their jobs were often working fewer hours, and productivity was slow to recover. At the time of writing, a new upward phase was beginning but, as discussed and indicated in Figure 6.1, it was significantly below the established trend. The Great Recession has left its mark, presenting a classic change to economic life, and demanding new ways of thinking.

As suggested in Chapter 5, it was driven by a staggering accumulation of new and old debt, much of which had been designed by innovative bankers.

In the aftermath, it was widely expected that the world's economies would deleverage, but this did not actually happen. In fact, debt continued to grow in nearly all countries, both in absolute terms and relative to GDP.

The key aim here in Chapter 6 is to investigate how a similar event might be recognised next time around, and what the Government might do to support financial stability. A greater understanding of the causes and effects of a financial recession have direct relevance to those concerned with real estate, as property bubbles form an integral part of most explanations. Ideally, it would be good to be able to foresee the next financial recession coming, as those whose careers are destined to be involved in property need to understand fully the twists and turns of the economic climate in order to be able to make informed and timely judgements. In short, the purpose of this chapter is to find out what went wrong the last time, and where we are headed.

In certain political arenas, there seems to be a suggestion that deficits and debts generally are bad. The age of austerity that followed the recession across most European states certainly amplified this impression. However, economically speaking, it would be wrong to infer that fiscal irresponsibility was the cause of the financial crisis. The statistical evidence is discussed and presented around Figure 7.1, but here we need to separate cause and effect, by recognising that the roots of the Great Recession are to do with the management of the financial system – or, in this case, the lack of it.

This might be difficult to grasp, especially given the loud and repetitive calls of the politicians, but austerity was a response to the crisis, not the economic cause. As a counterargument, it should be noted that people did not queue outside branches of Northern Rock (a relatively small retail bank that was the first to fail in the UK) for three days in September 2007 because the government was spending too much on nurses and teachers.

As most economists would point out, there is nothing wrong with borrowing, provided it is kept within certain limits. The idea that borrowing is bad is a myth that needs to be shattered. Without borrowing, society would not be able to buy houses, start up businesses or invest in infrastructure.

Living within a nation's means is consistent with borrowing – particularly at the level of the state. As Keynesian economists emphasised for much of the post-war period, running a state like a household is not a fair comparison. As you may recall from Chapter 1, macroeconomic management is founded on the proposition that an economy is distinctly different from the sum of its parts. What makes sense at the individual household level does not necessarily make sense at the national level. In Chapter 1, this principle was referred to as the 'fallacy of composition', but in this context it might make more sense to use an alternative phrase – the 'paradox of aggregation'.

## So what was the cause?

Up until the Great Recession, there was a tradition of accounting for financial crises as **exogenous** or, less formally, the outcome of an external shock to the economic system. As a consequence, they were considered impossible to forecast, as they were outside the main models of the economy. Recent events, however, have challenged this narrow-minded type of approach, and nowadays financial matters are recognised as an inherent part of the economic system. As the jargon describes it, finance has become an **endogenous** variable.

Historically speaking, therefore, economists have lacked a body of suitable work to address questions relating to severe financial recessions. This sounds almost unbelievable, but the only substantive exception was a lone voice in the 1970s and 1980s – Professor Herman Minsky – whose life work studied the linkages between the financial market and the real economy. Posthumously, his ideas have begun to find a place in the new movement within economics, right up to central bank level. Not only has Minsky provided an initial explanation of what happened in 2007/8, but his ideas also suggest a framework of what to look out for in the future. Indeed, his theories have spawned a new body of research that is highly relevant to professionals in the property industry seeking to identify the most appropriate time to invest. This new body of research is examined below, but first of all we acknowledge the corpus of Minsky's work and the emergence of the 'Minsky moment'.

## Herman Minsky (1919–1996) – ahead of his time?

As you no doubt recall from Chapter 4, there is a pressing need for the economics profession to merge the real economy and the financial economy – to identify the relationship between financial growth and real growth in modern economic systems. Yet it was more than 40 years ago that Herman Minsky began to develop a **financial instability hypothesis**. It was his life work, built on the premise that: 'The financial system swings between robustness and fragility and these swings are an integral part of the process that generates business cycles' (Minsky, 1974). As he explained it, a rich market economy, comprising expensive assets and supported by a complex financial system, is inevitably unstable. Without government regulation, the lending patterns that emerge through banking systems would ultimately cause an economy to go into a recession.

A further dimension of the Minsky hypothesis was his categorisation of debtors into three types: hedge borrowers, speculative borrowers and Ponzi borrowers (Minsky, 1992). To briefly summarise the character of each group in his type of language:

- Hedge borrowers are those who can fulfil all contractual payments – interest plus principal – from their current cash flows.
- Speculative borrowers are those who can meet the interest payments of a debt out of current income, but need to arrange further debt to cover the principal commitments when the debt matures.
- Ponzi borrowers have neither sufficient means to repay the principal nor the interest due on the outstanding debts from their current income. They borrow to pay interest and sell assets to pay the principal sum (Minsky dedicated the slightly unbelievable idea of this type of borrower to the infamous Carlo Ponzi, whose property scam had defrauded thousands of people during the Wall Street crash of 1929).

### Financial deregulation and the housing bubble

In many ways, Minsky's hypothesis and categorisation of borrowers has been exemplified through the history of the mortgage market. Commencing in the 1970s (around the time your grandparents were possibly buying a house), a standard mortgage was arranged so that the interest and capital (the principal) were paid off simultaneously. Twenty years later, in the 1990s (possibly around the times that your parents may have been buying their first house), it became acceptable to arrange an interest-only mortgage, on the basis that purchasers were confident that house prices would continue to undergo steady increases, so that the principal amount of debt could be paid off at maturity via an endowment policy (a type of investment arranged to grow to cover the original purchase price).

Although these arrangements might, at first, seem slightly odd, it is quite straightforward when you think about it, as the size of a mortgage is often determined by how much one can afford to pay each month. Following Minsky's typology, the speculative borrower managed to pay a higher price for a house than a hedge borrower with the same income. As a result, house prices steadily escalated from 1970 to 2007/8, and borrowers took on larger and larger amounts of mortgage.

### When the housing bubble became vulnerable

In the decade from the late 1990s through to 2008, a significant proportion of mortgage lending reached the last stage of the Minsky path towards instability. Using various teaser rates and interest-only arrangements as incentives, millions of people were encouraged to take out more debt than they could genuinely afford. Mortgages were even granted in excess of 100% of the value of the property. Thirty-year adjustable-rate mortgages were arranged, with exceptionally low rates to commence, and then reset to higher rates after two years or so. Payment holidays were granted for the first few months which, in effect, meant that no part of the mortgage debt was paid off at all during that period of the contract. House buyers were able to nominate the proportion of the principal debt that they could afford every month, on the basis that the amount of debt and interest payments would be amortised – paid off – at maturity.

All in all, mortgages were provided liberally and, during the first years of the millennium, banks seemed prepared to arrange a whole array of Ponzi-style mortgages. There certainly did not appear to be much discretion or scrutiny about who was being lent money and, in retrospect, it seemed that in some cases they were even designed to default.

### The Minsky moment arrived

Minsky had described reasonably precisely what happened between 1970 and 2008, and the momentum was greatly aided by the development of deregulated financial systems. From 1980 onwards, a whole range of complicated mortgages had been designed largely to help the banking community to make a lot of money. An immaterial consequence possibly led to a slight temporary increase in homeownership, but the cost to society from the debt overhang and subsequent recession was astronomical. This was certainly not the way that financial markets were seen to work in the mainstream texts studied at University. For centuries, the circular-flow model introduced in Chapter 4 (for example, see Figure 4.1) had accounted for banks as important institutions, providing a conduit between firms and households.

Banks were presented as catalysts to the system providing firms with funds to invest and grow. As the classic insightful joke made by those who lectured in the 1980s highlighted, whenever cash is routinely stuffed into a mattresses or glass jar in the larder, the economy does not grow very fast. In short, neoclassical economists presented the financial system as a means of efficiently linking markets for savers and investors. As such, businesses created job opportunities and stimulated economic growth. This conventional line of thought starkly contrasts with the more cynical view held today – that the financial system has become more concerned with feathering its own nest than supporting the broader economy. Something changed, and the system became corrupted.

To reassure you that this is not a case of being controversial for its own sake, we shall begin to draw this section to a close by referring to Professor Joe Stiglitz. He pointed out in his analysis of the Great Recession that: 'In all the go-go years of cheap money, Wall Street did not come up with a good mortgage product … [with] low transaction costs and low interest rates…. Instead, Wall Street firms focused on maximizing their returns, came up with mortgages that had high transaction costs and variable interest rates with payments that could suddenly spike, but with no protection against the risk of a loss in home value or the risk of job loss.

'Had the designers of these mortgages focused on the ends – what we actually wanted from our mortgage market – rather than on how to maximize their revenues, then they might have devised products that would have permanently increased homeownership. They could have 'done well by doing good' (Stiglitz, 2010: 4–5).

The experiences in the UK were little different. More than half of the outstanding mortgages – held by approximately five million households – were variable rate mortgages; meaning that they follow (or track) the Bank of England interest rate (a standard arrangement being two percentage points above base rate). Many of the mortgages had been arranged on an interest-only basis, although the more recent ones would be a standard repayment mortgage, which meant that the interest and capital repayments were combined. Either arrangement was all well and good while base rates were low but, whenever central banks start raising their rates, problems can quickly ensue. Furthermore, so-called liar loans had become increasingly common, as people were allowed to self-assess their ability to repay the mortgage, and fibbed about their income or failed to comply with written confirmation of their salary.

As the press cynically observed on both sides of the pond, in the period leading up to the 2008 financial debacle, NINJA loans were granted to people with *no income no jobs (and no) assets*. To paraphrase Alan Blinder's (2013: 70) neat conclusion to this irresponsible lending, although no one seems to know precisely how many NINJA loans were actually granted, it does not need a rocket scientist to remind us that the prudent number ought to be zero!

## Why did no one see it coming?

A new era demands new way of thinking, but the economics profession seemed hesitant to let go of their established theories and models. To briefly reiterate a major premise of this text, established academic economists, frequently appear to be wedded to the ideas that they learnt at University. These ideas were often highly mathematical, and often built around assumptions that markets always clear, and equilibriums are always reached. For example, financial systems were always seen to work, and the possibility of another Great Depression had been more or less dismissed. The odd recessionary hiccup was smugly excused as an 'external' event that was not predictable by logical and scientific modelling.

The arrogance of the situation was neatly captured by a royal event at the London School of Economics in November 2008 [2]. The story goes as follows: at a ceremony to open a new building, Queen Elizabeth curiously asked: 'how come nobody could foresee it?' Apparently, the nervous professor to whom the question was addressed – Professor Luis Garicano – initially fumbled the following response: 'At every stage, someone was relying on somebody else and everyone thought they were doing the right thing'. A more formal reply to the royal question, in the form of a three-page letter, spoke of a 'psychology of denial' that had gripped the financial and political world in the run-up to the crisis.

Faced with such a large-scale embarrassment, there was a clamour for economists to respond more positively. There was a collapsing debt mountain and slowly rising unemployment, alongside an agonised section of the rich and famous who had taken an enormous hit since the stock market had fallen by almost 25% in value. In sum, broad sections of the community were feeling the effects of the economic squeeze from the financial crisis.

## Let the facts speak for themselves

Fortunately, a significant number of economists came to the rescue by becoming less axiomatic and more empirical. They recognised that, to save the economics discipline from further disrepute, the subject could no longer remain detached from the experience of real life. It was necessary to acknowledge that the last decade had happened, that financial crises do come and go and, most importantly, that they emerge from within the system. As Roubini and Mihm (2011), two empirical economists of the new school, colourfully argue in their book about the future of financial recessions: crises are not black swans – 'rare and well-nigh impossible to predict' – but white swans – 'commonplace and relatively easy to foresee and to comprehend'. Evidently, if you look into the past, you can find literally dozens of them.

The new approach has done just that, and there is a whole body of evidence-based theory emerging. Two interesting examples – Jorda et al. (2014) and Rogoff and Reinhart (2009) –refer to extensive data from a number of countries, and are reviewed below. First of all, though, a word of warning: we are not endorsing data mining for its own sake; we are still engaged in economics, but starting from a different place. So, take care that facts do not become twisted to support precon-ceived ideas. As any good investigator would warn you, if you start off on the wrong foot, you inevitably run the risk of getting it all the wrong way round. The very nature of robust investigative research relies on maintaining a clinical approach to avoid conflict between fact and fiction.

## The 'Great Mortgaging'

Jorda *et al.* (2014) researched a long-run dataset that covered 17 advanced economies over the past 140 years, to investigate the causes and consequences of the growth of finance. They used the data to demonstrate that banks no longer lend primarily to businesses, as a result of the rapid growth in opportunities to provide loans for real estate. Whereas, in 1900, only 30% of bank lending was used to buy residential property, nowadays that figure is closer to 60%.

As Jorda *et al.* (2014: 2) were quick to point out: 'The intermediation of household savings for productive investment in the business sector – the standard textbook role of the financial sector – constitutes only a minor share of the business of banking today, even though it was a central part of that business in the 19th and early 20th centuries. We also find that household mortgage debt has risen faster than asset values in many countries, resulting in record-high leverage ratios that potentially increase the fragility of household balance sheets and the financial system itself'.

In other words, since the beginning of the 21st Century, most of the increase in the ratio of private-sector debt to GDP in advanced economies is due to rising levels of mortgage lending – not corporate borrowing, as had previously been the case. Far from channelling money to companies, modern banks resemble 'real-estate funds'.

## This time is different

Rogoff and Reinhart (2009) researched a larger and longer-run dataset, covering 66 countries over 800 years, with the intention of providing a broad summary of the history of financial crises. The subsequent book comprises nearly 500 pages, made up of 17 chapters and data appendices. An important motivation behind their investigation was, in their words, 'that theory gives little guidance on the exact timing or duration of financial crises, which is why we focus on experience'. The data refers to financial crises in various guises, covering a wide range of political systems, exchange rate arrangements, institutions, stages of economic development and historic circumstances.

Unlike much of the work of this modern genre, Rogoff and Reinhart did not limit their research to statistics that are simply readily available. This mean that when it comes to researching crises, they do not act like the proverbial drunk who searches for his keys under a lamppost, even though that is not where he dropped them; they act soberly, and venture into dark and difficult corners to search for their answers as far afield as the data will take them. As a consequence, they have to accept imperfect and incomplete data to spread their net across a wide range of experience. As far as is humanly possible, they take a good, long look at what the statistical records can tell them. To their credit, this distinguishes them from other academics who simply mine the data that they can easily get their hands on – which basically explains why so much work refers to the United States, the United Kingdom and a few other wealthy, advanced, nations.

The most relevant section of their book is laid out in Chapter 10 [3], which specifically looks at banking crises in Africa, Asia, Europe, Latin America, North America and Oceania (Australia and New Zealand) from 1800 to 2008. They found that the tally of crises is highest in the world's financial centres: France, the United Kingdom and the United States. Furthermore, this section of Rogoff and Reinhart's (2009) work also examines the pattern of housing prices and central government finances (specifically, tax revenue and public debt) around the time of major banking crises. The main finding is that debt is always dangerous, particularly government debt, not only when they borrow from foreigners, but also when they borrow from their own citizens. In fact, the data suggest that economic growth declines dramatically when a country's level of public debt exceeds 90% of gross domestic product.

## The student who debunked two professors

A good practice for students seeking to understand research is a replication exercise. This involves finding an academic paper to update and check the findings. Obviously, it can be done across any academic discipline, but it is most appropriate here, as Thomas Herndon, a post grad student in economics at the University of Massachusetts picked Rogoff and Reinhart's (2010) paper for his replication assignment and quickly made a name for himself, and his lecturers, because it appeared that he identified a number of errors in the *Excel* analysis. In fact, the published critique (Herndon *et al.*, 2013) went as far as suggesting that the findings drawn by Rogoff and Reinhart (2010) were based on a number of statistical errors.

This raised several questions about the conclusion that countries facing public debt to GDP ratios above 90% would experience a major decline in GDP growth. Indeed, the debate that followed raised doubts about whether debt caused slower growth, or slow growth caused debt. This type of chicken-and-egg – cause and effect – argument is typical of findings based on broad economic data from a number of sources, countries and years. As Tim Harford (2014: 120) concluded from this debate: painstaking economics research rarely produces 'cast-iron proof'. However, given the poor data they had to hand, I would be inclined to give Rogoff and Reinhart the benefit of doubt, and conclude that, in the circumstances, their work represents a 'best guess estimate'.

## Summing up

In the years before the financial crisis, it was considered good practice for the guardians of the financial system to use interest rate policy to lean again trends, raising interest rates when asset bubbles (such as housing) grew or, at worst, using them to clean up the mess after the bubble burst by cutting interest rates. Since the crisis, however, central banks have, in the light of the new empiricism, begun to try to distinguish between bubbles affected by 'irrational exuberance' and 'animal spirits', and those pumped up by debt. As a consequence, the rate of credit issuance has begun to challenge monitoring through interest rates. In brief, the divide between approaches before and after the financial crisis shifted from 'leaning' using interest rate policy, to 'leaning' through debt monitoring (for further details on monetary policy, see Chapter 5).

Another major shift has been the growing acceptance that financial systems are integral to economic systems. As the jargon introduced above defines it: *systemically important financial institutions* (SIFIs) are those who, because of their size, complexity and interconnectedness, can cause significant disruption to the global financial system and disorder to related economic activity (FSB, 2010). The implication is that such institutions may have become too big to fail, and need to be subject to far more supervision to reduce the possibility and impact of that failure. The significance of this development is explored further in the *Food for Thought* section of this chapter.

Finally, it has become apparent that we can no longer rely solely on economic models, as they do not seem capable of accounting for severe economic crises such as the Great Recession. The empirical alternatives, discussed above, are also problematic, as they require shrewd judgement to be effectively used. At the current time, however, this seems to be a more realistic alternative than relying on the presumptuous nature of mainstream models. Also, empiricism opens up the debate. Broadening this still further are the behavioural economists who add that financiers and investors are motivated by crowd psychology – 'herd behaviour' – rather than 'rational expectations'. As Richard Thaler (2015) pointed out in his aptly titled book *Misbehaving: The Making of Behavioural Economics* [4]: 'compared to the fictional models of academic economics humans do a lot of misbehaving, and as a consequence traditional economists have made a lot of bad predictions'.

## Central bank: Lender of last resort

As introduced in Chapter 5, a central bank is a powerful and important economic institution. Its policies and actions directly affect the quantity and allocation of credit available across the various sectors of an economy and the rates of interest charged for the related loans. It also manages the exchange rates used for international transactions. In turn, these tools influence consumer expenditure, business investment, levels of employment, the rate of growth, income distribution, the trade deficit, real estate markets and so on.

Now we need to add one final piece to the central bank jigsaw and, to put this in context, we need to go back 150 years. As already discussed, financial crises are not new or unusual events on the world stage, and this was neatly highlighted by Walter Bagehot's classic *Lombard Street*, which was published in 1873 and written, in part, as a reaction to a financial crisis in 1866 that collapsed a City of London wholesale discount bank – *Overend & Gurney*.

*Memory Lane*

In Britain, economic crises had occurred – with some regularity – in 1816, 1825, 1836, 1847, 1857, 1866, 1873 and 1890. Often, the root of the problem was triggered by the financial system. As detailed in Chapter 5, as financial markets became more sophisticated, there was less need for cash. In 19th Century terms, this was achieved largely through the development of bonds, equities, and cheques. The central part of the explanation was described in the section on money creation (on page 103), where we detailed how banks can quite suddenly be caught short of liquid funds if too many depositors demand their cash back at once.

Such an event had occurred in 1866, when *Overend & Gurney* came under the threat of bankruptcy. The Bank of England stepped in to save the day by lending them the funds they required to continue in business. Although this act of good faith averted a general run on the banking system in England it was, at the time, executed by a private company, albeit that its list of stock holders read like a roll-call of the 'great and the good' of the City of London. The significance of this event, however, is that it gave rise to the idea of a Central Bank as a 'lender of last resort'. The Bank of England was nationalised in 1946.

During the 20th Century, the role of the central bank was extended to managing and resolving general monetary problems. This was achieved by becoming a banker's bank, being the sole issuer of a nation's currency and accepting the role of being the Government's bank. This latter role was often motivated by a need to finance debts, particularly those arising from wars.

Slowly, the idea spread across the world, with international functions of central banks evolving in much the same direction in most countries, although it is fair to say that they often followed the examples set by the United Kingdom and the United States. The Great Depression of the early 1930s provided a further incentive, as it highlighted the need for central banks to have the tools to effectively stem the contraction of bank credit in a slump. Further incentives followed in the post-war period in the 1940s and 50s, as the emergent economies of Asia and Africa recognised the importance of a central bank in controlling the monetary system and contributing to the broader economic policies of government.

In other words, the development of the central bank system has been largely circumstantial – reflecting the various histories and doctrines of each country. For instance, it is interesting to think what would have happened to central bank powers if the Fed had not chosen to make an exception of Lehman Brothers by letting them collapse in September 2008.

Having a central bank to stand behind the financial system is critically important and, in the wake of the financial crisis of 2008, they have undergone a transformation. No longer do they simply set interest rates and provide discretionary support in times of financial crises. Nowadays the powers of central banks have been radically extended to include: the supervision of a more broadly defined financial sector; identifying and fixing reserve requirements; specifying the terms on which a household can obtain a mortgage; managing government debt; administrating foreign exchange restrictions; and lastly, but by no means least important, ensuring that banks do not go bust again.

## Where to look in the future

To sum up, excessive debts can lead to systemic problems. It does not matter if the debts are accumulated by the government, banks, corporations, or consumers, they always carry a risk of turning bad or not being paid, and the larger they get, the more vulnerable the financial network becomes. The risks are no doubt exacerbated by the fact that most governments will bail out banks to prevent a collapse in confidence in the broader economy. Therefore, banks may change their behaviour and take more risks, and behave more like casinos than utilities. Indeed, some argue that banks should not be bailed out, because it encourages them to take greater risks and creates future moral hazard.

As a consequence, economists are slowly recognising that, to assess the health of an economy, the level and nature of debt that exists need to be carefully scrutinised. Regulators need to keep track of the development of various types of bank credit, such as: mortgage lending for real estate; corporate loans to business; private credit provided through various channels to households; and national debts organised for governments. As the research community grandly refer to it: datasets that review long-run disaggregated bank credit need careful monitoring.

Monitoring levels of indebtedness, however, is fraught with difficulty. First, care needs to be taken that the financial sector is distinguishable from the private and public sectors, in order to avoid double counting, as the debt provided to households, companies, and governments can easily be represented as financial debt. Another way of looking at this is to acknowledge that financial institutions around the world carry large amounts of debts on their books, to the tune of $199 trillion in 2014. Of this amount, $45 trillion (around 20%) represented debts between financial institutions.

Second, as you may recall from Chapter 5, we briefly examined the broad range of institutions and instruments that make up a modern financial system, to highlight the challenges presented by monetary supervision and enforcing policy. The respective forms of debt instruments were neatly drawn together in Table 5.1, where the broad range of institutions and instruments that modern monetary policy needs to embrace were clearly identified. The spectrum of debt covered a range of credit markets, from mortgage loans and government bonds, to online agreements and student loans.

In the last three decades, the financial world has changed in so many ways. The financial liberalisation that commenced in the 1980s – what was called the 'Big Bang' – led inadvertently to the 'Big Crash'. The financial sector had been lulled by the opportunity of huge profits to take on a distinct expansion of debt, the significance of which was beyond the grasp of mainstream economic models. As a consequence, when the global financial credit bubble finally exploded, it was beyond comprehension – it called for a new way of thinking. Key to this was an appreciation of the risks of a systemic breakdown that could follow on from a rapid build-up of debt. The 'Minsky Moment' had well and truly arrived.

The challenge we are still struggling to confront lies in spotting the tell-tale signs of the next financial recession. For instance, it is nearly ten years ago since the financial crisis commenced but, as we go to press, there appears to be a possibility of a further instalment of the debt saga unfolding (*Economist*, 2015). Some of the signs are apparent in the disaggregated bank credit datasets that researchers scrutinise but, as we have stressed many times, statistical relationships cannot be regarded as all-embracing. Remember, to see all the signs of a forthcoming financial recession, one needs to look beyond the data.

**Part B**

## Food for thought: Where is the next crisis coming from?

Financial recessions may be identifiable as a familiar part of the economic historic landscape, but they are still difficult to predict. The obvious problem facing economic forecasters is that the events that trigger them rarely manifest themselves in the same way. As we have seen, the locus of events in the recent recession stem from the mortgage markets of America and Western Europe, whereas the previous financial crisis, in the late 1990s, was initially set off by problems with cross-border capital flows and strongly fluctuating exchange rates in the emerging markets of South East Asia. Such global financial events impose great hardship on the world's economies. Rents, business profits, investments, wages, consumption and debt repayments all become problematic aspects of a financial crash. Hence, there is a strong determination to learn lessons to secure more stability in the future.

One of the aims of the *Food for Thought* sections, and this book itself, is to overcome the tendency of automatically continuing with the mainstream approaches and making the same mistakes over and over again. As Kaletsky (2010: 181) perceptively remarked: 'The concept of a single correct model of how the economy operates is an absurd delusion'. It is a new financial world, and we need to be aware of new innovations.

A classic example of developments in the world of finance is high-frequency and high-speed trading. This phenomenon was brought under the spotlight by the publication of Michael Lewis's book *Flashboys* in 2014. The book described high-frequency trading on stock exchanges as a process dependent on pre-programmed algorithms – or, in plain English, a system designed to carry out transactions of stocks at intervals of 650 milliseconds or less.

To paraphrase (Lewis, 2014: 9): in the old days (before, say, 2007), the speed with which a trader could execute had human limits. Human beings worked on the floors of the exchanges so, if you wanted to buy or sell anything, you had to pass through them. Nowadays (since 2007), stock exchanges are simply stacks of computers in data centres. The speed with which trades occur is no longer constrained by people. The only constraint now is how fast an electronic signal can travel between exchanges.

As a result, a new transatlantic cable is being laid to connect New York and London and another across the Arctic Ocean to link London and Tokyo – all just to cut a few hundredths of a second off the time it takes to receive data or send an order. Kevin McPartland of the Tabb Group, which compiles information on the financial sector, estimated that companies spent $2.2 billion in 2010 on high-speed servers and fibre-optic cables to link traders into a global network. Such large-scale investment into trading infrastructure makes it abundantly clear that there are distinct financial advantages in securing the highest possible trading speeds.

For example, Lewis (2014) describes in detail how one financial group spent $300 million to lay a cable in the straightest possible line from Chicago to New York, cutting through mountains and under car parks, just so the time taken to send a signal back and forth could be cut from 17 milliseconds to 13 milliseconds. In return, the group charged traders a subscription of $14 million a year to use the line. Traders were willing to shell out on such high fees because the advantage of a few milliseconds is rumoured to be sufficient to generate annual profits in the region of $20 billion. Even if Lewis is allowed some fictional licence to exaggerate, the difference between high-frequency and slow-moving traders (such as mutual-fund companies, pension funds and everyday retail investors) is obviously immense.

As Lewis (2014) points out several times in his book, it only takes 100 milliseconds to blink your eyes; but in a fraction of that time, a high-frequency trader can send trading instructions that enable them to be ahead of the market. In this way, they can make a small fortune and exploit all those with slower (blinking speeds) connections. In essence, Lewis inadvertently spoilt the standard textbook image of the stock exchange as a perfect market – open, transparent, competitive, and fair.

Rigging markets by gaining access to price information a fraction of a second before all other investors is hard to swallow and certainly leads to greater volatility. Arguably, it might seem a natural extension of the traditional system, when guys in coloured jackets bellowed at one another on the floor of the stock exchange, acting on the basis that 'their word was their bond'. The new, faster, impersonal world that Lewis's book brought into the spotlight seems hard to believe. However, in its review, *The Economist* (2014) managed to form a neat and useful everyday analogy: high-frequency traders are like 'the people who offer you tasty titbits as you enter the supermarket to entice you to buy; but in this case, as soon as you show appreciation for the goods, they race through the aisles to mark the price up before you can get your trolley to the chosen counter'.

Inevitably, such sophisticated high-frequency trading begs the question whether it is legal for a handful of insiders to operate at faster speeds than the rest of the market. The FBI, and the Securities and Exchange Commission in America, the European Commission and The Bank of England, are currently investigating the situation. The fear is that sophisticated technology to buy and sell stocks at super-fast speeds undermines the integrity of the market, as it benefits speculators and costs investors. In their defence, high-frequency traders argue that they are not doing anything wrong, as their speed of operation between buying and selling actually helps the markets, by improving liquidity, reducing spread, lowering trade costs and improving price discovery.

Both sides of the argument are pertinent as, according to some accounts, more than 60% of US financial trading and a third of European trading already filters through a high-frequency platform. Nine times out of ten, they are not real traders in any normal sense, but software algorithms. As Orlowski (2015) concisely summed it up, 'the process of matching buyers and sellers [has] moved away from the hand signals used by pit traders to lightning-fast electronic trade matching algorithms'. This makes them not only difficult to identify and monitor, but also complex to regulate. As indicated above, the regulatory authorities are currently looking into high-frequency trading, but it is a difficult task for enforcement agencies to grapple with.

## *Are systemically important financial institutions taking over control?*

The example of high-speed trading is not a means of staking a claim to fame; its significance has already been rehearsed several times in the media. It is restated here simply to highlight the global power of financial arrangements, and to make it crystal clear that effective economic forecasting requires a finger on the economic pulse. In future, economists will need data to confirm what is being sensed, training in economic thought, a modicum of cynicism about tried and tested theories, and a good deal of intuitive judgement. As we have concluded before, blindly employing existing models to forecast future economic activity will no longer suffice. The shelf-life of neoclassical models is drawing to a close. To paraphrase Professor Robert Schiller: Forecasters are *some good* at predicting the time path of a normal recession based on fluctuations that they have seen many times, but they are no good at all predicting the kind of financial recession that comes along once in a while and severely fractures key financial institutions (Schiller, 2012: 111/2).

# Part C
# Measuring and Forecasting

*New Economic Thinking and Real Estate*, First Edition. Danny Myers.
© 2016 John Wiley & Sons, Ltd. Published 2016 by John Wiley & Sons, Ltd.

# Chapter 7
# Central Government and Fiscal Policy

The storyline of this text seeks to account for the years of recession that followed the financial crisis, and this entails tracking the economy from the Great Moderation to the Great Recession and beyond. The Great Moderation provides the backdrop, as it represents the period from the early 1990s. The Great Recession represents our central plot from 2008 to 2014, and for the period beyond we need to extrapolate, as a forecast is the best we can do. This will form an important part of Chapter 8.

The **Great Moderation** was a period of relatively steady economic growth that represented a kind of plateau before the fall – and what was truly 'great' about it was its duration. In broad terms, it represents a period of around 20 years in most industrialised countries. The precise timing and nature of the phenomenon varied from place to place, but it was certainly a recognised feature of most OECD countries. In the UK, the Great Moderation describes the period from **1992 to 2007/8** – the longest continuous period of expansion in the UK. As pointed out above, however, the Great Moderation was not simply experienced in the UK; it occurred around the same time in many other advanced economies. For example, in the USA, it commenced and finished slightly earlier, with 1984 being the commonly agreed start point and mid-2007 being the end.

In more precise terms. the 'Great Moderation' describes the stable period when the variability of real GDP growth and inflation both fell markedly, and recessions did not really occur. In other words, there was an extended period when swings in GDP growth and levels of price inflation were more or less non-existent although, in some countries, there were some short periods of exception when economic expansion slowed and/or inflation was raised slightly. In general terms, however, the Great Moderation represented a long period of calm before the storm.

In stark contrast, the Great Recession of 2008 to 2014 (and, in some countries, continuing through 2015) created a very different type of economic landscape,

*New Economic Thinking and Real Estate*, First Edition. Danny Myers.
© 2016 John Wiley & Sons, Ltd. Published 2016 by John Wiley & Sons, Ltd.

increasing the level of complexity and prompting a need for new economic thinking. For instance, in some circles, it was feared that economic growth may never recover and the age-old question of stabilising inflation had morphed into how best to avoid the problem of deflation. There was also the new dilemma of how to stimulate demand with inflation rates that had been near to zero for more than six years. The dynamics of the economy had certainly changed, and economic management demanded new economic thinking.

In fact, it seemed as if we were sliding towards a new economic order where the 'norm' was represented by ongoing unemployment and no significant economic growth. This possibility had been captured by the adoption of a phrase that was first coined in 1938 by the then President of the American Economic Association, Alvin Hansen – **secular stagnation**. The secular stagnation hypothesis was revived to suggest that the economy from 2013 to 2020 will be characterised by sub-par growth, very low inflation, and even possibly deflation, with nominal interest rates at, or close to, zero. Inevitably, this would have a profound impact on monetary and fiscal policy.

Thus, to continue our story, this chapter specifically clarifies the nature of macroeconomic variables and how they may be managed by manipulating fiscal policy. This knowledge is essential to anybody who wants to understand and manage property, as the demand for buildings is always derived from what is happening in the broader economy. There is also an obvious requirement that property economists should have the ability and confidence to interpret economic statistics relating to the wider economy. Hence, macroeconomic targets are conceptually introduced in this chapter, and the statistical detail is examined in the next. From the point of view of economic comprehension, therefore, it would be logical to regard Chapters 7 and 8 as a related pair.

## Macroeconomic targets

A good starting point is to recognise that all governments, regardless of their political persuasion or nationality, seek to achieve the same economic goals. In other words, there is an international consensus about the main economic targets to strive for – namely, a sustained rate of economic growth, price stability, full employment, and a positive trade balance with overseas partners. Each of these macroeconomic targets is reviewed below, along with some statistics, in Table 7.1, to outline the recent economic performance of the UK economy. Finally, we add

**Table 7.1**  UK macroeconomic statistics

|  | 2004 | 2007 | 2009 | 2011 | 2014 |
|---|---|---|---|---|---|
| Inflation[1] | 1.7 | 2.1 | 2.9 | 4.2 | 0.5 |
| Unemployment[2] | 4.7 | 5.2 | 7.8 | 8.1 | 6.2 |
| Economic growth[3] | 2.6 | 2.5 | −5.2 | 1.1 | 2.3 |
| Balance of payments[4] | −22.9 | −37.3 | −45.2 | −27.4 | −92.9 |

[1] *Consumer Price Index (percentage increase on previous year, December to December)*
[2] *Labour Force Survey (percentage annual unemployment, seasonally adjusted)*
[3] *Annual percentage increase in real GDPA*
[4] *Current account (total for whole year, £ billions)*

some remarks about the new macroeconomic problem of income distribution but, as this is not currently measured on a regular basis by the ONS, no data is given in Table 7.1. We do, however, address forms of international measurement relating to income distribution in Chapter 8.

## Sustained economic growth

The number one long-term objective of all governments is to achieve steady increases in productive capacity, and ultimately to become the richest economy in the world. In the 2014 World Bank league tables, the United States was comfortably number one, nearly twice the size of its nearest rival China. After Japan and Germany in third and fourth places respectively, came the United Kingdom and France, with less than two hundred billion dollars of GDP separating them (see World Bank Development Indicators [1]). The **gross domestic product** or GDP represents the total money value of all production in a country that has taken place during one year. The figures are used worldwide as a proxy for a country's prosperity. Since the more money a country makes, the higher its GDP growth, the assumption is that increases in GDP mean that the citizens of that country are enjoying a higher standard of living (some discussion of this was introduced in Chapter 2's Food for Thought section).

In simple terms, gross domestic product can be regarded as the annual domestic turnover – or, to extend the analogy, a giant till ringing up all the transactions taking place inside a country. In order to portray the rate of change of actual output accurately, GDP must be corrected for price increases (or decreases) from one time period to another. When this is done, we get what is called 'real' GDP. As such, a more formal measure of economic growth can be defined as the rate of change in real GDP over time (usually one year).

As the footnotes indicate, the growth data in Table 7.1 has been corrected accordingly, and it shows that the real gross domestic product had been on a positive upward path in the years leading up to 2008. In fact, as stated in the introduction, the period 1992 to 2007/8 were years of steady growth in the UK, and this steady upward trend was the norm in most Western economies. In 2009, the UK, along with most other Western economies, recorded a year of severe recession and, although the data in subsequent years suggest a period of slow recovery, it is worth remembering that economic growth figures are always relative to previous years. Thus, when there has been a big slump in the numbers, you need to pay attention to the actual totals and not become bamboozled by the percentage rates of change from one year to the next. For instance, in real terms, it took almost six years for GDP in the UK to return to its 2008 level, despite annual growth figures indicating some kind of economic recovery. Further coverage of GDP and methods of its calculation are outlined in Chapter 8.

## Price stability

Stable prices are crucial for confident business planning, facilitating contracts and enabling the exchange rate system to function smoothly, whereas persistently rising or falling prices cause problems to the economy. As a result, price stability is a primary objective of most governments. It is no longer believed that tolerating higher rates of inflation can lead to higher employment or output over the longer term. In fact, the fashionable argument seems to be quite the reverse – that a period of **disinflation** (a slowing down in the rate of price increases) could increase consumer spending and provide a stimulus for growth, especially if there is spare capacity in the system. Hence, when you ask an economist to identify the correct level of inflation, they rarely give a clear cut answer. At times, it seems too high and at others it seems too low; it seems to go through phases of being 'too hot' or 'too cold'. It all depends what is happening elsewhere in the macroeconomy

As a general rule, however, America, Britain and the Eurozone have a government target to keep inflation around 2% – that is, not below 1% and not above 3%. With this target in mind, the **consumer price index** (CPI) is monitored on a monthly basis. A sample of annual CPI statistics for the UK economy is presented in Table 7.1. As the table shows, before the Great Recession, the *general* trend was around the 2% target, and this was regarded as encouraging – not so much an end in itself, but due to its significance in supporting all other government objectives. Since December 2014, however, the trend in the UK and beyond has started to fall below target. In fact, in some countries, where the recession had hit particularly hard (such as Italy, Greece, Spain, Portugal and France), the monthly rate of change in price actually turned negative – into **deflation** – with prices across the board persistently falling each month.

Inflation below an already low target is problematical enough but, when prices changes actually start to fall into the negative zone, the problems are arguably worse. Deflation is particularly problematical, because money made tomorrow is worth less (how much less will depend upon the percentage rate of deflation) than the money made today. This stymies debts, investment, consumption expenditure, tax revenue and earnings – in fact, any decision where payments are, or can be, deferred. To take one of the more worrying problems as an example, debts created before a period of deflation become harder to service, as the real value of money used for repayments weakens as deflation sets in.

Deflation becomes even more problematical when the short term interest rate offered by the central bank is close to zero, as was the case across much of Europe in 2015. For example, in 2015, the ECB operated a base rate of 0.25 and the Bank of England had an equivalent rate of 0.5 – which had been its set position for seven years! Such low interest rates tend to confuse those educated to follow the traditional neoclassical approach of boosting demand and employment by lowering interest rates. When interest rates are already dangerously close to zero, there is little room to manoeuvre. In some cases, it seems that the only option for increasing demand is to employ **quantitative easing**, as outlined in Chapter 5. This dilemma also underlines the need for new economic thinking. Further explanation of the measurement of inflation is detailed in Chapter 8.

## Full employment

Full employment does not mean that everybody of working age is employed because, in any dynamic economy, some unemployment is unavoidable. For example, there will always be individuals moving in and out of employment as they change from one job to another, and there will always be seasonal, technological and overseas factors that cause fluctuations in the jobs available in different sectors. The real problems arise when there are large numbers of unemployed for long periods of time, as a large pool of unemployed labour represents wasted resources. This is particularly worrying when the unemployed are young – say, between 16 and 25.

Unemployment has many costs, not just in terms of loss of output, but also in terms of human suffering, loss of dignity and self-esteem. There is also a loss of income for individuals, increased pressure with respect to government spending on social benefits, and a reduction in tax revenue. From an economic perspective, unemployment may be viewed as unused labour capacity. Hence, most governments record the number of workers without a job, although the precise way this is measured changes from time to time. At present, 'official' unemployment in the United Kingdom is estimated in two ways: by the labour force survey, based on an internationally agreed process recommended by the International Labour Organisation (ILO) – the **ILO unemployment measure**; or through the number of people registering for unemployment benefits, known as **claimant unemployment**.

Unemployment is either expressed as a percentage rate – the number of unemployed as a percentage of the total workforce of 33 million – or as an absolute number. As Table 7.1 suggests, unemployment was not particularly problematic before the financial crisis (with a 'norm' of approximately 5%). However, as the table records, it reached more worrying proportions through the recession and is now settling at a 'new norm' of around 6%. It is worth remembering that 1% difference in the UK represents more than 330 000 people. In short, unemployment is an increasingly sizeable problem, with more than two million people unemployed in the UK in 2014.

The figures are further complicated by a marked increase in the number of 'zero hour contracts', part-time work and low-paid self-employment. In each of these cases – including self-employment – people are finding themselves in jobs that do not fully utilise their abilities or their available time. As a result, many of the newer employment opportunities that presented themselves after the Great Recession have been concentrated in low pay sectors.

Unemployment problems are no longer cyclical (i.e. they will not be resolved with time), but structural – more long-term. For instance, much of the Eurozone labour market is complicated by rigid rules relating to employment, convoluted systems of taxation, and excessive amounts of 'red tape'. As defined by the language of the debate, the problems lay in the ways that labour markets were 'structured'.

In fact, in August 2014, when the world's central bankers gathered for their annual conference at Jackson Hole, Wyoming [2], the labour market was an obvious choice of topic for that year's event. It was particularly apt because most economies were challenged by unemployment problems, and were beginning to think about raising the dominantly low interest rates. To do this effectively, the central bankers needed to judge how far their economies were from full employment. As the various papers that were presented made clear, judgements concerning the size of the employment gap were complicated by shifts in the rate of productivity, by mobility problems, and deflationary pressures. Thus, determining how close an economy is to full employment (full capacity) is a new problem that haunts many economies.

The traditional economists honestly believed that, in the long term, the market would ensure that everyone who genuinely wants to work would find a job at current rates of pay. If some people remain in the labour pool, the neoclassical economist would argue that it is because something is causing the market to fail – that something is stopping the unemployed from accepting the wage rates that would clear the market. These barriers to labour markets clearing could be imposed by trade unions pressures, or government subsidies or benefits. This debate, however, leaves open the question of what level of full employment is acceptable in the post-crisis world, and how it will be achieved. It currently raises the question: is there sufficient demand for everyone to work?

Understanding the nature of unemployment statistics forms an important part of the feasibility study for many types of property development, as it varies across occupations, regions, social class and time. Therefore, learning more about the detailed measurement of unemployment (as laid out in Chapter 8) will help in evaluating specific real estate markets and the broader macroeconomic environment.

## External balance

All international economic transactions are recorded in a country's **balance of payments** statistics. The ideal situation represents a position in which, over a number of years, a nation spends and invests abroad no more than other nations spend or invest. Economic transactions with other nations occur on many levels and, for accounting purposes, the transactions are often grouped across two or three categories: current account, capital account and financial account. Of these three, the most widely quoted is the current account. This involves all transactions relating to the exchange of visible goods (such as manufactured items, which would include building materials), the exchange of invisible services (such as overseas work undertaken by consultants), and investment earnings (such as profits from abroad).

Clearly, in any one year, one nation's balance of payments deficit is another nation's balance of payments surplus. Ultimately, however, this is not sustainable and, in the long run, debts must be paid. The data in Table 7.1 show a worrying trend insofar as the UK current account figures are all negative amounts.

However, in addition to buying and selling goods and services in the world market, it is also possible to buy and sell financial assets, and these are recorded separately in the financial account. The UK's annual position on its financial account is usually positive. A further qualifying remark regarding foreign trade is to recognise that balances of payment figures are notoriously difficult to record accurately and, of all the statistics shown in Table 7.1, the balance of payments estimates is subject to the biggest amendments. In practice, therefore, statistics relating to the external balance need to be considered in a broader historical context.

Equally, a trading bloc such as the EU will be made up of nations with deficits and surpluses. This was particularly well illustrated in the Eurozone after the Great Recession, with Greece, Portugal, Spain, Cyprus, Italy and Ireland suffering from significant current account deficits, while Germany, France and the

Netherlands could boast a healthy surplus. This dual experience was, however, particularly complex, because all 19 countries use the Euro, and the traditional escape route for a nation mired in a deep slump is to reduce its exchange rate – to encourage exports by making them relatively cheaper, and discouraging imports by making them relatively more expensive. Obviously, such an option was not possible among a group of countries who have agreed to share a common currency and a common monetary policy. On the other hand, those who strongly support the Euro argue that the system was set up to support such problems by encouraging flows of capital from surplus to deficit countries.

The Great Recession, however, tested the monetary union to its limits, as the poorly performing economies with balance of payment deficits desperately needed a looser monetary policy than those in the stronger economies boasting of balance of payments surpluses. For example, if Greece had control of its own currency in the summer of 2010, it could have reduced its value and made itself an irresistibly cheap and sunny destination for holiday makers from all over the world. However, as discussed in Chapter 5, the ECB does not run a separate monetary policy for each individual country. It is either one monetary policy and one exchange rate, or no common currency at all!

Interestingly, at the outset of the Great Recession, the UK and US both experienced several of the problems that characterise a debt crisis, and were in some ways comparable to Greece, but they both certainly fared much better during the recovery period. Many economists believe that this was due to Britain and the USA having their own currency and their own central banks managing their own monetary policies. Without doubt, flexible exchange rates assist countries to achieve economic stability, and monetary independence helped to place America and Britain at the forefront of the recovery. UK balance of payment accounts are looked at in more detail in Chapter 8.

## Equitable distribution of income

As explained right at the start (in the first Food for Thought section), since the Great Recession, the question of income distribution has taken on greater macroeconomic significance. In basic economic terms, income is derived from two sources, either as a reward for selling factors of production (as described in Chapters 1 and 4) or as a transfer from the state in the form of benefits (aspects of which are examined in the next part of this chapter). The question of *distribution*, however, is determined by how governments tax this income, and the patterns of expenditure that they make on goods and services. Hence, there is some debate regarding whether this issue is a political or economic one.

The crux of the problem is that most modern governments agree on the principles of a market-led economy, yet there is increasing recognition that the rewards and opportunities are not distributed fairly. Furthermore, since the global financial crisis, there has been a heightened awareness that poor growth and employment problems are closely associated with income inequality. Hence, there is recognition among economists that Governments have a responsibility to decide how fiscal policy and benefits can be used to redistribute income between the haves and the have-nots. This often entails selecting goods and services which have special merits to be provided or strongly subsidised by the state, such as the provision of education, health, housing and pension services. In this context, the objective of an equitable distribution of income describes a situation relating to 'fairness', 'social justice' and 'inclusion' – in short, a society that does not allow economic power to concentrate unfairly or limit the opportunities of human resources.

The traditional set of economic objectives discussed above are all entwined with the theories and laws of production, but the laws of distribution can no longer be isolated from the bigger picture. For example, it was widely reported in 2014 that the richest 1% owned 48% of the world's net household wealth (up from 44% in 2009). On the basis of these trends, the richest 1% were forecast to earn more than 50% of the wealth by 2016. Meanwhile, at the other end of the wealth spectrum, 80% of the poor share 5.5% of the world's wealth!

Interestingly, the radical journalist George Monbiot (2015) regards the question of income distribution as a state conspiracy against those on lower incomes, in which: 'the very rich no longer fall and the poor no longer rise'. He qualifies this odd arrangement by pointing to government policies such as: the benefit cap (that limits the amount of money paid to those who need to claim benefits for housing and food etc.); the freeze on council-tax banding since 1991; the lifting of the inheritance tax threshold; the various tax incentives to encourage the private rental market; and the forced sale of high-value council houses.

Complimenting Monbiot's view, *Private Eye* (2015) [3] produced a map of land and property registered in England and Wales in the name of offshore companies – seeking tax benefits – between 2005 and July 2014. The holdings amounted to 1.2 million acres. The beneficiaries were Russian oligarchs, oil sheikhs, British aristocrats and newspaper proprietors.

This perspective may be regarded as cynical, but it serves to highlight the political nature of economic decisions, and why the rich might prefer a less regulated system. It also distinguishes income distribution as a thorny question that will not go away without government intervention. As new economic thinking has consistently endorsed since its birth, equitable income distribution is clearly a macroeconomic objective that can no longer be ignored. As recent IMF research concludes, it is evident that you have to live on the right side of the tracks to get on in life, and that does not sound ethically fair (Ostry *et al.*, 2014). As a consequence, at the international level, there is considerable work being done on the measurement of income distribution, and the highlights of this are reviewed in Chapter 8.

## Central government

All nations have some form of centralised government to coordinate the various functions of a state – welfare, legal, financial and so on. The level of efficiency in carrying out these functions is obviously subject to debate, although *Transparency International* [4] (an independent organisation set up in 1993) tries to provide an annual assessment of the level of corruption at the government level. Their Corruption Index assesses 175 countries and territories on a scale from 0 (highly corrupt) to 100 (very clean). No country has a perfect score and, rather worryingly, two-thirds of countries score below 50. This suggests that on a global level corruption is still a problem.

Notably, most rich countries are relatively clean, with the USA and most members of the EU ranking in the top 25%, with the possible exceptions of Italy, who scored 43 and ranked 69th, and Greece, who scored 40 and were ranked 80th alongside China in the 2013 Corruption Perception Index [5]. Given the nature of the exercise, the real extent of the problem is hard to pin down, but at least the index tries to measure the perceived levels of government corruption in countries worldwide in a consistent manner. It also serves as a good reminder of the challenges to moderate the abuse of power and underhand dealings when attempting to manage state business.

## Public finance: A Greek tragedy

The ways that a central government organises its income and expenditure has a significant impact on the performance of an economy. To take the classic example of Greece in 2014, when its government admitted to a gaping black hole in public finance, two out of three Greeks chose either to understate their earnings or to fail to disclose them altogether. As a result, something like 25% of Greeks cheated the government of its legal income, which was a significant tad above the European average of 20%. Obviously, given the damage done by the Great Recession, the Greek government needed to bring more of the underground activity into the open, to boost official central government income. In journalistic terms, the shadow economy needed to be brought into the sunlight, to raise government revenues and avoid the hole in Greek public finance getting deeper and deeper.

On the expenditure side, 25% of the Greek labour force were officially unemployed and needed to receive government benefits to have food and shelter. Even though Greek payments to the unemployed remained low compared to other European states, unemployment benefits continued to entail significant state costs. A similar scenario can be added for the bills to pay for occupational pensions, education, and health, where much of the expenditure is determined by demand. Also, we should not overlook military expenditure, as this is the one area where the Greek government spends comparatively more than its European partners. Obvious questions are: how can this government expenditure be funded, how fairly can it be allocated, and how much of it is truly required?

Already, by 2014, the amount that the Greek central government had borrowed represented 175% of GDP yet, as pointed out, it seemed that the nation's workers had relatively little commitment to paying their fair share towards funding public services. Government levies of 43% on labour costs, compared to an OECD average of 26%, were no doubt a further disincentive to Greek citizens to coming forward and contributing to government funds.

This Greek tragedy (excuse the pun) has been used as a case study to introduce the problematical nature of public finance when managing an economy. There is, in fact, a close relationship between this chapter and Chapter 5 – the one dealing with central banks and monetary policy. The common theme that unites each of these two chapters is **stabilisation policy**, which is designed to manipulate economic activity to bring an unstable economy back towards an even keel.

During the years of the Great Recession, this involved: a greater reliance on markets and managing demand by keeping interest rates at low levels and/or pumping money into the economy through quantitative easing; bailing out financial institutions; and cutting taxes or increasing government expenditure.

## Fiscal policy

In all nations, fiscal policy emanates, on the government's behalf, from the Treasury or Finance Department. It consists largely of taxation (of all forms) and government spending (of all forms). The word 'fiscal' is derived from the Latin for 'state purse', and this is most appropriate, as taxation is the main source of income from which governments finance public spending. In other words, fiscal policy is concerned with the flow of government money in and out of the state coffers. An indication of the scale of the various receipts and expenditure are shown in Figure 7.1

The line that plots spending from 2002 to 2014 shows a reasonably steady rate of expansion throughout the period. There is, however, a detectable rate of increase from 2008 onwards, as the impacts of the recession create a need for extra welfare spending. More or less the exact opposite is portrayed in the pattern of government income, which experienced a sharp dip from 2007 to 2009 as tax revenue from income and profits were cut back. Obviously, the gap between income and expenditure represents a deficit. As suggested in Chapter 6, one does not have to read much between the two lines to see that the increase in government deficit was the *result*, not the *cause*, of the recession.

A key element of any fiscal framework is to make sure that both sides of the government balance sheet are managed efficiently. Any public sector debt must be held at a prudent and stable level in relation to GDP and, in principle, borrowing is only acceptable to cover capital expenditure. The idea behind the capital expenditure

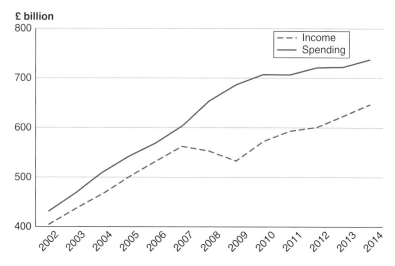

**Figure 7.1** UK Government income and expenditure.
*Source*: OBR, *Public sector finance databank*, April 2015.

Part C

rule is that a government, like a private company, should not attribute to one year the full cost of projects expected to generate gains over several years. In short, a government should only borrow money to fund investments if it benefits future generations. This distinction between current and capital spending makes public accounting tricky, and some countries (e.g. Brazil, Costa Rica, Germany, Japan, Kosovo, Liberia, Malaysia, Pakistan and the UK) have drawn a distinction by referring to capital and current account budgets by enforcing two rules, namely:

1.  The **golden rule**, which states that, over the economic cycle, the government should only borrow to invest, not to fund current spending.
2.  The **sustainable investment rule**, which states that, over the economic cycle, public sector debt, expressed as a proportion of GDP, must be held at a stable and prudent level.

A significant proportion of the public sector's resource spending is demand-determined (such as expenditure on welfare, pensions and health), whereas capital spending in the public sector tends to be politically determined, in the sense that it is committed years in advance. For example, the hospitals and schools built under PFI schemes incur annual payments that were determined many years ago. Thus, the Government's objective to balance the annual public sector accounts always presents a considerable challenge.

The fiscal challenge was a prominent problem during the years of the Great Recession, as there were steady increases in the size of the annual budget deficit. For example, in 2010, the forecast for the UK Government's annual budget deficit – the gap between its spending and its income – was proudly expected to be below £40 billion by 2014 but, as things turned out, it was actually nearer to £100 billion. As suggested by Figure 7.1, tax revenues and national insurance receipts had declined, expenditure on welfare benefits had gone up, and some banks had been bailed out. The cost to the state of this downhill slide into recession was obsessively charted month by month. In fact, the opposition party, trying to score political points, suggested that the losses were equivalent to £4000 for every taxpayer.

Moreover, these experiences were shared on both sides of the pond, and America's fiscal deficit, recorded at $1.4 trillion in 2009, actually exceeded the GDP of many smaller countries at that time. Internationally, the debt numbers made explosive headlines and the global response led to fiscal austerity. In simple terms, this involves curbing government activity so that it becomes less expensive. Policies of austerity, however, like most fiscal options, are fraught with problems.

As evidence, central governments are notorious for missing public finance targets. Although the impression given in a lecture hall is that the central government is in control of the purse strings, in practice, public finance is never that easy to manage. Two further case studies will amplify the nature of the problem.

*Public finance: a French farce*

This time we draw on a case from France, where the dilemma demonstrates the tension between the central government and *local* government. As in many countries, the local town hall is facing a budget squeeze. Argenteuil, for example, is noted as being poorer than the average town: its unemployment rate is nearly 20%, and many of its residents live in subsidised housing. The local budget also supports gardeners, parks, education, crèches, the maintenance of a medieval chapel, a cultural centre (comprising a 500-seat theatre and two cinema screens) and so on. The local government debt in 2014 amounted to €300 million.

Yet, each year, central government transfers to this large French town were being cut – in 2015 by €3.5 million, and by a further €8.5 million in 2016. In effect, the central government of France was relying on the local government to secure budget savings, but they could never be sure that the town halls would adjust services accordingly. Similar scenarios are also being played out in the UK in towns such as Birmingham and Newcastle [6].

## Public finance: taxation

All governments rely on a mix of revenue streams, and most significant of these are the monies that flow from various forms of taxation. Most notable are the taxes on wages, consumption, profit and property, respectively referred to as income tax, expenditure tax, corporation tax, and property or land value tax. The combination and structure of these taxes varies considerably between countries. Anglo-Saxon (Australia, America, Canada, New Zealand and the UK) economies tend to favour taxes on wages, profits and capital gain, whereas Asian states (China and India) prefer to raise money from expenditure taxes such as VAT. There is no accepted formula of the best way to raise government funds, but few nations have fully explored the possibilities of land or property as a tax base.

## Property taxes

The following example is based on the UK, which has two taxes that impact upon residential property: **stamp duty land tax** (SDLT), a tax on transactions; and **council tax**, an annual levy imposed on property that is scaled by its value. Detailing each of these in turn will help to clarify some of the characteristics of property as a tax base.

In the simplest of terms, stamp duty is a transaction tax on properties with a value greater than £125,000. To be more precise, it is charged at a rate of 2% on buying a residential property costing between £125,000 and £250,00, and increases incrementally from this base. The current rates are shown in Table 7.2.

Another way of describing the banding of SDLT is as a 'slice' system, where successive bands of the purchase price are taxed at increasing rates. For example, on a house valued at £275,000 you pay nothing on the first £125,000, as stamp duty only kicks in on values over £125,000; 2% on the next £125,000 slice (i.e. £2,500); and 5% on the remaining £25,000 (i.e. £1,250), making the total stamp duty on this transaction £3,750. The 1.2 million residential property transactions that took place in 2014/15 raised a total of approximately £11 billion.

Council tax, on the other hand, is an annual levy on property used to part-fund services provided by local authorities, such as policing, fire services, support for the elderly and vulnerable, parks maintenance, refuse disposal and street cleaning. It is charged as an annual levy (but usually paid monthly) on each of the 28 million residential properties in the UK. The actual amount is set and collected by the

**Table 7.2**  Rates of stamp duty

| Purchase price of property | SDLT rate | Amount of tax to pay |
|---|---|---|
| Up to £125,000 | Zero | Zero |
| Over £125,001 to £250,000 | 2% | £2,500 to £5,000 |
| Over £250,001 to £925,000 | 5% | £12,500 to £46,250 |
| Over £925,001 to £1.5 million | 10% | £46,250 to £150,000 |
| Over £1.5 million | 12% | £180,000+ |

Source: Adapted from HMRC, November 2015.

**Table 7.3**  Council tax bands in England, 2015

| Council tax valuation band | Ranges of value (at 1st April 1991) |
|---|---|
| A | Up to £40,000 |
| B | More than £40,000 and up to £52,000 |
| C | More than £52,000 and up to £68,000 |
| D | More than £68,000 and up to £88,000 |
| E | More than £88,000 and up to £120,000 |
| F | More than £120,000 and up to £160,000 |
| G | More than £160,000 and up to £320,000 |
| H | More than £320,000 |

Source: Adapted from Valuation Office Agency, June 2015.

local authority, following a formula administered centrally by Department for Communities and Local Government (DCLG). As such, it raises more than double the amount that SDLT raises each year – in the region of £28 billion in 2014/15.

The precise system of calculating the council tax due on each property each year is complicated by the fact that the calculations are based on property values that are historic, and the systems vary across the devolved powers of England, Wales, Scotland and Northern Ireland. For instance, the properties in Northern Ireland and Wales are based on property values dating back respectively to 2005 and 2003, but in England and Scotland, the property values used as the calculation reference still date back to a valuation exercise that was carried out in 1991. The absurd consequence of this is that when a new property is built, someone has to work out what it would have sold for 25 years ago.

To complicate this further, each residential property is categorized into one of eight bands, according to its historic value. As an example, the current bands used across the 417 billing authorities in England are shown in Table 7.3. The same banding system (A–H) is used in each of the devolved nations, but the range of values differs. For instance, in Scotland, the 1991 values start at £27,000 in band A and finish with band H for properties with values in excess of £212,000. In other words, the council tax principles are the same across the UK, but the valuation band ranges and the formulas used in each of the four devolved nations is different.

Typically, households end up spending around £1,500 per year (i.e. around £125 per month). The houses in the most expensive bracket pay on average somewhere in the region of £2,536 (i.e. around £211 per month). The precise amount varies from one local authority to the next, but it is never equitable, in the sense that those who reside in a band H valued property will pay at most three times as much as someone living in a band A property, even though the value of the band H property may be ten or more times higher. Finally, to highlight how out of touch the data is with house prices today, it is interesting to note that there is only one band for properties valued (in 1991) above £320,000. Council tax stops increasing after this point.

Understandably this may all sound rather confusing, which this is no surprise, as property tax – particularly council tax – is riddled with inequities, anomalies, inconvenience and problems of transparency. In short, the only desirable quality that UK property currently displays as a taxable resource is that its difficult to avoid. In its current configuration, council tax is by and large regressive, in the sense that it takes no account of the ability to pay. It is, crudely, an annual tax charged according to the value of the property in which one resides, so it affects those on lower incomes disproportionately (even though council tax benefits try to correct for this at the extremes). By comparison, stamp duty is relatively more progressive, as the duty is cranked up in incremental portions as houses become more expensive, so those who can buy the most expensive homes contribute the most, and there is no upper limit.

### Tax summary

There is some theoretical understanding that, in an ideal world, taxes should be efficient, fair and simple. That is: tax systems should not influence economic decisions such as the choice over what to produce, what to consume or where or when to work; the greater burden should fall on those who can afford to pay; and the system needs to be convenient, certain and difficult to evade. However, there are trade-offs. For example, VAT causes less distortion to making choices, but hits poorer people harder as they spend a higher share of their income than the rich. Equally, income tax can be applied incrementally, causing those on higher incomes to pay more tax, but this burden can prove to be a disincentive to choosing between work and leisure. Similarly, corporation tax can become so high that firms that are sufficiently mobile may find it beneficial to locate elsewhere – preferably in a tax haven. By the same token, taxes on things that cannot be moved easily, such as property, have less impact on personal decisions. In sum, a well-designed tax system needs to tick many boxes. It needs to be fair, efficient, hard to evade, and easy to enforce.

### Public finance: cosmopolitan solutions

Different countries arrive at different political and cultural solutions to fiscal problems. For example, Britain is still a relatively centralised country (with the exception to the rule being property tax), whereas other countries have greatly devolved powers and local governments make fiscal decisions. As suggested by the French case study above, this has its advantages and disadvantages. In the devolved federal structures, it is hard to avoid dilemmas between central and local government, especially when it comes to raising taxes or reducing public spending. On the other hand, it avoids asking a central government employee to choose between a new bypass and a new bridge, or imposing a mansion tax on houses of a certain value in a local area that they barely know or understand.

At the central government level in the UK, there is a general goal to reduce public spending to 36% of GDP by 2020. Also by this date, it is envisaged that the budget will be in surplus, and tax increases will be a thing of the past. There is a post-recession commitment that hauntingly takes us back to the neoclassical view of the world that respects and protects the private individual, the private firm and private property, to the extent that governments have begun to shy away from taxing these resources. In short, in 2020, the UK central Government will still have hold of the public purse strings, but its fiscal grasp is destined to weaken.

## Austerity economics

What makes **fiscal austerity** particularly difficult is its shrinking and costly impact on the economy. Not only does it destroy output, but it also has seriously damning effects on the level of employment. As a consequence, the large number of countries that followed the austerity route from 2010 to 2014 found themselves in a Catch-22 situation. Reducing public sector debt by imposing cuts on government spending, such as welfare benefits, had led to an increase in unemployment and a consequent loss of revenue from income tax. Governments were stuck between a rock and a hard place.

*How an economic fairy tale led to a nightmare*

Ha-Joon Chang's analysis of the economic predicament made a case that favoured a fiscal deficit. He pointed out that between 2008 and 2010, the recession reduced government revenue by 2.4% of GDP, while spending on benefits increased by 3.2% of GDP. Hence, by adding the two together, the recession triggered a deficit equivalent to 5.6% of GDP. He suggests that this increase in debt would be better accounted for by spending on projects that raise productivity – such as infrastructure, R&D, training and early learning programmes for disadvantaged children. As he concludes: 'A government budget should be understood not just in terms of bookkeeping but also demand management, national cohesion and productivity growth. Jobs and wages should not be seen simply as a matter of people being 'worth' (or not) what they get, but of better utilising human potential and of providing decent and dignified livelihoods' (Chang, 2014).

Politicians who were understandably worried by the unusually high levels of public debt and the consensual mainstream economic response at the time supported austerity economics, especially as it was felt that, in the given conditions, the effectiveness of stimulus measures would be muted. New economic thinking, however, did see some value in rekindling Keynesian ideas. The emerging debate was, interestingly, captured by the IMF in their annual publication, *World Economic Outlook*. It began in October 2010, when the IMF published an admission that, over the last couple of years, the fund had severely underestimated the severity of the economic contractions in a large number of countries. In other words, they admitted that shrinking budgets had done more damage to economies than previously assumed. According to their calculations, the fund had miscalculated by a factor of three! (WEO, 2010: Box 1.1: 41)

Four years later, the IMF staff went even further by suggesting that those advanced economies where low growth and high unemployment prevailed should consider making a plan to increase investment in public infrastructure. In fact, the WEO report (2014) included a short (12 page) primer on the *Economics of Infrastructure*. This pointed out that, given the low borrowing costs and weak demand in several countries, the time was right for investment in public infrastructure. Furthermore, it reiterated the Keynesian idea that infrastructure investment is not only an essential factor of production, it also can raise output in the short and long term. In fact, according to their analysis, based on 17 advanced countries, an increase of one percentage point of GDP in investment spending raised the level of output by about 0.4% in the same year, and by 1.5% four years after the increase. Finally, it concluded that debt-financed projects could achieve these output effects without increasing the debt-to-GDP ratio. In short, public infrastructure investment could pay for itself if done correctly (WEO, 2014: Chapter 3).

These observations were particularly controversial, as most of the loans and support that had been distributed by the IMF to advanced economies trying to recover from the 2008 crisis had been made on the proviso that they would support a regime of 'fiscal consolidation' – which is a euphemism for cuts to government spending. In other words, austerity had been supported by the IMF rescue programmes from 2007 to 2010 but, as the recession dragged on, their views on the severity of the economic contraction in a large number of countries led them to consider the power and appropriateness of fiscal expansion.

### Is there a doctor in the house?

This somewhat muddled, but honest, academic approach is often explained by resorting to medical analogies. The sick patient, being akin to countries in financial trouble, goes to the IMF – the doctor – who prescribes a treatment (and gives money). The IMF's prescriptions are given with certain conditions and instructions ands although the economy may not immediately recovers the benefits should become apparent in the long run. As the saying goes, 'no pain no gain'. These medical analogies are particularly apt for a subject that wants to be regarded as scientific, as even the most experienced doctor will have some questions regarding the working of the human anatomy. There are many things that both professions do not entirely understand and cannot predict about problems that are inherently systemic.

To extend the analogy, economists are uncertain about the pace of cutting borrowing; they know that going 'cold turkey' on more debts will destroy jobs and wreak havoc on the economy in the short run. Indeed, the IMF was created on the understanding that lending to countries in difficulty, such as an addiction to spending, might require a period of temporary support. However, like doctors, they will be unsure about the size (dosage) and timing of the prescribed package of treatment. Doctors are also aware that every patient responds differently to treatment, depending on their genetic makeup, their age and their general level of health. The same type of principle applies to countries, depending on their culture, stage of development and overall economic performance. It is not surprising, therefore, that even the most highly trained doctors and economists might make mistakes and incorrectly diagnose problems.

Like any analogy, the medical comparison can only be taken so far. The economy, for example, does not just deal with one entity. When pain is inflicted by a doctor, it primarily hurts one person but, when economic policy causes problems (economic pain), it is a matter of which parts of society benefit and who bears the cost. The medical analogy is illuminating, as it reminds students that, given the broad range of variables that are inherent to an economic system, or an economic problem, it cannot be treated mechanistically by crunching numbers. Knowing what policy to support, and how hard to enforce it, is also a matter of judgement, and will vary from case to case and time to time.

Currently, there is an ongoing policy debate about whether economic resources are best managed by the central government, the local government or the market. Although it is possible to argue that, prior to 2008, the market had gained the upper hand, in the wake of the recession, regulators have returned as a means of preventing further financial crises and to recover fiscal and broader economic stability.

## Food for thought: An ageing population

As discussed in this chapter, concerning fiscal matters and macroeconomic objectives, the Great Recession has left significant scars on central government budgets. Securing a fiscal balance had proved to be difficult at the best of times but, since 2008, the governments of rich countries have been burdened by falling tax revenue and increasing welfare payments. Furthermore, they are all now potentially facing a new set of miserable crises, this time in health, social care, pensions, and housing, due to the problem of an ageing population.

An ageing population literally means that the average age is increasing, the primary reason being that people are living longer. For example, the Office for National Statistics (ONS) forecasts, from the 2011 census data that, by 2021, the number of people aged 65 and over will have increased by 24%, and those aged 85 and over will have increased by 39%. By 2031, there will be an increase of 51% – half as many again – of those in the 65-plus bracket, and double the number of people who are older than 85. In actual numbers, this translates to 278 000 more British pensioners per year. The problem is that the working population, whose tax will presumably be used to support the older generation, will only grow on average by 29 000 per year. This suggests a decrease in the ratio of workers to pensioners by a factor of more or less 10 : 1.

Acknowledging that the age structure would become more top-heavy, and that countries would harbour increasing numbers in the 50-plus bracket, has been discussed since the 1950s. To date, however, relatively little has been done to address the problems. As with other global issues, such as climate change, much trust was placed in the ability of markets to quickly and efficiently accommodate change, and resolve any problems. Regardless, the UN has spent more than a decade encouraging governments to consider a broad range of economic, political and social reforms, 'to assure the well-being of the growing number and proportion of older persons in most countries of the world' (see UN, 2013: 1). Inadvertently, therefore, international organisations such as the United Nations are promoting new economic thinking by encouraging governments to support structural changes to address intergenerational issues. There are many such nuggets that could be examined, but here we only have space to explore three such challenges.

## Is the UK ready for ageing?

First is the question of retirement pensions. Young, rational and capably minded workers give virtually no thought at all to how they will live out their later years, or how they will fund them. Given a trade-off between present and future consumption, people would rather have jam today in preference to jam tomorrow. This dilemma is universal, even though many know from sad family experiences that increasing numbers of old people end up living their elderly years alone, suffering medical conditions, and managing problems with memory, etc. (in fact, already more than half of the very old live alone). Yet, the majority, left to their own devices, do not put enough aside for an old age pension; and Governments do not have the funds to fill all the pension pots that are opening up.

Fortunately for the politicians, economists who understand behaviour and the notion of the 'greater good' have begun to offer a solution; one that you will experience, if you graduate to work in the UK, US or New Zealand, where legislation now binds anyone taking up a new job to 'automatically enrol' into a company pension scheme. If you do not want to participate, then you have a short period of time to opt out (whereas, in conventional retirement-saving plans, workers often had to opt in).

The simplicity of this policy is quite deceptive; it subtly makes pension saving the default option, as it becomes more difficult to avoid. The new legislation was formulated by those who understand the psychology of personal finance, as it draws attention to recognising the costs of ageing and the need to plan for the future. As behaviourists have emphasised, people do not necessarily make rational long-term plans in relation to saving for a pension; they need to be 'nudged' along. The market alone does not provide the necessary incentives.

## Is the UK ready to care?

The second challenge draws from the House of Lords report (2013), which was commissioned to consider public service provision in the light of demographic change, and to make recommendations. According to the report, the current system is working towards 'breaking point', with rather muddled boundaries drawn between mental care, health care, community care and social care. As the report stated: 'Social care and its funding are already in crisis, and this will become worse as demand markedly increases. The split between healthcare and social care is unsustainable and will remain so unless the two are integrated. Sufficient provision of suitable housing, often with linked support, will be essential to sustain independent living by older people' (House of Lords, 2013: 8).

To the uninitiated, this might seem like a crazy situation but, due to historical reasons, there were, and still are, marked divisions between mental health and physical health, primary care and secondary care, and so on. The divides may not make sense from a patient's point of view and, from an institutional perspective, they no doubt result in inefficient and inappropriate services. However, this is still representative of the state of play around 2016. The market, left to its own devices, is unlikely to resolve it quickly enough. The question that it triggers, therefore, is how can things be improved?

For instance, there has been considerable talk about the value of providing communal housing for the elderly. Several interesting examples of co-housing in America and Scandinavia already exist – some dedicated to senior citizens, and others open to all ages. An important feature of these community-based developments are shared facilities and amenities, such as large communal rooms, extensive dining facilities, assisted bathing rooms, offices and rest rooms for support staff, shops, and even mini-cinemas. As potential developers, many of you will recognise that the costs for such developments may well be prohibitive, as much of the floor space is given over to common areas.

The only ways that such specialist developments could be funded – privately or with government support – is via a high service charge for those living within the 'gated' communities. On the other hand, it could be argued that people living in an organised supportive community could reduce some of the burdensome care costs that the state currently pays. It seems cheaper and nicer to have neighbours who can look out for one another. Whether this was the precise level of development or sophistication that the House of Lords report envisaged when it recommended 'an urgent need to deliver a greater amount of specialist housing for older people' is not clear.

What is apparent, however, is that any such recommendation would need to resonate across several fragmented parties at the same time. In practice, it would mean getting at least nine agencies and departments on board, such as the Department of Health, Department for Communities and Local Government, the Homes and Communities Agency, local authority Housing Departments and Adult Care Services, Local Planning Authorities, Health and Wellbeing Boards, as well as house builders and housing associations. In the current age of austerity, it is unlikely that such harmony across so many divides – and budgets – will be achieved, as each agency needs to 'cut their cloth' to take account of more straitened times, and avoid any discord with the paymasters at county hall or Westminster.

## Is the UK ready for structural reform?

To deliver a new economic model for an ageing society requires significant structural reforms. As the above policy recommendations demonstrate, the Government needs to intervene to introduce new legislation and arrange a welfare system where people 'pay in' when they are young and healthy and 'draw out' when they are older and need support. These are not new roles; any government that is genuinely concerned about the 'greater good' will design interventions and organise transfer payments. A common example is the collection of taxes from young workers, to fund care and pension provisions in old age.

Economic decisions are nearly always muddied by political, moral, cultural and philosophical questions. For example, the scenario above about communal homes is one of many possible solutions offered to overcome the loneliness, helplessness and boredom that old age can inflict. However, new ideas always battle against cultural inertia, institutional rules and regulations. In many ways, traditions stifle innovation and change. While mainstream economists imply that markets and economic growth can rally against these barriers, new economic thinking recognises the need to set decisions in a broader context.

As those at the forefront of the movement know too well, this is all easier said than done. A good example is Adair Turner, who is currently a senior Fellow of the Institute for New Economic Thinking. His public profile was considerably raised days after the collapse of Lehman Brothers in September 2008, when he was appointed as Chair of the Financial Services Authority and, subsequently, Chair of the International Financial Stability Board. Since these appointments, he has had to considerably review his ideas and re-examine the first principles he had been taught at Cambridge University in the 1970s. He is now convinced that economists should analyse the world as it actually is, and human beings as they actually are, and avoid taking simplifying assumptions too literally. His writing challenges conventional economic wisdom about the role of free markets and unfettered growth (Turner, 2012). It is fresh thinking such as this that gives structural reforms a greater chance of taking place in society.

# Chapter 8
# Measuring and Forecasting Economic Activity

Those who have reached this chapter as the final stage in the textbook will have picked up by now that real estate markets are best understood in a macroeconomic context, and that requires not only a good grasp of what governments are attempting to achieve with policy (as laid out in Chapters 5 and 7), but also a strong and confident appreciation of data. Obviously, you need to remember that the demand for real estate – particularly commercial real estate – is derived from economic activity in the broader economy. Consequently, as has been emphasised right from the start, current graduates seeking jobs in surveying – or any other profession, for that matter – need to be savvy with data. They need to be grounded in the practical reality of the economy and commercial life. Final year students should be able to engage with and question articles in the press and, as a professional surveyor, you would not be expected to continue to rely on commentary from a website.

By the end of this chapter, however, you will be aware of the range of official data that the ONS (Office for National Statistics) releases on the economy, and other data that is available to support the daily work of a surveyor. In an odd phrase used in the literature supporting the new thinkers, when graduates seek employment beyond the walls of academia, they need to be 'oven-ready'.

Unfortunately, there is not one set of data that you can trust for all purposes, and during your careers, you will need to draw from different sources when providing information to developers, finance institutions or clients in the private or public sectors. As implied in Chapter 3, an economy consists of thousands of micro-markets, each too small to be picked up by broad-brush indices. Thus, surveyors have a distinct advantage, as they are well placed to pick up local knowledge and see and hear business developments in specific markets. In other words real estate – particularly commercial real estate – is rarely required for its intrinsic qualities, but more commonly for what it contributes to the production, and consumption, of goods and services.

*New Economic Thinking and Real Estate*, First Edition. Danny Myers.
© 2016 John Wiley & Sons, Ltd. Published 2016 by John Wiley & Sons, Ltd.

The aim of this chapter, therefore, is to understand economic statistics from the primary source, as knowing how data is collated and what they mean is half the battle. In fact, a good preparatory exercise is to study one official data series in detail, carrying out a kind of literature review to get into the rigour of sampling, collation, reliability, revisions, rounding and so on. To some extent, these data characteristics will be introduced as we overview each of the main macroeconomic objectives, but there is nothing to beat first-hand experience so, if you get the opportunity, do try and follow this recommended exercise.

Each data set presents a snapshot of the market cycle from a slightly different angle. As a consequence, within the matter of a few hours, an economic forecast, or the value of real estate, can alter as a response to the announcement of new economic information. Indeed, financial analysts are often criticized for short-termism – for over-responding to the changes presented in the data, and not seeing the bigger long-term picture. It takes a lot of nerve to buck these trends, but the aim of this chapter is to encourage you to avoid herd-like behaviour, and to have the confidence to go with your gut reactions.

This is more difficult than it may first appear, because of the fanfare of noise that often accompanies a change of direction in the data. Journalists and broadcasters like to make headlines out of them, and politicians compete to interpret them in a favourable light for their party. The important point here is that surveyors also need to be able to form a view from this cacophony of signals, and to be able to form their own impression. This chapter explains what lies behind the numbers, clarifying what they actually measure, how they are computed, how they evolved, and how they relate to real estate markets, and so on. For brevity's sake, we begin by just concentrating on the official data relating to the macroeconomic objectives that were introduced in the previous chapter.

## Some general principles to watch out for

Although each statistical series is designed to be objective, accurate and reliable, it is a major challenge to present economy-wide activity in a representative and comprehensive manner. Statistical processes can be misleading, and may misrepresent precisely what is happening unless you fully understand the footnotes, the headings and the small qualifying remarks that accompany the publication of official data. Therefore, we begin this section by making some general comments about statistical conventions that need to be understood.

### Definition

First of all, you must be entirely clear about what is actually being measured, as the aim of any statistical series is to portray a specific level of activity reliably. For instance, simply changing the format, or the way that certain data is collated, does not alter the *actual* level of inflation, output, trade or whatever. For example, governments are notorious for making changes to the ways that official unemployment figures are recorded. These changes are commonly designed to reduce the official unemployment figures, but all that has changed is the way unemployment is recorded; the changes do little more than provide a 'cosmetic effect', as the same number of people are still looking for work!

## Seasonality

Another statistical device that is commonly applied to data is seasonal adjustment. This suggests that the figures have been statistically 'smoothed' to allow for any changes in seasonal opportunities that occur from month to month. To take another employment-related example, during the winter, the construction sector typically experiences higher rates of unemployment than during the rest of the year so, to seasonally adjust the calculation, this specific period is excluded from the annual average. This enables us to identify if the specific set of figures is unusually large or small for that period. The figures pronounced on by the media are usually of the **seasonally adjusted** variety.

## Precision and revision

Do take care when looking at published data, as frequent use is made of the term *estimate*. This not only acknowledges that economic statistics are rarely 100% accurate, but also highlights that statisticians are keen to revise data as new information becomes available, or new techniques are applied to a particular data series. This is often the case between the first release of data and subsequent revised publication, and sometimes this stage is indicated by use of the term *provisional* or *preliminary*. Some of the more academic literature on the topics may even draw a distinction between planned and realised outcomes – or, as economists prefer to call it, *ex ante* (from before) and *ex post* (in retrospect).

A pertinent example of revised methodology complicating the interpretation of data can be seen in the various assessments of the strength of recovery from the 2008 crisis. In this text, we draw on official ONS data, which acknowledged that it took six years for the UK economy to recover. However, as we go to press, data the ONS has revised its method of calculating GDP and has identified a stronger pace of growth between 2011 and 2013, which suggests that the recovery may have been achieved a year earlier. The GDP figures that are being referred to, however, do not account for changes in population size and, once GDP per head becomes a focus, the recovery is again seen to take six years (this is discussed further below).

The recurring point is that data needs to be trusted as reliable, robust and comprehensive. This becomes increasingly difficult as the scale of measurement broadens across the economy and complies with international standards. For example, in the foreword of the *UK National Accounts (The Blue Book)*, 2015 edition, the ONS point out that: 'Very few statistical revisions arise as a result of "errors" in the popular sense of the word. All estimates, by definition, are subject to statistical "error". In this context the word refers to the uncertainty inherent in any process or calculation that uses sampling, estimation or modelling'.

In other words, revisions tend to be based on new statistical techniques, or the incorporation of new information – but they are not due to human or system failures. The bottom line, however it is explained, is that very few data sets are completely reliable. That is why economists tend to adopt qualifying terms, such as 'indicative', 'predicted', 'estimated', 'provisional', 'discontinued', and/or 'subject to change'.

## Measuring economic growth

As explained in Chapter 7, measurement of economic growth relies on the monitoring of changes in Gross Domestic Product (GDP). This can be done from one year to the next, or every three months. Although the conceptual idea of total output and its related implications might still be a little bewildering, it has become the world's most ubiquitous indicator of economic progress. It is widely used by policymakers, economists, international agencies and the media as the primary scorecard of a nation's economic health and well-being

It basically does what it says on the tin: **Gross domestic product** (GDP) measures the *gross* (total) *domestic* (home) *product* (output). To express it formally: GDP represents the total money value of all the production that has taken place inside a specific territory during one year.

A detailed breakdown of the GDP figures is given in the *National Accounts*. In the United Kingdom, these are released quarterly on the Web and published annually. They provide a systematic and detailed description of an economy's performance. In the past 20 years, the totals have significantly increased in size, progressing from GDP figures expressed in billions to the recent totals that exceed a trillion. However, the national accounts are far more important than just indicating changes in GDP. They form an important reference for those who wish to broaden their understanding of the relationships between the various sectors of the economy and its measurement. For our purposes, it is not necessary to delve into the minutiae of this system; we just need just to establish a number of general points, to allow sufficient confidence to discuss the role of real estate within the broader economy.

### Gross Domestic Product (GDP)

Before considering any figures, we must fully understand what they convey, and the significance of any changes in their size. In simple terms, gross domestic product (GDP) can be regarded as the annual domestic turnover or, to employ the analogy used in Chapter 7, the result of a giant till ringing up all the transactions that occur within a specific territory. No distinctions are made between transactions that enhance well-being and those that diminish it. GDP is merely a gross tally of all the goods and services produced and bought from one geographical area. No distinction is drawn between productive or destructive activities, or between sustainable ones and unsustainable ones; the GDP simply totals all output, and assumes that every monetary transaction adds to social well-being by definition.

An alternative measure is **gross national income** (GNI). This is similar to GDP, but includes a net figure for employment, property and entrepreneurial income flowing in and out of a nation's economy from overseas. In other words, GNI aggregates all the activity that generates income to a specific nationality. As a very general rule, however, GDP and GNI represent similar amounts, and rarely differ by more than one or two per cent in most high-income economies.

In the years before the Great Recession, the difference was always positive. However, in the past couple of years, following the increased problems of international trade and debt, the balance between the total of monies produced in the economy were slightly decreased, once the international flow of property and entrepreneurial income and other transfers with the rest of the world were taken into account. For example, in 2014, the difference between the GDP and GNI totals in the UK were about 33 billion, with GDP accounting for around £1816 billion (i.e. approximately £1.8 trillion) and GNI totalling £1783 billion. The difference, however, between these two national accounting identities may be substantially larger in less developed economies.

A further adjustment that needs to be made to national account totals is to allow for inflation. In other words, when figures are adjusted from current prices to constant prices, it is possible to calculate the **real value** of any change in economic activity between one year and the next. Effectively, economic growth can only be declared if *real* GDP has increased. If real GDP has declined, this is described as a **recession**. In the majority of years following World War II, the recorded figures have been positive.

However, this text is focused on the exceptional events following the credit crisis that commenced in 2007/8 and, in terms of *real* GDP (RGDP), these were years of stark change. Across the globe, a general pattern of transition was witnessed, as countries moved from an extended period of positive economic growth to the 'short sharp shock' of recession. A period of negative growth, discussed throughout the book since Table 1.1, was presented in the introduction. In a historical context, it is easy to see how the era earned its reputation as the 'Great Recession'.

Because the recession following the financial crisis was so deep and protracted, the property world of new factories, shopping centres and houses struggled to recover to pre-recession levels. The halving of economic growth had dire consequences for those looking for opportunities to invest in properties. In most cases, the standard of living did not rise for the average consumer during the Great Recession. Employment opportunities were limited, average wages were reduced, and the burden of debt became increasingly apparent.

The UK shares a common set of accounting conventions with other countries, and this allows international comparisons of GDP and GNI to be relatively straightforward. As an example, figures for five selected economies are given in Table 8.1. The final two columns show GDP growth in previous years. The row showing the average annual rate of economic growth for from 1990 to 2000 highlights the pace of change during the period prior to the Great Recession and, as you can see, the average growth was around 2.7% per annum across the three selected high-income countries. In sharp contrast, the rate of growth associated with the next decade appears to be about 50% slower. Similar annual figures for France, Italy Spain, Greece and Portugal indicate an even slower rate of recovery. In relative terms, Norway, the United States and the United Kingdom can be seen to be getting back on top. From an investment perspective, some countries are looking more attractive than others, as the pace of change is broadening out.

## Conclusion

To close this section, we need to add one or two small caveats about national accounting data. First, the figures recorded in national accounts are official activities 'put through the books'. Alongside these formal, legal activities, there are informal, illegal, activities, such as unofficial work carried out for cash in hand, which is difficult to include. In the widest technical sense, however, national accounts should include all productive output. Thus, although some economic activities are hidden and difficult to measure, estimates are made. For example, since 2014, estimates relating to the smuggling of alcoholic drink and tobacco products, prostitution and drug peddling, and the output, expenditure and income directly generated by each activity, have become officially recognised as an official part of the European system of accounting.

Second, it should be mentioned that economists are beginning to question whether national accounts are a good measure of welfare, since they clearly glorify the materialistic society in which we live. Expenditures triggered by accidents, contamination, natural disasters, prisons, wars and corporate fraud count the same as socially productive investments in housing, education, healthcare, sanitation or mass transportation. National accounting is an assessment of financial condition that is arrived at by adding up all 'business activity', regardless of its nature, so it tends to lump together income and expenses, assets and liabilities. As a result, GDP numbers fail to capture our true overall well-being as a nation. Monetary values certainly do not encompass everything that we care about; some things always remain beyond price.

## Measuring income per head

In a broad sense, worldwide economic activity tends to be on an upward path and, as the bottom line of Table 8.1 suggests, the world as a whole appear to be benefitting from economic growth. It should be noted, however, that if the population producing the GDP is rising by a similar percentage, there is no reason to suppose that the well-being of individuals has increased. For example, in 2014 the headlines suggested that GDP in the UK had risen by 7% since the recession, but the population of the UK had also grown during the six-year period, so any implicit improvement in living standards had been more or less cancelled out. In fact, detailed UK quarterly real GDP indicate that the average income per head [1] fell in the years between 2008 and 2014, by around £100 per month – so, on the whole, people in the UK did not become better off.

A similar scenario applies to the data reported from China and India, which have shown relatively large increases in economic growth throughout the 21st century. As Table 8.1 indicates, figures since 1990 record average economic growth of 8–9% per annum, albeit from a low starting-point. However, more importantly, in terms of assessing income per head, each of these countries has a population in excess of a billion people (in fact, more than two and a half billion people live in India and China added together). To facilitate international comparison, therefore, it is necessary to remember to take into account the population size of a country. This is achieved by expressing GNI on a *per capita* basis – by dividing total GNI by the total population to arrive at an amount per head (see the dollars *per capita* column in Table 8.1).

**Table 8.1**   GNI and GDP for selected economies

| Selected countries | Gross national income (GNI) | | Gross domestic product (GDP) | |
|---|---|---|---|---|
| **High and middle income** (In rank order) | Billions of dollars | Dollars per capita | Average annual % real growth | |
| | **2014** | **2014** | **1990–2000** | **2000–2014** |
| Norway | 529 | 103,050 | 2.0 | 1.1 |
| United States | 17,601 | 55,200 | 3.6 | 1.7 |
| United Kingdom | 2,129 | 34,710 | 2.6 | 1.5 |
| **High income average** | | | **2.7** | **1.4** |
| China | 10,069 | 7,380 | 10.6 | 10.3 |
| India | 2,036 | 1,610 | 6.0 | 7.6 |
| **Middle income average** | | | **8.3** | **9.0** |
| **World** | **78,260** | **10,858** | **2.9** | **2.6** |

*Adapted from World Bank Development Indicators (July, 2015: Tables 1.1 and 4.1).*

The statistics in Table 8.1 are taken from the World Development Indicators [2], a comprehensive annual set of data produced by the World Bank. The current publication lists data for 206 national economies in alphabetical order. In previous years, however, this data was presented in rank order according to GNI *per capita*. The concept of 'rank order' demonstrates the importance of these figures, as they are used to create a type of league table, in which (in 2014) the United States come ahead of the United Kingdom, since the gross national income (GNI) divided by the population is higher. On a *per capita* basis, the US and the UK are among the top ten richest countries in the world, with the Swiss, Scandinavian, Dutch and Irish joining the pack. Norway, however, has a population of little more than five million, who share a $529 billion economy, making it the richest country in the world with a *per capita* income in excess of $100,000.

At the other extreme, India and China, with their large populations, are relatively poor. Following conventions defined by the World Bank, neither India nor China can currently be considered to be near a high-income economy, as their annual *per capita* GNI is a constraint. At the extreme, some of the very poorest people of the world have to survive on an annual income of less than $600 *per capita* (which is possibly less than some students in the Western world earn each month, even while they are studying).

This analogy between Western students and the poor of the world highlights how difficult it is to imagine what life must be like below the poverty line. Yet it is well documented by the United Nations and the World Bank that more than one billion people in the developing world continue to live on less than $1.25 a day. Half the world's adult population – approximately 2.5 billion individuals – do not even have a bank account. Putting an end to people living with less than $1.25 a day had been an explicit goal of the World Bank, but slowly the emphasis is shifting away from the crude traditional practice of focusing on *per capita* GDP growth. More and more economists are recognising that, while GDP growth rates are useful summary measures of a society's economic progress, they are unable to capture the distributional aspects of growth. Indeed, it is entirely possible for a country to be growing rapidly on average, while the poor within the country see their incomes stagnate. Hence, a new way to define the goal of poverty reduction is to foster income growth of the bottom 40% of the population in every country (World Bank, 2014).

## Measuring income distribution

The distribution of money income can be graphically represented with a **Lorenz curve**, named after the late Max Otto Lorenz, a US-born statistician, who proposed it early in the 1900s. The Lorenz curve shows what proportion of a country's total money income is accounted for by different proportions of its families. Look at Figure 8.1. On the horizontal axis, we measure the *cumulative* percentage of families – lowest-income families first. Starting at the left corner, there are zero families; at the right corner we have 100% of families; and in the middle we have 50% of families. The vertical axis represents the cumulative percentage of money income. The 45° line represents perfect equality; 40% of the families obtain 40% of total income, 60% of the families obtain 60% of total income, and so on.

Of course, in the real world, perfect equality of income never exists, and no nation would have a straight line Lorenz Curve. Rather, it would be some curved line, like the one labelled 'actual money income distribution' in Figure 8.1. For example, the bottom 40% of families in the United Kingdom – those identified by Ed Miliband as the 'squeezed middle' – received approximately 20% of the total incomes earned in 2011. The difference between perfect money income equality and the Lorenz curve is the inequality gap.

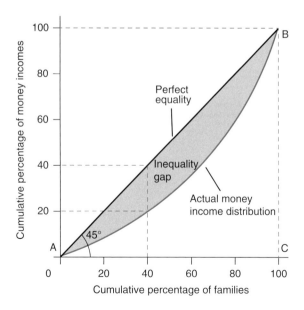

**Figure 8.1**   The Lorenz curve.

The Lorenz curve is therefore useful for showing the change in income distribution over time since, the further the curve drops below the 45° line, the greater the level of inequality. For instance, in the last 30 years, from 1985 to 2015, across most OECD countries, the curve moved outwards away from the 45° line, suggesting that the scale of inequality was increasing (OECD, 2015). The problem with comparing Lorenz curves from one year to the next or between countries is the general imprecision. This problem is partly overcome by using Gini coefficients.

## The Gini coefficient

A measure of the degree of income inequality is the **Gini coefficient,** devised by the Italian statistician Corrado Gini (1884–1965). A diagram showing a Lorenz curve, such as the one in Figure 8.1, can also demonstrate the concept of the Gini coefficient. We compare the area between the straight 45° line and the Lorenz curve of actual income distribution, with the entire area under the diagonal – that is, with the triangle that represents half of the box in Figure 8.1 and is labelled ABC. In other words:

$$\text{Gini coefficient of inequality} = \frac{\substack{\text{Area between diagonal line and} \\ \text{Lorenz curve of actual money income distribution}}}{\text{triangular area under diagonal line}}$$

What does this mean? It means that the Gini coefficient will range from 0 to 1. If we had perfect equality, the Gini coefficient would be 0, because there would be no area between the diagonal line – a line indicating absolute equality – and the curve of actual distribution of income. The greater that area becomes, however, the greater becomes the Gini coefficient and, hence, the measure of inequality. A Gini coefficient of 1 would, therefore, represent complete inequality. These are purely theoretical extremes; no society, however, egalitarian it may aspire to be, could achieve making everyone perfectly equal, which is what a Gini coefficient of 0 represents. In practice, any country with a Gini coefficient above 0.5 is actually very unequal.

Another way of looking at this is that the greater the level of income inequality becomes, the higher the Gini coefficient. For instance, in 1985, the Gini coefficient for the average OECD country was around 0.29; by 2011/12, it had increased by three points to 0.32. To be specific, the Gini coefficient had increased in 16 out of 21 OECD countries for which long-time data were available. In Finland, Israel, New Zealand, Sweden and the United States, the figure had increased by five points to 0.37. The only exceptions to this general rule of increasing inequality were found in Greece and Turkey where the Gini coefficient had fallen slightly (OECD, 2015).

The OECD's concern was that growing income inequality had reduced GDP growth in many industrialized countries. Their chosen explanation was that poorer citizens tend to spend every extra penny (euro or dollar) they get – or, as economists' jargon expresses it, poor people's 'propensity to spend' any extra income is much higher than that of the rich, who tend to save extra income. As a result, much of the extra money taken in by the wealthy tends to sit unspent in the form of financial savings, rather than being spent and generating economic activity in the real working economy.

The implication of this analysis means that the greater the level of income inequality, the less is spent, and the level of GDP declines. Also of concern in some quarters is the glaring fact that, in recent decades, the rich have acquired increasingly large slices of the economic pie, and the opportunities that go with it. These dual tensions have raised the profile of monitoring income distribution, and slowly it is becoming a government objective. As discussed in Chapter 7, governments have it in their powers to redistribute income and wealth through the taxation and welfare systems, but it is fair to conclude that the debate has not yet reached the level of consensus that is shared over the other macro-objectives. As a result, the monitoring of data relating to income and wealth does not yet share the same the level of sophistication, acceptance and support that the other objectives currently enjoy. As Professor Stiglitz (2013: 357) remarks in his bestselling (500 page) treatise on inequality: 'The economics is clear: the question is, what about the politics?'

Admittedly, the Great Recession did not create inequality; but it has made it worse, to the extent that economists can no longer ignore the question of income distribution. Hopefully, it will also gain a place in the hearts and minds of more politicians, so that the appropriate monitoring and policy decisions can be put in place. There is certainly hope at the end of the line, as the corporate bosses and politicians who met at the World Economic Forum in Davos, in 2015, to discuss topical issues, also homed in on inequality. As a journalist reported it: 'It might be hard to stomach that the overlords of a system that has delivered the widest global economic gulf in human history should be handwringing about the consequences of their own actions'. However, even they can sense the threats to economic stability unless something is changed (Milne, 2015).

## Measuring inflation

As introduced in Chapter 7, an important objective of a stable and competitive economy is a low inflation rate and, in most high-income countries, this means keeping prices rises within a band between 1–3%. If prices rise at 2% a year, most shoppers can more or less ignore their slow ascent. As economists often suggest, a touch of inflation is often helpful, as it gives bosses an excuse to nudge unproductive workers – as a pay freeze actually translates in real terms to a 2% cut in purchasing power. More importantly, in the current climate, it keeps economies away from deflation and the depressing choices – of hoarding cash and delaying purchases – that falling prices can bring.

The magic number for central banks to achieve, therefore, is a target rate of inflation of around 2% – that is, consumer prices should not be allowed *persistently* to increase beyond that level. The italicised word (in the previous sentence) is important, as any increase in the price level must be 'sustained' to be categorised as an inflationary situation. Continuous annual price rises were experienced in the UK and across Europe in the 1970s (when everyday prices were tending to increase by approximately 12.5% a year) and the 1980s (when prices were raised on average by around 7.5% per year). These were decades marked by inflationary problems.

**Table 8.2**   Annual average UK inflation rates

| Period | % change in price |
|--------|-------------------|
| 2000–2004 | 1.2 |
| 2005–2007 | 2.2 |
| 2008–2012 | 3.3 |
| 2013 | 2.6 |
| 2014 | 1.5 |
| 2015 | 0.03 |

*Source*: Office for National Statistics, November 2015.

Part C

Table 8.2 shows the annual average change to the *consumer price index* for the period 2000–2015, and this suggests that for the greater part of the period, the problem of continuous price increases has been tamed. For example, the 3% ceiling was only exceeded during the years 2008–2012. Since the beginning of 2013, however, relative to the years immediately following the crisis, there was a distinct whiff of **disinflation** in the air; that is, prices continued to rise each year, but the overall rate had begun to slow down. The forecast for inflation in 2015, on the basis of the data released in mid-November, was less than 0.1% (the precise number shown in Table 8.2 was correct up until October 2015). The general slowdown in the pace of price increases was regarded by some politicians as a sign of good news, as it offered the opportunity for wages to rise at a faster pace than retail prices. Thus, spending and living standards could theoretically increase.

**Deflation**, on the other hand, which is characterised by persistently falling prices and indicated by negative rates of change, is far more worrying. Deflation is, in effect, the complete reverse of inflation, to the extent that it typically results from a fall in aggregate demand; in response to which, firms reduce prices in order to sell their products. Inevitably, as a form of price instability, deflation has distinct adverse economic effects. For example, consumers and businesses may put off spending decisions because they expect prices to be lower in the future. Negative inflation also presents the Government with particular difficulties of macroeconomic management because, once inflation rates fall below zero and become negative, the Bank of England monetary policy committee cannot reduce interest rates to stimulate demand.

The target, therefore, is to achieve price stability by navigating a careful course between excess inflation and negative deflation. The measure – of inflation and deflation – involves representing changes in price over a period of time. The statistical device best suited for this purpose is index numbers. These are a means of expressing data relative to a given **base year**. They enable the cost of a particular range of products to be expressed as a percentage of the cost of the same group of products, compared to a previous time period. The basic principle is portrayed by Figure 8.2.

## Cost of living indices

The most commonly used price index in the UK is the **Consumer Price Index** (CPI). The best way to think of this is to imagine a 'supermarket shopping basket'

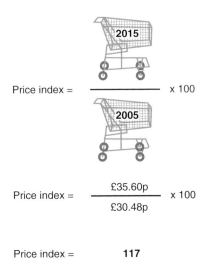

$$\text{Price index} = \frac{2015}{2005} \times 100$$

$$\text{Price index} = \frac{£35.60\text{p}}{£30.48\text{p}} \times 100$$

$$\text{Price index} = \mathbf{117}$$

**Figure 8.2**    Calculating a price index. In the example, two baskets of goods are compared and a base year of 2005 is selected. 2015, expressed in relation to 2005, gives a price index of 117 – in other words, an increase in price of 17%.

full of goods and services on which people typically spend their money, so it includes everything from food to entertainment. The purpose of the CPI, therefore, is to track changes in the cost of living.

For the sake of accuracy, the cost of the basket should be calculated with reference to all consumer goods and services purchased by all households, and the prices measured in all shops and internet sites that supply them. In practice, however, this is impossible, so the CPI is calculated by collecting a sample of prices from various retailers in various locations. The current sample – involving shops and online price quotes – represents a selection of 700 goods and services. The prices of these indices are collected across 150 geographical areas in the UK. As a result, the ONS monitors more than 100 000 prices each and every month.

Another important objective is to make sure that the basket is representative of the current consumer goods and services typically purchased by households. Hence, the basket is reviewed each year to keep it as up to date as possible and to reflect changes in buying patterns. Items are dropped from the basket when they become difficult to find, or are no longer typical of what most people spend their money on, and they are replaced by more up-to-date items. For example, when the index commenced, in 1947 – almost 70 years ago – the basket included men's and women's hats, ladies' stockings, vinyl records, bars of soap, cod liver oil, ox liver, mutton, mangles and gas fires. By 2015, these items had been dropped in favour of canvas shoes, e-books, internet services for streaming videos (e.g. Netflix) and music (e.g. Spotify), liquid soap, plant food, baby wipes, e-cigarettes, avocados, kiwis, fruit smoothies, pre-packed salad and fish fingers, and so on.

The annual review of the basket needs to consider not just the list of items to be priced, but also where they are commonly bought. Hence, in recent years, more and more internet and technology-based goods and services have been added. The essential goal is for the prices of goods and services purchased by the typical household to be consistently assessed and monitored. The level of detail that informs these regular reviews should be noted, as it underlines the level of importance attached to the official measurement of economic variables.

In pursuit of accuracy, in early 2013, the ONS launched **CPIH**, a new experimental measure of consumer price inflation, to include the cost of home ownership (which is detailed below). As you may remember from Chapter 3, these costs represent a significant expense for a large majority of households in the UK, but they do not form part of the CPI basket. The costs of utility bills and of minor repairs and maintenance are the only explicit reference to housing accounted for by the main index.

A further technique applied to the 'shopping basket' of items is **statistical weights**. This is important, as it provides a means of recognising that some items are more relevant than others in terms of their share of the average household's expenditure. In other words, statistical weights reflect an understanding of what households typically spend their money on. The simplest example is that the statistical weight for food is far higher than that for tobacco and alcohol, as changes in food prices affect everybody, whereas tobacco and alcohol prices only affect smokers and drinkers. In fact, in 2015, the statistical weight for food was about three times greater than tobacco and alcohol, which means that a 5% increase in the price of food would have three times as much effect on the total cost of the basket, when compared to a 5% increase in tobacco and alcohol.

In the main index, expenditure on housing and household services (such as housing rent, repair and maintenance and utility bills) is not given any more statistical significance than the weight of the items representing spending on transport, recreation and culture, and restaurants and hotels. In direct comparison, in the calculation of the CPIH basket, the housing and household services category – the cost of owner occupation – not only includes some more items but, as a group, they carry more weight than any other group. In fact, in 2015, broadly speaking, housing was statistically given more weight in the CPIH basket than transport, recreation and culture and spending in restaurants and hotels all added together! The suggestion here is that a typical household spends the largest majority of its income – around 28%, according to the CPIH structure of weights – on housing and related occupier costs.

The main distinction, however, between the CPI and CPIH is in their use and origin. The CPI has its origin in a system that is common to the European Union (EU). It was previously called the **harmonised index of consumer prices**, and it provides a direct comparison with other members of the EU. It has been used by the UK government to target the **official rate of inflation** since January 2004. As you may recall, the current target is to keep the inflation rate around 2%, subject to a margin of 1% on either side. The CPIH, on the other hand, is a far more recent development, providing an experimental and uniquely British measure of the cost of living. As outlined above, it was only introduced in 2013, but already it has begun to grasp imaginations, and it is often the preferred inflation rate to headline in the British press.

To sum up, the contents of the baskets used for CPI and CPIH are very similar, but not identical. The prime distinction is that the CPIH basket includes an item to represent an owner-occupier's housing costs – sometimes abbreviated as OOH in the official literature. This does not, however, explicitly account for mortgage costs from month to month as, not only would this be difficult for households that are in different contracts, started at different times, but also because, ultimately, it would limit the transferability of CPIH from extending to the rest of the EU in due course.

Instead of mortgage interest payments, CPIH uses an approach called 'rental equivalence' to measure owner-occupiers' housing costs. Rental equivalence is based on the rent paid for an equivalent house, as a proxy for the costs faced by an owner-occupier. In other words, it answers the question, 'how much would I have to pay in rent to live in a home like mine?' (it might also be worth reiterating that housing costs, such as 'actual rents', repair and maintenance and utility bills, are included in both cost of living indices). These subtleties form the main technical differences between CPI and CPIH.

Finally, it is worth noting that neither of the indices referred to so far capture changes to actual house prices. Although this may be inconsistent with some users' expectations of measures of housing costs, the inclusion of an asset price and, therefore, capital gains, would make the index less suitable as a measure of the everyday costs of consumption. To measure changes in house prices, or other real estate assets, there are a number of specialised indices to refer to.

### Specialised indices

There is a broad range of specialised indices, and the same methodological principles apply. For example, the Investment Property Databank (IPD) compiles a property price index by comparing specific capital and rental values for 11 000 commercial properties on a regular basis. Its data goes back to a base year in 1981.

Similarly, there are a number of specialised house price indices. The largest two mortgage lenders – Nationwide and Halifax – publish a house price index each month, based on comparisons of the prices of four different house types across 13 regions of the UK. These two financial institutions base their indices on the mortgage offers they have made in the previous month. Houses costing over £1 million are excluded, as it is assumed that this may distort the average picture.

A more comprehensive, but less up-to-date, measure comes from the Land Registry. This index is based on stamp duty land tax (SDLT) transactions. It therefore covers every property deal in England and Wales. However, it is slow to reveal what is happening in the market, since SDLT is paid at the end of the property transaction, and that can be four or five months after the sale price has been agreed; house prices can rise by as much as 20% within three months. Recently, the websites *Hometrack* and *Rightmove* have added two further indices to the set. They collect information at the local level from estate agents on asking prices and agreed prices, and they also cover far more properties than Nationwide and Halifax. All of these indices are monitored and revised by the Department of Communities and Local Government to form a further measure of house prices – the CLG house price index.

Each house price index produces a marginally different estimate of house price inflation. This is because the indices are dependent both on the sample data that has been used to make up each specific basket and the way that each index is subsequently calculated.

House price indices are important, because they are used by the Government and the monetary policy committee as an indicator to assess the economy.

Many other institutions and professional bodies also produce specialised indices that are relevant to the property sector. For example, the Royal Institution of Chartered Surveyors produces the **Building Cost and Information Service** (BCIS). This comprises a building cost index and a tender price index.

The building cost index measures changes in costs of labour, materials and plant – that is, it covers the basic costs faced by contractors. The basket is compiled from nationally agreed labour rates and material prices. The index also includes forecasts to help predict any changes in prices that may occur in the period between submitting a tender and project completion. This is useful, because the long time duration of large contracts means that work is often let at fixed prices before work commences. The building cost index also forms part of the data that informs the viability exercises outlined in Chapter 2.

The tender price index involves an analysis of successful tenders for contracts worth more than £250,000. It includes movements in wage rates, discounts, plant costs, overheads and profit – that is, it indicates the basic cost of construction work to the client. In effect, the tender price index is a measure of the confidence in the industry about its current and future workload. When demand for the industry's services is high, not only do contractors' margins increase, but so do the margins of their suppliers and wage rates, and one would expect to see rises in the tender price index. Conversely, when demand for the industry's services decline, all these factors decrease and, thereby, exert downward pressure on the price index.

The gap between these two indices suggests something about market conditions. For example, during the Great Recession, the two indices converged. The explanation is simple: as less work was available, contractors reduced their bids to the bare minimum – in some cases even below cost – just to win the contract. As the market picked up and became more buoyant, tender prices increased, as contractors could take advantage of the opportunity to more than cover their costs.

## Summing up indices

The important aspect in the compilation of any price index is to assure that the prices being recorded are for comparable items. Apples must be compared with apples, not with oranges, and the baskets that are used for comparisons must be consistent! As indicated at the start of this section, a change in the measure of inflation does not alter the *actual* inflationary pressure in the economy; it remains the same, regardless of the index used to measure it.

# Measuring unemployment

In conceptual terms, the numbers of unemployed are measured as a percentage of economically active people who are able and willing to work but cannot find a job. The data can also be expressed as an absolute number, but the percentage rate is preferable, because it measures the proportion of the economically active population who are unemployed. It therefore takes account of changes in population sizes over time and between cultures.

At first sight, the notion of unemployment seems reasonably straightforward, as surely it includes anybody who does not have a job. However, it is not always that simple. For example, how would you classify: Someone over 65 who claims a pension? Someone who is long-term sick and cannot work? Or someone who only works three hours a week, but wants more work?

These are difficult questions, and they go some way in introducing why definitions of unemployment need to be commonly accepted to be useful. The International Labour Organisation [3] – an agency of the United Nations – classifies all people aged over 16 into one of three groups: in employment, unemployed, or economically inactive. In very general terms, anybody who carries out at least one hour's paid work in a week, or is temporarily away from a job (e.g. on holiday), is in employment. This includes people who are on government-supported training schemes and people who do unpaid work for their family's business. Following on from these very specific criteria, anybody without work who has actively tried to find a job in the last four weeks, and is willing and able to start work in the next two weeks, is considered to be unemployed.

### The economically active and inactive

Those who are neither in employment nor officially unemployed, such as those involved in full-time education, those in early retirement, housewives, and those who are not at present seeking work, are defined as **economically inactive**.

The **economically active** represent people who are employed, as well as those who are unemployed. Or, to put the emphasis the other way, the economically inactive should not be confused with those who are *registered* as unemployed!

The statistics presented in Table 8.3 clarify the distinction between the different groups that make up the labour market.

### ILO and claimant unemployment

As stated in Chapter 7, there are two separate measures of unemployment regularly published in the UK – one recommended by the International Labour Organisation (ILO), and the other, distinctly British, method based on a claimant count.

The **ILO unemployment measure** has the distinct advantage of being used by most countries in the world, and it provides an international standardised approach. The

**Table 8.3**  The labour market in 2015

| | |
|---|---:|
| Total population aged 16 and over | 51,939,000 |
| minus those classed as economically inactive | 19,053,000 |
| **equals total economically active** | **32,886,000** |
| minus unemployed (ILO definition) | 1,852,000 |
| **equals total in employment** | **31,034,000** |

*Source*: ONS labour market statistics, August 2015.

important recurring feature is that each country is required to conduct a quarterly Labour Force Survey (LFS). In the UK, this involves interviewing around 40,000 households (i.e. approximately 80,000 people aged 16 and over to 74), every three months (results for single months are also produced, but these estimates are not as robust). The survey defines unemployment as those without jobs who say they have actively sought work in the last four weeks, or who are waiting to take up appointment within the next fortnight. It is worth adding, however, that since the measurement is based on a sample survey, figures can be no more than an estimate of the actual level of unemployment.

Although the ILO measure is not so easy to calculate, and is subject to some sampling error, it has the advantage of being used internationally, and has become the official measure of unemployment in the UK. This enables international comparisons to be made, since each country uses the same definition, the same survey techniques and a similar sample size.

Table 8.4 shows several examples of unemployment figures from EU and OECD countries (based on data available in June 2015). As each estimate is derived from the ILO survey method and stated as a percentage of the labour force, they form a good source of comparison – that is, by consistently using a percentage rate of unemployment, the figures are always expressed relative to the size of the nation's work force. Thus, in Greece, more than a quarter of the labour force were unemployed, compared to less than 5% in Germany. Germany,

**Table 8.4**   Comparisons of unemployment, 2015

| *Unemployment rates published by Eurostat* | |
| --- | --- |
| **European Union** | **Unemployment rate (%)** |
| Croatia | 15.3 |
| Cyprus | 16.2 |
| Germany | 4.7 |
| Greece | 25.6 |
| Spain | 22.5 |
| United Kingdom | 5.6 |
| Total EU[1] | 9.6 |
| Eurozone[2] | 11.1 |
| *Unemployment rates from OECD* | |
| Canada | 6.8 |
| Japan | 3.4 |
| United States | 5.3 |

*Notes:*
[1] The 'Total EU' series consist of all 28 EU countries.
[2] The Eurozone consists of 19 EU countries using the Euro.
*Sources:* Eurostat and OECD, July 2015.

however, has a larger economically active population than Greece, so the actual numbers of unemployed are greater in Germany. Relative to its size, however, Greece has a far more significant problem, as 1.25 million people out of its 5 million labour force were unemployed in 2015, and half the number were under 25. Across the EU as a whole, more than 20 million were unemployed in June 2015, and 17.5 million of that number were in the 19 countries using the Euro. In the United States, 5.3% represented more than eight million people – 8 292 000, to be precise!

Alongside the ILO measure of unemployment, an additional measure, the **Claimant Count**, is often quoted in the UK. The Claimant Count is based on a monthly total of those receiving unemployment benefits, such as Jobseeker's Allowance (JSA) or Universal Credit (UC). The data is relatively easy to collect, since it is based on a computer count of all those officially registered as 'willing and able to work but presently claiming benefits'. This measure is recognisably suspect, as it excludes all those who are not eligible for benefits, such as all men aged over 60 or anyone who registers as desiring work at commercial agencies but not with the job centres because, owing to marriage or similar circumstances, they are not eligible for benefit. Finally, it will include some fraudulent claimers of benefit, who work as well as 'sign on' although, nowadays, the numbers involved in this illegal practice are minimal, as the system has been tightened up in the last few years.

## Summing up

The review of labour market statistics discussed above distinguishes between those who are employed, unemployed, or economically inactive. In other words, the data is designed in such a way that it shows the proportion who are engaged in paid work, and indicates the extent to which people would be engaged in such work if their personal circumstances were different, or if jobs that attracted them were available. Unfortunately, since the recession, workers have had to take – and stick around in – less than ideal jobs, like fast food and retailing, even though they are qualified for far more. This failure of the job ladder, however, is not revealed by the data, and does impact all workers equally.

Obviously the actual labour market is far from static, with people moving between different categories, as their personal, and overall economic, conditions change. The data merely provides a snapshot of those who are unemployed and those who are economically active. The members of each group will not be static, as there are constantly large numbers of people joining and leaving the pool of unemployed labour. Those joining the pool are referred to as the *inflow*, and those leaving it are referred to as the *outflow*. If the inflow and outflow are equal, the unemployment rate remains the same. If the number leaving jobs and flowing into the reservoir of the unemployed exceeds new appointments, the unemployment rate rises.

To judge the severity of unemployment problems, therefore, we need to be able to examine more details relating to the duration, region, gender, age, and qualifications of the unemployed, and estimates of such data are published each month. This is important, as property developers need to assimilate as much insight as possible into an area to understand its viability for development.

## Measuring international transactions

As suggested in Chapter 7, figures relating to trade and investments across national boundaries are notoriously difficult to record accurately. Furthermore, there are many cultural barriers to developing successful strategies to invest in property and construction abroad. As a consequence, it tends to be only the larger firms and institutions that get involved with commercial real estate at the international level.

In terms of measurement, the economic transactions between UK residents and the rest of the world are presented each year in the **Balance of Payments** (Pink book). At the simplest level, these international accounts provide a measure of all the money coming into the country from abroad, less all of the money going out of the country during the same period. Examples of such transactions include: the export and import of goods, such as oil, food, raw materials, machinery, equipment, computers, white goods and clothing; the export and import of services such as international transport, tourism, insurance, computer software, accountancy and legal activities; and income flows relating to investments and the ownership of financial assets.

In other words, the balance of payments records a nation's international trading position, plus its lending and its borrowing. Dealings that result in money entering the country – such as from exports – are credit (plus) items, while transactions that lead to money leaving the country – such as the payment for imports – are debit (minus) items. To take one of the few straightforward examples from the Balance of Payments Tables, it is recorded that in 2014 the construction industry added £1965 million to UK export income (by being responsible for building on overseas sites). On the other side of the balance sheet, in the same year, the UK imported construction services debiting £2185 million from the books. In sum, there was a Balance of Payments deficit of £220 million from construction activities alone.

### *The London property market and overseas investment*

Of all the measurements discussed in this chapter, Balance of Payment data is the least reliable. To take a topical example, the press seemed obsessed during 2014/15 with blaming wealthy foreigners for the unaffordability of homes in London. The cliched story ran along the following lines: overseas investors buy everything in sight, pricing everyone else out of the market. They don't buy flats because they want to live in them – they 'buy to leave' and sell for a vast profit at some future date. The headlines painted a picture in which the super-rich foreigners saw London properties as 'safe deposit boxes' where they could stash their spare millions and watch them grow.

It is, however, hard to find data to substantiate these rumours. There have been numerous attempts by agents (such as Knight Frank [4] (2013) or Savills [5] (2013)), and an authoritative study carried out by Molior (2014) (researchers in the residential development industry, specialising in London), commissioned by the British Property Federation (BPF). Although the statistics presented by Molior (2014) need some kind of health warning (as the work draws heavily from confidential information held by developers, agents and private individuals, such as thousands of Land Registry title documents, telephone interviews and sales data from specific residential schemes), it was systematic and authoritative, and provided a useful counterpoint to media reporting.

Part C

For example, Molior (2014) asserts that around 60% of the 21,300 new homes built in London in 2013 were purchased for investment purposes (such as 'buy to let' or 'buy to sell'), leaving 40% for owner occupation. More importantly, only 15% of the investment purchases were actually made by overseas buyers (defined as buyers who normally reside outside the UK, to distinguish them clearly from the buyers who were born overseas but normally reside in the UK, as is the case for 37% of people who live in London). To reiterate, 3,195 of the 21,300 sales recorded by Molior during 2013 were purchased by buyers normally resident overseas. Furthermore, there was little evidence to support the rumour that the overseas buyers were leaving properties empty.

Identifying who actually invests in the London property market, therefore, is a difficult question and, when it is measured by rental stream, it is further complicated by exchange rate variations, price changes and methods of valuation. Fortunately, at the introductory level, much of the relevant analysis of property economics resides within the boundaries of one nation, so it could be argued that this set of macroeconomics statistics is possibly less important than others. For instance, the construction data referred to above represents less than 2% of the traded service activities recorded on the credit or debit side. However, international transactions generally can have considerable implications on an economy's performance, and should not be entirely ignored at any level of study. Thus, the formal accounting process needs to be dealt with, albeit relatively quickly.

### Taking stock of an external balance

The balance of payments forms a record of transactions with the rest of the world and, as such, they take account of dealings between residents and non-residents. Following international conventions, the transactions can be broken down into two main groups: the **current account** and **capital and financial accounts**.

The most significant flow is the balance of payments on *Current Account*. This provides a record of all transactions arising from trade in goods and services, investment and employment between UK residents and non-residents. Technically speaking, therefore, the current account balance should not be confused with a simple **trade balance**, since it also includes **primary and secondary incomes** such as wages, investments and current transfers (such as aid and gifts). In effect, the current account records how much money is flowing into the UK and how much money is flowing out. It is similar to a current account at a High Street bank, where the balance shows income in relation to expenditure. If, at the end of the month, the balance is positive, the nation has a surplus which can be placed into a separate savings account. If, however, the balance is negative, the nation has a deficit and this needs to be funded by either drawing on previous savings, or by taking on some debt. Overall, the UK has consistently run a current account deficit every year since 1984, and it is this set of data that is commonly referred to in the newspaper headlines and media.

To sum up, therefore, the current account basically measures flows. If a country records a current account deficit, it means that the residents are consuming more and/or earning less than they are producing, or gaining in some form from abroad. The most recent figures suggest that, in 2014, the UK's current account deficit was £92.8 billion. Although that is a huge amount by any reckoning (and it would be more than enough to pay for the construction of the 2016 Olympics venues in Rio de Janeiro several times over), it is important to keep things in perspective, and think of a current account deficit in relation to the size of the related economy as a whole. In 2014, the current account deficit was 5% of UK GDP, which is the largest it has ever been, but this is not as bad as the press commentary might imply.

Regardless, debts need to be honoured, and that means that the UK must either sell some of its assets or increase its liabilities. These two respective actions are achieved via the 'capital' and 'financial' accounts.

The *Capital Account* records the flow of funds into and out of a country associated with non-produced fixed assets, such as copyrights, and the purchases or sales of land. Also, this account includes simple transfers of capital, where there is no specific *quid pro quo* to offset the transfer of ownership, such as institutional payments or grants to or from the EU or IMF, or the forgiveness of debt. By comparison with the transactions recorded on the current account, these specific capital manoeuvres are relatively small in scale, and the amounts involved rarely constitute more than 2% of the whole balance. As a consequence, it is highly unlikely that the current account and capital account would ever tally – and this brings us to a third set of accounts.

The *Financial Account* deals with transactions relating to the net acquisition of financial assets and net incurrence of liabilities. To extend the analogy of personal finance introduced above, the financial account combines savings, investment and credit card accounts, alongside borrowing from friends and family. Formally, it comprises cross-border transactions involving the ownership of shares, debt securities, derivatives and other financial instruments, as introduced in Chapter 5. As already inferred, it provides a lion's share of the funds required to counterbalance a current account deficit. For instance, in 2014, the financial account balance stood at £89.4 billion, which funded 96% of the current account deficit.

Obviously, significant problems occur if the public sector has few financial reserves, or faces limits on how much it can effectively borrow or raise in tax income. For instance, when the Greek government's finances collapsed in April 2010, it had already borrowed to the hilt in the international financial markets. Furthermore, evasion and corruption were endemic in Greek society, and this made it difficult to generate significant funds in taxes from the collapsing economy, or to find anybody within Greece willing to lend it money. As a result, Greece experienced a genuine balance of payments crisis.

## Summing up

In very general terms, the *Pink Book* reveals a series of balances, such as the current account balance, and the capital and financial account balances. It is possible, therefore, to envisage more than one 'balance' of payments. When all the statistics are put together, a number of discrepancies inevitably occur and the three accounts never perfectly balance. To correct for this, a balancing item (referred to a *net errors and omissions*) is included in order to bring the accounts into an exact balance – to synchronise them with one another. The main reason for them being out of sync is that the data is obtained from a number of international sources, and there are often time delays before items are recorded. Inevitably, therefore, there will always be some omissions. The statistical discrepancy, or balancing item, also justifies the large-scale revisions that the figures are commonly subject to over a number of years, so initial balance of payments estimates are provisional in the most generous of senses.

## Measuring business fluctuations

In Chapter 1, we defined macroeconomics as focusing mainly on aggregate behaviour; that is, events that many firms tend to experience. In subsequent chapters, we pointed out how, in a recession, although many firms and industries perform poorly, this does not mean that all firms are doing badly. During a recession, some firms will get lucky by introducing a new product that consumers really want. In short, in some sectors, the recession will bite more than others.

The measurement data used to investigate the nature of business fluctuations centres on identifying the turning points. For this to make sense, it might be helpful to quickly review the economic cycles introduced in Chapter 6. In Figure 8.3, we revisit the various phases that characterise business fluctuations, and we use recent economic activity as a reference point.

Beginning on the left-hand side of the graph in Figure 8.3, a **depression** is characterised by heavy unemployment, low consumer demand and surplus productive capacity, plus low business confidence. Such a situation has not been officially recorded since the 1930s. Prior to the Great Recession, the UK economy had not experienced a prolonged period of negative growth – only relatively short blips, such as the one experienced in the early 1990s. The **recovery**, or expansion phase, is easy to identify, as employment, income and consumer spending all begin to increase; investment also increases and business expectation becomes more favourable.

In a very general sense, the economy of the UK had experienced one long period of expansion from 1995–2008. Thus, there was more than a decade of uninterrupted economic growth; the economy was on a definite upward path. At the peak of the **boom**, industries are working at full capacity and bottlenecks begin to appear in the supply chain, which leads to price increases. After an indefinite time

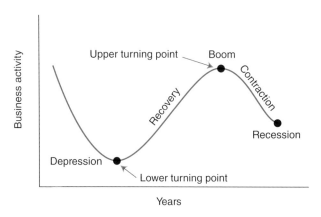

**Figure 8.3**    Phases of economic activity.

period, the economy begins to slow down, or contract, as it moves towards the final phase shown in Figure 8.3: the **recession**. At this point business expectations are not so good; consumption, employment and investment all begin to fall, and a significant number of firms are in receivership. From 2008–2014, recessions were a common phenomenon across many economies and, to this day, it remains the largest recession the world has ever known.

Table 8.5 shows the average length of the economic cycle and the related periods of contraction and expansion experienced in the United States since 1854 (the figures are derived from data recorded by the National Bureau of Economic Research – NBER – which is an American research agency that is officially responsible for determining the beginning and end of economic cycles in the United States). The table highlights that between 1854 and 1945, the average expansion lasted 31 months, and the average contraction 20 months. Since the Second World War, however, expansions have lasted almost twice as long – an average of 59 months – and contractions have shortened to an average of only 11 months. As a rule of thumb periods of expansion are lasting longer and contractions are getting shorter.

As a consequence, the average length of one cycle, measured from one recession to the next, has extended in time from 48 months to 70 months (i.e. from four to nearly six years). In historical terms, therefore, the period of contraction – from peak to trough – has become less and less problematical. As explained at some length in Chapter 6, the business cycle dating committee stated that the Great Recession began in the United States in December 2007, and officially reached its lowest point in June 2009 (NBER, 2010 [6]). In technical terms, this limited the official phase of contraction to 18 months, which is the longest period of economic contraction experienced since 1945.

Equivalent UK data shows a peak to trough decline, of approximately 6% in economic activity from 31 March 2008 to the end of June 2009 (i.e. five consecutive quarters). From then onwards, economic growth was erratic for about three years, with several quarters between 2010 and 2013 recording broadly flat or declining GDP; in fact, during this time the average quarterly growth was around 0.25%. Since 2014, however, GDP began to grow more steadily in the UK, with the economy slowly returning to levels that existed before the downturn. The relevant data is presented in Figure 8.4.

As can be seen in Figure 8.4, GDP in the UK was relatively steady, up until the financial crash that affected global economic growth from 2008 onwards. Some countries managed to recover more quickly than others, with Canada, Germany and the United States being the first to stabilise. As the UK data shows, the 2008

**Table 8.5**  Recessions and expansions, 1854–2009

| Historical cycles | Contractions* | Expansions* | Length of cycle* |
|---|---|---|---|
| 1854–1919 (16 cycles) | 22 | 27 | 48 |
| 1919–1945 (6 cycles) | 18 | 35 | 53 |
| 1945–2009 (11 cycles) | 11 | 59 | 70 |

*Average duration measured in months
Source: NBER, August, 2015.

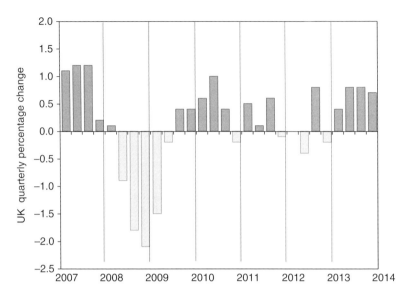

**Figure 8.4**   UK quarterly GDP growth, 2007–2014.

recession dragged on for a long time and recovery was worryingly slow. Figure 8.4 confirms that the bottom had literally fallen out of the UK market (with an average change in quarterly growth from January 2010 to April 2014 of less than 0.4%).

Other countries, however, were still feeling the repercussions seven years later, with Greece, Spain, Italy, Portugal and Holland still struggling to recover in 2015. In these countries, the journalistic phrase 'Great Depression 2.0' would have been more descriptive of the recessionary phase. All told, a significant number of people had lost their jobs and income and, in many places, the economy lost so much momentum and gathered such vast amounts of debt that it is debatable whether these countries would ever fully recover. It is an interesting time to be studying economics, especially in the context of real estate, as surveyors need to understand what data can and cannot tell us about the broader macroeconomy, in order to stay ahead of market developments and give shrewd investment advice.

## Identifying the turning points

One way to measure business fluctuations is to assess the trends in the economy by calculating changes to GDP from one calendar quarter to the next. The first quarter begins on January 1 and ends March 31, and so on (in some instances, data refers to a financial year that runs from the end of March through to the beginning of April of the following year – in which case, it will be footnoted or form part of the heading). Forgive me if you find all this too trivial, but I generally find that these prefatory remarks about calendar and financial years are useful when preparing students to take their first steps at interrogating actual data. As a test, try to review the last nine quarterly national accounts of any one of the countries listed by the OECD (there are 34 member states to choose from, but more than 40 major economies are regularly reported). In other words, select *one* country from the *OECD quarterly national accounts database* [7] to identify its current economic trend and when that phase commenced. In effect, there are two broad questions: can you identify the current direction and speed of travel of a specific economy? – and, secondly can you put a *precise* date on the economic turning point?

## Interpreting business fluctuations

There is a collection of economic statistics that can indicate where we are, where we have been and, most importantly, where we seem to be going. Their origin date back to the 1960s, and they are still referred to as **cyclical indicators**. They enable governments to predict changes that are happening in an economy, based on a composite set of statistics that are regarded as running ahead of the general economic trend. This is because things do not happen simultaneously; some indicators may point in an upward direction, while others portray a downward trend, especially at the 'peaks' and 'troughs' (the turning points) of a cycle.

Statistics that precede the general trend of the economy by changing six to twelve months ahead of the main trend are referred to as **leading indicators**. This group is broken down into two subgroups: a longer leading index (which looks for turning points about one year ahead); and a shorter leading index (which indicates turning points approximately six months ahead). Examples of leading indicators are housing starts, new car sales, business optimism and the amount of consumer credit. **Lagging indicators**, by contrast, alter in retrospect, usually about one year after a change in the economic cycle. They confirm what we already know and, in forecasting terms, are not so important. Examples of lagging indicators include unemployment, investment in building, plant and machinery, levels of stock, and orders for engineering output. Economic statistics that are thought to trace the actual cycle are called **coincident indicators**, and the obvious example is GDP figures.

## Forecasting the economy

The interpretation of economic events is a complex process, especially as macro-economic policy instruments can affect several variables at once. To take the simplest example, some cynical forecasters are quick to suggest that the sight of an increasing number of cranes on the skyline, visible from their office window, means that we are about to witness the start of the next recession. However, this is a ridiculous suggestion, as there are many other variables that need to be used as a basis for forecasting. Indeed, the art of forecasting involves completing a picture using as much existing data as possible, and combining this analysis with anecdotal evidence to arrive at an overall view.

In the years leading up to the Great Recession, economic models – often computer-based – used mathematical equations to confidently link up a number of economic variables. Good examples are the Treasury forecasts, which are informed by 36 independent models managed by institutions in the city and beyond.

**Table 8.6**  Economy forecasts 2015 to 2019

| Average projections | 2015 | 2016 | 2017 | 2018 | 2019 |
|---|---|---|---|---|---|
| GDP growth (%) | 2.6 | 2.5 | 2.4 | 2.4 | 2.3 |
| CPI (%) | 0.1 | 1.4 | 1.9 | 2.0 | 2.0 |
| ILO unemployment (%) | 5.5 | 5.1 | 5.0 | 4.9 | 4.9 |
| Claimant unemployment (mn) | 0.97 | 0.89 | 0.88 | 0.87 | 0.89 |
| Current account (£bn) | −28.4 | −24.4 | −22.4 | −18.4 | −17.7 |

*Source*: Adapted from HM Treasury 2015.

Table 8.6 shows the August 2015 forecast for the UK economy up until 2019. The table summarises the averages; it does not show the range of estimates making up the forecast. For example, the highest and lowest forecasts for the percentage change of GDP in 2016 were 3.0% and 1.4%; the respective figures for CPI ranged between 2.7% and 1.2%.

Understandably, it is difficult to predict accurately the behaviour of millions of consumers and businesses to the last detail, and economic forecasts inevitably contain a margin of error. To acknowledge this fact, the Bank of England uses the phrase 'data uncertainty' to describe the difficulty of making policy judgements when statistical indicators are subject to revision and sudden changes due to events. To paraphrase an analogy used by Norman Lamont during his time as the Chancellor of the Exchequer in the early 1990s: forecasting an economy on the basis of current statistics is like driving a car with the front and side windows blackened, and just a rear view mirror to see where the car is going. Furthermore, there are also problems relating to time-lags, since it often takes years for a specific monetary or fiscal instrument to fully work through an economic system. To continue the analogy of driving a car: the brake and accelerator pedals may only take effect some time after they are applied!

## Problems of forecasting

As discussed at several points in this text, relying on a mathematical computer-based model is no longer entirely acceptable (although forecasters like to point out in their defence that understanding half of a picture is better than not seeing any of it at all!). Economists of the new school are keen to stress that economic models did not help us to predict the severe economic downturn that started in 2007/8 and, as a result, extrapolation is no longer as valid. The problems with mainstream forecasting models are that they tend to imply that economic systems are linear, continuous, rational and mechanistic. However, variables change, unforeseen events do occur, and small but important statistical assumptions soon scale up. To clarify these problems, we use two case studies.

### Case 1:    the law of small numbers

Given the scale of today's economy, a small adjustment to a forecast can upset predictions immensely. For example, in the March 2015 budget, the Chancellor of the Exchequer, George Osborne, forecast that his plans could achieve a small budget surplus of £7 billion by 2018/19. However, this was predicated on the basis of certain economic assumptions, namely that inflation returned to the Bank of England's 2% target, and that economic growth during the period 2015–19 would be in the region of 2.3–2.4% (OBR, 2015 [8]).

However, by making some small, but significant, tweaks to the numbers, forecasters can go horribly wrong. For example, say inflation does not return to the Bank of England's 2% target, but stabilises around 1%; and that the economy continues to grow, but at a slightly lower rate such as the 1.8% per annum that had been the norm between 2010 and 2014.

The result is that the forecast budget surplus quickly evaporates and becomes a large deficit. Indeed, by plugging these figures into a model, the forecasted £7 billion surplus by 2018/19 turns into a hole of over £120 billion in the UK's public finances.

Which of the two sets of data is the more realistic scenario is arguable, as both are a forecast. The important point is that seemingly tiny differences in cumulative figures matter, especially when the starting point is an annual deficit of £91 billion. Furthermore, there is still some conjecture regarding the next move in interest rates, as they could go either way at any time.

*Case 2:    The law of changing conditions*

In the past, it was frequently suggested that a university degree is a sound investment, on the basis of the extra income that a graduate earns, compared to those who stop their education when they leave school. The classic line of argument was that students benefit by at least £100,000 in salary during their career by graduating. Indeed, up until 2008, I was guilty of peddling out this scenario on a regular basis to fresher students attending their first lecture, using it as an example of opportunity cost, and hopefully reassuring the audience that they had made a shrewd choice by deciding to study at university.

The problem is that the £100,000 return on investing in education is based on conditions and data from 30 years ago. Therefore, given that the variables have changed so considerably, it is no longer fair to extrapolate. For example, in the past, there were far fewer students attending university (up to 10 times less), as the number of full-time students has risen from slightly over 200,000 in the mid-1980s to more than two million today. As a consequence, many students now have to accept non-graduate employment that is often part-time, or on zero-hour contracts. Furthermore, the costs of studying have significantly increased, with tuition fees and loans becoming a standard part of the student experience. In sum, the only sensible response is to take all economic assumptions with a pinch of salt.

## Forecasting property markets

Most official statistics in the UK are based on a history and consensus of conventions, many of which have been agreed internationally. For example, the various statistical series of macroeconomic data (detailed above) have been comprehensively measured since the Second World War. As we have seen, the majority of it refers to national, aggregated data. In direct contrast, the collection of property data is still a relatively young science, not yet 40 years old. It tends to be unofficial, informal, local and disaggregated. When it is used by surveyors, it is often focused on a specific asset at a specific address.

As a consequence, information relating to property is nowhere near as comprehensive as data that refers to the broader economy. In fact, data relating to commercial property, rents and capital returns and the like are commonly reliant on confidential private records. Some of these spill over into the public domain via the *Estates Gazette*, a professional magazine that is published weekly (and was commented on in Chapter 1 at some length), and various specialist reports. The reports, published annually, or in some cases quarterly, tend to be based on actual transactions and market intelligence gathered by agents, such as, Jones Lang LaSalle (JLL), CBRE (CB Richard Ellis) Savills, Strutt & Parker, and Cushman & Wakefield (who merged with DTZ in September 2015 to form one of the world's largest real estate services firms, with offices in more than 60 countries).

Finally, there are two specialist organisations collecting property data that is made available for a fee, namely the Investment Property Databank – IPD – (who specialise in producing price indices for commercial property) and CoStar (who provide a range of data relating to UK commercial markets). Most universities have arrangements for these subscription-based data sets to be accessible to students via their intranets.

In 1993, the Governor of the Bank of England remarked that he was surprised at the relative lack of consistent comprehensive data on the property markets and the lack of research into the functioning of that market. Eighteen years later, a high-profile government-led inquiry into the causes of the financial crisis in the United States focused on similar data issues. To paraphrase some of the findings: in the decade preceding the collapse, there were many warning signs ... house prices were inflated, lending practices had spun out of control, and too many homeowners were taking on mortgages and debt they could ill afford. In other words, 'alarm bells' were clanging inside financial institutions, regulatory offices, consumer service organizations, law enforcement agencies and corporations throughout America and Europe, but they were left largely unchecked (FCIC, 2011: 3 to 4). The problem was that the relevant data that could have been used to monitor the residential markets was not consistently or comprehensively collated or analysed.

It is often alleged, however, that there is a relationship between changes in property values and indicators of inflation. The empirical evidence certainly suggests that there is some kind of cause or effect relationship, as property prices in both the commercial and residential markets correlate with the headline rate inflation. The difficulty lies in identifying the line of causation; that is, do property values lead to inflation, or is it inflation that drives up property prices? To restate the question in more formal terms: do property values represent leading or lagging indicators of inflationary pressure in the economy?

If you follow the research question, you will discover that the data record is somewhat mixed. Residential property values and inflation data are easy to source, and there does seem to be a close relationship between the two. Presumably, that is why the Government and the Bank of England are so sensitive to its well-being. In fact, the monetary policy committee studies the housing market as part of its monthly data research. It regards sharp rises in residential property prices not only as a sign of inflationary pressures in the economy, but also as a direct cause of such pressure – in short, a leading indicator.

However, much less is heard about commercial property prices. The sources of data are not as comprehensive, and the indices are not regularly produced, so there is no evidence that commercial property plays a causative role in the inflationary process.

The effects of the commercial property sector on general inflation could work through two channels. First, although commercial property prices do not feature directly in the consumer price index, they could impact on retail prices through their effects on business costs. The lengthy periods of fixed rent review, however, mean that changes to rents would not show up until long after the rental agreement is signed. In this respect, it is best to think of commercial property values as lagging economic activity, rather being a key driver of it.

Second, there is the long-term impact on wealth that follows on from changes in the capital value of commercial property. A substantial proportion (approximately 50%) of the commercial property sector is owned by investment institutions, so the effect of revised capital values is reflected in loan-to-value ratios, negative equity and loan defaults. In other words, a poor investment performance of institutional funds will ultimately pay out less in pension funds and life insurance to their clients. These effects will be distributed over long periods into the future, and will not be instantly visible to the beneficiaries, let alone realisable by them. The evidence, therefore, suggests that the impact of commercial property values on consumer prices and the wealth of society are more than likely to be experienced in the long term.

The residential sector, therefore, appears to be a confident leading indicator of inflationary pressure, while commercial property values tend to lag behind the trend. Furthermore, it is too complex to confidently use as an official lagging indicator.

Aside from the complexities of certain statistical relationships, there is another problem that is commonly attributed to all types of economic forecasting – namely, the dilemma of always having to look backwards to look forward. In other words, if statistics allow us to be confident of what has happened in the past, can they, through extrapolation, enable us to forecast the future with equal confidence? The accepted answer is that statistics alone are not enough. Experience, intuition and other qualitative information are equally important, especially as things change. As emphasised above, no two cycles are the same; history does not repeat itself. Any serious property forecast, therefore, must combine statistical analysis with a confident, reflective personal knowledge of the marketplace.

To draw from one of the hundreds of interviews used as evidence in the American-led inquiry into the financial crisis: Warren Peterson, a builder in Bakersfield (a city in California) told the commission that he was confident that he could pinpoint when the world changed to the day. Peterson was a house builder, building as many as 30 units per year, and each Monday morning he would arrive at his office to find a bevy of real estate agents, sales contracts in hand, vying to purchase one of the new houses he was building. The stream of traffic was constant. But then, one Saturday in November 2005, he was at the sales office and noticed that not a single purchaser had entered the building. He called a friend, also in the home-building business, who said he had noticed the

**Part C**

same thing, and asked him what he thought about it. 'It's over,' his friend told Peterson. And then came the crash and, up until 2011, Warren Peterson had only built one new home since late 2005 (FCIC, 2011: 24 and 156).

The closing moral to our story, therefore, is that although mainstream texts often imply that having a lot of statistics is a means to finding out about the economy, data is not the be-all and end-all. Economic data needs to be approached with caution because, when you look at it in isolation, the answers always appear half-baked. If you really want to know – and feel – what is going on in a market-place, you need to keep your ears and eyes open – what some call 'old-fashioned shoe-leather research'. By this, they mean getting out on the streets and talking to agents, mortgage brokers, local investors, and anyone else who may be able to provide insight into the real estate asset or market in question.

## Food for thought: The new (High Street) economy

It does not seem appropriate to publish an economics textbook in 2016 relating to new economic thinking and real estate without prompting some thoughts about technology, as it affects economic life on so many levels: the way we pay our bills; the way we shop; the way we transact business; the way we forecast the future; and so on. As a consequence, it has impacts on the levels and nature of employment, the ways that income and wealth become distributed, and the character of competitive prices. Most significantly, in the context of this book, it affects the use and value of different forms of real estate.

As we have already documented, the economy experienced a profound set of changes during the Great Recession. These gave rise to a series of economic events, such as a jolt to business confidence, a slowing of consumer expenditure, a widening of inequality and a major reform of the financial system. What we now bring to the party is the paradigmatic shifts caused by the technological developments that have been running alongside these economic changes since Sir Tim Berners-Lee invented the World Wide Web in 1989, which allowed the internet to progress from a specialist data-transfer system into a mass-market tool used by hundreds of millions around the world.

During this time, the internet has transformed every part of our economic and social culture – the ways we communicate, shop, find things out, watch videos, book tickets, make payments, etc., etc. A Pew survey in the United States, carried out by Fox and Rainie in February 2014 [9], found that 90% of Americans believed the internet had been good for them. Critics, however, (such as Jaron Lanier [10], Doc Searls [11], Astra Taylor [12], Ethan Zuckerman [13], Nicholas Carr [14] and Andrew Keen [15]) have tried to persuade us to take a long hard look at the weird, dysfunctional, imbalanced world that we have been building with digital tools.

The critics argue that while the internet is a technology that appears to liberate, inform and empower people, this is only half the story. As Keen (2015) argued: '(The) unregulated network society is … compounding economic and cultural inequality, and creating a digital generation of masters of the universe. This… may be rooted in a borderless network, but it still translates into massive wealth and power for a tiny handful of companies and individuals.'

To give some measure of the scale of importance of these developments, each day the world's internet has three billion users, who send something like 200 million emails, undertake four million Google searches, share 2.5 million pieces of Facebook content, publish 277,000 tweets, post 200,000 new photos on Instagram [16] and spend somewhere in the region of $100,000 on Amazon (Keen, 2015).

To put it bluntly, the digital age of the internet, the smartphone and social media has changed the face of the urban city centre. The digitally interconnected world has given rise to completely new methods of commerce and retail. This is not only to do with the ways that businesses communicate with one another, their workforce and their customers, but the way that commercial and retail space is utilized. Not surprisingly, there is an ongoing debate about the significance of the **new economy** and its implications for B2B (business to business), B2C (business to consumers) and M2M (machine to machine) transactions.

Already, by July 2015, the ONS had estimated that the average weekly spend online was £821 million pounds, which accounted for slightly more than 12.5% of all retail spending (excluding petrol and diesel). By 2018, most forecasts expect the equivalent weekly spend online to exceed a billion pounds and represent more than 20% of all retail spending.

## From bricks and mortar to virtual online

Traditionally, retailers depended on shopping centres and High Streets for the bulk of their sales. Nowadays, however, it is increasingly important to hold warehouse stocks to support home delivery and click-and-collect. In short, as we progress into the future, bricks and mortar will increasingly play only a supporting role to online activity.

Debenhams already have already claimed, in October 2015, that it aimed to grow its online sales to 30% of its business by 2016. John Lewis was at a similar point with their online balance. This means that big department stores are now doing more business online than at their flagship stores in London's West End – Oxford Street. It also worth noting that, although stores like these are closed on Christmas day, money is still gained by online orders.

Inevitably, such online developments have transformed industrial and retail real estate markets. Whereas it used to be important to have stock in the back of the shop, it is becoming equally important to support home delivery and click-and-collect – e-commerce – by renting cavernous warehouses in which pickers can drive fork lift trucks to collect different products. The most notorious examples are the huge warehouses run by Amazon in various parts of Europe and Asia.

As a result, warehouses are rising at a staggering pace. Jones Lang LaSalle, a property-services firm, reports that, since 2012, the amount of industrial space (of which 75% is warehousing) has grown at twice the pace of retail space. Hence, industrial rents are rising, while retail rents are still recovering from the recession. Interestingly, the world's biggest industrial-property owner, Prologis [17], (boasting facilities in 21 countries, leased to more than 4700 customers) claim that 30% of their current projects are built for tenants whose sales are tied to online orders.

Such developments have been well documented in several reports. Of particular relevance is the retail report put together by Bill Grimley and his team in

2013, to prompt thought in the political arena about the future of the High Street in town centres. The report drew evidence from more than 500 busy town centres across England. In total, the industry in 2014 still comprised around 100 000 companies, contributed in the region of £200 billion to the economy, and employed 4.5 million people. In short, High Street shops were worth more to the economy than the government's health, education and defence budgets added together (Grimley, 2013:1).

## Hot-desking

These online developments have also had an indisputable impact on the demand for commercial space. As noted above, any economy based on IT has implications for the ways businesses communicate with one another, their workforce and their customers. To take an oft-quoted example, 'hot-desking', 'agile working' or simply 'working from home' has reduced the amount of office space required per employee. In fact, according to the British Council for Offices (BCO) in the period from 2009 to 2014, workspace per person was reduced, on average, by two square metres (see Murgatroyd, 2014).

In the past, a typical office might have comprised of 80% fixed workplaces, 15% meeting space and 5% other support space (post and computer rooms, etc.). In a modern office, however, the space allocation is far more dynamic. Offices today are likely to have a greater variety of workstation settings, but in a smaller proportion of the overall space budget. The main factor causing the shift is a growth in meeting space – client entertainment, formal meeting rooms and areas for collaborative working to cater for a mobile labour force.

It is currently estimated that about 40% of the world's top companies employ 45% of their workforce outside the boundaries of the formal workspace. Given that rents and rates (which are primarily driven by demand for space) represent the bulk – about 60% – of occupancy costs, these modern ways of working using mobile technology can significantly cut business costs, so they are popular with employers. Surveys suggest, however, that more than a quarter of companies that have introduced 'hot-desking' report a drop in staff morale, and staff are still the largest cost that most businesses face. So, perhaps, it is time to take a close look at the evidence for whether hot-desking really boosts productivity, or whether it just undermines the team spirit.

## The pub

As a final case study, we examine what has happened to the stock of pubs since 2008. Rumour has it that up to 50 pubs per week were being closed in the UK as the recession plummeted to its lowest point between January and June 2009. However, these types of statements do exaggerate a trend that does, in fact, date back to 1980. In approximate terms, half of the 21 000 pubs that had disappeared in the 35 years leading up to 2015 had closed before 2008. Furthermore, there is an economic argument to suggest that the trend will continue, and thousands of more pubs will close before 2020.

A general explanation for this slowdown in trade is cultural as, since 1980, homes have become warmer and more comfortable, and the reality is that nowadays people prefer to share a bottle of wine in front of the television, or use social media to contact family and friends, than spend the evening in a pub. As Snowdon (2014) explained in his report drafted for the Institute of Economic Affairs: 'The shift from the pub to the home and other venues has been a long and gradual one. In the late 19th century, music hall, day trips on the railway, dog-racing and professional football challenged the pub's virtual monopoly as a working class leisure activity. Cinema, bingo, radio, television and the internet followed in the 20th Century'. The pace of decline, though, was accelerated by the Great Recession that began in 2008, causing a notable slowing down of expenditure as real wages dropped. Economists, however, have been quick to point out that there is no consistent relationship between disposable incomes and the number of pubs. Thus, it would be fair to conclude that recessions may be just one of the nails in a pub's coffin.

Another set of reasons for the pub trade to be in decline is to do with the availability of relatively cheap alcohol in supermarkets. This specific trend is greatly amplified by alcohol taxes, the burden of business rates, late night levies and (again, unlike supermarkets) the VAT that pubs have to charge on food. Combined, these factors make every pint and sandwich sold in a pub far more expensive than its equivalent at home.

A further factor that dented the pub trade was the smoking ban. A survey of publicans (carried out in September 2008 by the Federation of Licensed Victuallers Associations – FLVA) reported that, while 54% of pub customers smoked in 2006, the number had fallen to 38% in 2008, following the introduction of smoking bans in Scotland (March 2006) and the rest of the UK (April and July 2007). The FLVA survey also noted that there was a net reduction of 74% in smokers' visits to pubs, whereas there was only a 6% net increase in non-smokers' visits to pubs.

These trends are supported by a mass of other data showing that the smoking ban was highly damaging to the pub trade. For example, one survey by the Association of Licensed Multiple Retailers estimated that the smoking ban had cost pubs on average £6000, each due to spending on providing new outdoor smoking areas. Other surveys are less specific, but most acknowledge that the impact of the smoking ban has been one of the main problems facing the pub trade (Snowdon, 2014: 28 and 30).

## Do the maths

As the profits of the pub landlords' dropped and the property market collapsed, creditors encouraged the various pub companies (such as Enterprise Inns, Admiral Taverns, Punch Taverns, and Faucet Inns) to sell off their pubs, pay back their debts and secure a return on their investments.

Some of the pubs that were sold reopened under new ownership as pubs, cafes or restaurants, but the vast majority were redeveloped into residential flats. Although planning wise residential use was more difficult to negotiate, it was well worth the hassle. To quote some actual figures from a set of transactions carried out between 2011 and 2014 for a pub in the London Borough of Camden (the Parr's Head on Plender Street), it was sold by Admiral Taverns in May 2011 for roughly £500,000 to a private developer. A plan for the conversion of the property into six flats was approved in November 2011. Sixteen days later, the pub, now with planning permission for residential use, was sold on to another developer for £1.3 million (i.e. more than twice the price that had been paid six months earlier). Early in 2012, building work began on the site and, one year later, six flats were put on the market. In 2013/14 prices, these were sold for a total of £2,965,000 – at just shy of £3 million. This represents somewhere in the region of 50% profit, after allowing for redevelopment costs.

## Chicken-or-egg conundrums

Although traditional economists might be inclined to develop a theoretical regression model to estimate how many pub closures were caused by each of the factors discussed above, the calculations would be highly speculative. The causes of the post-2008 closure of pubs interact in many complex ways, and there is not enough evidence available to isolate the impact of each. In a nutshell, the message is that real estate markets – like all markets – are driven by many variables. Indeed, the precise point of using the pub case study to close this *Food For Thought* section is that it serves as a good reminder that it is not technology alone that is changing the face of the High Street. For example, are people buying more alcohol from the supermarket because it allows them to shop and play video games online at home, or are people buying more alcohol from supermarkets because other factors, such as the smoking ban, has made drinking in a pub less appealing?

Obviously, such questions cannot be answered precisely, and this is the beauty and the beast that makes economics such a fascinating subject to study. In a word, new economics is 'pluralistic', and only distantly related to the limited 'dismal science' of its classic and neoclassical founders. Economics has been transformed into a more vibrant, dynamic and realistic study, based on empirical and psychological evidence, increasingly concerned with being a force for a fair and, crucially, less dismal world. In short, it has become a 'bright science'. Providing it is applied perceptively, and with a degree of humility, it can create rewarding insights into an economy and its markets – regardless of complex conundrums.

# Afterword

For those who have studied this textbook chronologically – from front to back – it should be apparent that the basis of mainstream economics has become questionable and deeply flawed at the extremes. The after-effects of the 2008 financial crisis not only cast a long shadow over the economy for the past eight years, but also caused a groundswell of new ideas and approaches to ripple through the discipline. Inevitably, given the nature of the subject matter, there has always been some controversy about the appropriate policy, theory and outlook. The Great Recession, however, has significantly sharpened the divide between heterodox and orthodox economists. It is as if the financial crisis of 2008 also gave birth to a crisis in economics.

The initial seeds that helped to formalise this new economics were conceived by a gathering of 150 top academics at Kings College Cambridge in April 2010 [1]– the first symposium of the Institute for New Economic Thinking [2]. The specific choice of venue to host the event was symbolic. John Maynard Keynes had been a Fellow of Kings during the global economic crisis of the 1930s and (as outlined in Chapter 1), he was an advocate of government intervention, rather than the free market. His ideas provided some solution to an economic slump. As we have witnessed, the path of history was not smoothly and dramatically repeated. Definite solutions have not emerged but a debate has opened up, and a refreshed, broader and relevant curriculum is now available.

Inadvertently, this text has already drawn from some of those presenting papers at the Cambridge meeting in 2010 – namely:

- **Adair Turner** [3], Chairman of the UK Financial Services Authority from 2008 to 2013, where he played a leading role in the redesign of traditional and shadow banking regulation. He is the current Chairman of the Institute for New Economic Thinking and, in October 2015, his definitive book – *Between Debt and the Devil* – was published to much acclaim for providing an authoritative critique of society's addiction to debt and real estate and the banking system that feeds it).

- **Joseph Stiglitz** [4], Professor of Economics at Columbia University, recipient of the 2001 Nobel Memorial Prize for his contribution to the economic consequences of information asymmetries, and a prolific author of articles and books. His most recent title (published in 2013), *The Price of Inequality*, clearly identified the gap between the rich and poor as a worldwide economic policy issue that could no longer be ignored by mainstream economists. As a founder member of the advisory board and curricular development at the Institute for New Economic Thinking, he has been well placed to champion inequality as one of the important new issues).
- **Anatole Kaletsky** [5], economist and journalist currently based in London writing for *The Economist*, *The Financial Times*, *The International Herald Tribune*, *Prospect* and *Reuters*. He was Chairman of the Institute for New Economic Thinking in 2014 and author of a major post crisis polemic, *Capitalism 4.0*, in which he kick-started the debate, in 2010, regarding the future of the global market economy and the economic thinking that lies behind it.
- A considerable intellectual debt is also owed to **Ha-Joon Chang** [6], a young Professor of Economics at Cambridge University, the author of several accessible paperback books and an occasional contributor to *The Guardian* newspaper.
- **Robert Schiller** [7], Professor at Yale University, recipient of the 2013 Nobel Memorial Prize in economics – for his empirical analysis of asset prices – and author of several books, the most recent titles being about behavioural finance.
- **Andrew Haldane** [8], Chief Economist at the Bank of England, where he is also currently Executive Director of Monetary Analysis and Statistics and a member of the Monetary Policy Committee. He has already authored more than 100 research papers on monetary and financial policy issues, many of which are written in an accessible and humorous style.

As the citations imply, their work has had an explicit influence on the text – see references for details.

As outlined in the introduction and Part A of the text, the economic establishment has been seriously challenged, because the crisis did not fit the mainstream perspective of rational agents, efficient markets and equilibrium. Subsequently, in Parts B and C, it was emphasised that a blossoming and sophisticated financial network tended to make dynamic market economies increasingly unstable. As a consequence, the importance of fiscal and monetary policy emanating from the central government and central bank has begun to take on far greater importance. In conclusion it is apparent that, to qualify as a good economist, it is no longer possible to rely on elaborate models based on various probabilities and assumptions. Nowadays, it is necessary to have the insight, and the confidence, to draw one's own conclusions from data and experience. To put it bluntly, you cannot expect to rely solely on a set of models to forecast changes in the value of real estate or other financial assets.

Indeed, as the manuscript was being finalised for publication into a text – in October 2015 – Angus Deaton was awarded the Nobel Prize in Economics for his distinctly empirical-based work on inequality. For more than 30 years, he had studied household data to build up a realistic picture of how individuals actually behave in everyday life, rather than assuming how they might behave according to some theoretical model. As the awarding body observed: 'Previous researchers in macroeconomics … relied on aggregate data [whereas] today's researchers usually start at the individual level and then, with great caution, add together individual behaviours to compute numbers for the entire economy.' In short, Professor Deaton was awarded his prize for an empirical approach that has turned economics into a new type of science.

Interestingly, Professor Angus Deaton was not the first radical to have his work internationally recognised by a Nobel Prize in Economics [9]. Professors Stiglitz and Akerlof had also been awarded a Nobel Prize in Economics, in 2001, for their extensive work exploring alternative approaches. Their main contention was that markets are not necessarily either efficient or stable, or that the economy, and our society, is not well described by the standard models of competitive equilibrium used by mainstream economists. In fact, their main claim to fame is for acknowledging that market participants often act in ways that cannot easily be reconciled with rationality. Their ideas concerning 'information economics' demonstrates that, even if markets are competitive, they are almost never efficient when information is imperfect or asymmetrical (some people know something that others do not – as pointed out in the section on 'Ideology' in Chapter 5).

Finally, it is worth noting the role of students [10]. Much of the movement for change in Economics has been spurred on by students who are keen to graduate with worthy and credible degrees for employment in 2020 and beyond. One such group is the Post-Crash Economics Society (PCES) [11], based at Manchester University. They published a 60-page report in April 2014 which provided a detailed, evidence-based argument, outlining the shortcomings of an economics education based solely on one paradigm – the neoclassical school. Their report emphasised how alternative perspectives have been marginalised, and how this limits innovation and constructive criticism, which is regarded as vital for economic understanding. Furthermore, the report made it clear that the study of ethics, politics and history are almost completely absent from current syllabuses. The Manchester students' views are shared by similar societies at Cambridge, the London School of Economics, Sheffield, Glasgow, Essex, and University College London, and further afield in the USA, Chile, France, Brazil and Holland.

For the majority of readers today, the full value of *new economic thinking and real estate* will not be confirmed until they reach their first job. As anyone who has genuinely studied the preceding pages will know, the recurring advice has been that economists must keep their feet firmly on the ground. They should deal with the world as it is, and not as they would prefer it to be. As Paul Krugman (2009) [12] commented in one of his regular *New York Times* columns: 'economists will have to learn to live with messiness. That is, they will have to acknowledge the importance of irrational and often unpredictable behaviour, and face up to the often idiosyncratic imperfections of markets'.

In other words, an elegant economic 'theory of everything', is based on simplifying assumptions that can be modelled mathematically to produce definite answers, is no longer credible. Since the unforeseen financial crisis of 2008, the tunes that economists dance to have changed considerably, and the new beats and moves that are being introduced will resonate loudly into the future.

# Glossary

**affordable housing:** Accommodation that is cheaper than equivalents available in the local market. Examples include subsidised accommodation for rent, shared ownership and, in some market situations, cheap housing for sale. It is an aim of local planning policy to assure the provision of appropriate quantities of housing in this category.

**affordability:** A measure of house prices in relation to incomes after tax. Also see *affordable housing*.

**aggregate demand (AD):** All planned expenditures for the entire economy summed together.

**aggregate supply (AS):** All planned production for the entire economy summed together.

**asset:** Anything of value that is owned.

**asymmetric information:** A situation where two parties to an economic transaction have unequal knowledge of the risks involved in making that transaction.

**balance of payments:** A summary of one country's trade dealings with the rest of the world. It is compiled as an account of inflows and outflows recording visible and invisible trade, investment earnings, transfers, and financial assets.

**bank deposit multiplier:** see *credit creation*.

**Bank for international Settlements (BIS):** This international financial organisation was established in 1930 to facilitate collaboration between central banks in their pursuit of monetary and financial stability. Its importance was raised by the financial crisis of 2008 and it is increasingly recognised as 'the bank for central banks'.

**base rate:** The rate of interest that UK financial intermediaries use as a reference point for all other interest rates for lending and receiving deposits. For example, large financial intermediaries will borrow from one another at interest rates close to the base rate.

**base year:** A year chosen as the point of reference for comparison to other years.

**basis point:** A unit of measure used in finance to describe a precise change in the value or rate of a financial instrument. To be precise, one basis point is one hundredth of a percentage (i.e. if a yield rises from 3.40 to 3.60, it has risen by 20 basis points).

**BIS:** see *Bank for International Settlements*.

**boom:** A period of time during which overall business activity is rising at a more rapid rate than its long-term trend.

**Building Cost and Information Service (BCIS):** A service set up by the Royal Institution of Chartered Surveyors in 1962 to facilitate the exchange of detailed construction costs. The information is taken from a wide range of differing contracts and traders. Indices and data are revised on a quarterly basis.

**building regulations:** A government code of practice that specifies the type and minimum quality of materials to be used in a building. The regulations are enforced by local authorities.

**business rates:** The commonly used term for non-domestic rates – charged on commercial properties such as shops, offices, warehouses and factories. The funds raised are used for the provision of local services.

**capital:** All manufactured resources, including buildings, equipment, machines and improvements to land.

**capital account:** A record of international transactions relating to the acquisition/disposal of non-produced, non-financial assets.

*New Economic Thinking and Real Estate*, First Edition. Danny Myers.
© 2016 John Wiley & Sons, Ltd. Published 2016 by John Wiley & Sons, Ltd.

**capital gains tax:** This is paid when a profit is made by selling an asset; the tax is imposed on the difference between the purchase price and the sale price, not on the total sum received.

**capital value:** The monetary worth of an asset; the price it could be purchased for.

**cartel:** Any arrangement made by a number of independent producers to coordinate their buying or selling decisions. The members of a cartel agree, in effect, to operate as if they were a monopoly. See also *collusion*.

**central bank:** The official guardian of a country's financial system. Usually owned by the government, and broadly manages monetary policy. Since the birth of the Euro in 1999, the monetary policies of 19 respective central banks have been delegated to the European Central Bank in Frankfurt.

**ceteris paribus:** The assumption that all other things are held equal, or constant, except those under study.

**claimant unemployment:** This is a record of the number of people claiming unemployment-related benefits on one particular day each month.

**coincident indicators:** Economic statistics that are used by economic forecasters to track movements in the economy. For example, changes in output and the stock levels of raw material confirm that an economy is changing.

**collusion:** An agreement, written or unwritten, between producers to determine prices, share out markets and/or set production levels.

**commercial bank:** A privately owned profit-seeking institution, sometimes referred to as a joint stock bank to highlight the fact that it has shareholders. High Street banks, such as NatWest, HSBC and Barclays, are examples of commercial banks. Also referred to as retail banks.

**community infrastructure levy:** A type of tax that allows local authorities to charge developers a tariff to contribute towards infrastructure requirements.

**consumer price index (CPI):** A monthly measure of the change in the overall costs of goods and services purchased by the average household. Since January 2004, it has been the official target used by the UK Government to monitor inflation. The CPI is similar to CPIH, but there are subtle differences in coverage and methodology.

**corporate social responsibility:** Contribution of businesses to sustainable development, achieved by taking into account their economic, social and environmental impacts in the way they operate.

**cost-benefit analysis (CBA):** This is a way of appraising a proposed development. It involves taking into account the external costs and benefits, as well as the conventional private costs and benefits. This is done by estimating monetary values for aspects such as health, time, leisure and pollution.

**council tax:** A levy imposed on all domestic properties (i.e. around 28 million taxable units in 2016) to raise funds for local services. The rate of payment varies slightly from one group of properties to the next, according to one of eight valuation brackets.

**CPIH:** A consumer price index introduced in 2013 which includes owner occupiers' housing costs (OOH). CPIH does not currently meet international standards. See also *consumer price index*.

**credit creation:** The process by which banks expand their lending by a multiple of the deposits they receive, based on a belief that not all customers will want to withdraw their deposits at the same time.

**credit crunch:** A situation that emerged in the financial markets in 2007, in which lenders began to raise the cost of borrowing and restrict the supply of loans.

**current account:** A balance of international transactions in respect of trade in goods and services, income and transfers.

**cyclical indicators:** Economic statistics that are used by economic forecasters to analyse the state of the economy. See entries for: *leading, lagging* and *coincident indicators*.

**deflation:** This is a persistent fall in the general price level of goods and services – the opposite to inflation – leading to negative rates of change.

**demand function:** A symbolised representation of the relationship between the quantity demanded of a good and its various determinants. It looks like an algebraic equation, but it is actually just notation.

**demand schedule:** A series showing various possible prices and the quantities demanded at each price. In effect, the schedule shows a rate of planned purchase per time period at different prices.

**depression:** The term given to a serious and prolonged economic slump, the most famous example being the great depression of the 1930s. In modern terms, it could be described as an extended recession.

**deregulation:** A term popularised since 1979 to describe a situation in any industry where statutory barriers to competition are liberalised or removed.

**derived demand:** Demands created to help satisfy other markets. For example, the demand for factory buildings is derived from the demand for manufactured goods. The term highlights a distinction between investment goods and consumer goods.

**developer's profit:** The amount which covers the risk element between start and completion of a project, plus an element of profit on the venture. A developer's profit has two elements: the return for undertaking a project, and a compensation for the risk involved.

**direct policy:** A phrase used to distinguish direct government intervention from broader macroeconomic policies. Direct policy tends to be of a legislative nature.

**direct relationship:** A relationship between two variables that is positive, such that an increase in one is associated with an increase in the other, and a decrease in one is associated with a decrease in the other.

**discount rate:** See *repo rate*.

**disinflation:** A term coined in the early 1980s to describe the trend of a fall in the rate of inflation.

**economic growth:** An increase in an economy's real level of output over time, normally measured by the rate of change of national income from one year to the next.

**economic rent:** A surplus earned by any factor of production that is over the minimum necessary to incentivise it to work.

**economically active:** A statistical category that refers to the population who are either in employment or unemployed.

**economically inactive:** People who are neither in employment nor unemployed. These include those who want a job but have not been seeking work in the last four weeks, those who want a job and are seeking work but not available to start, and those who do not want a job.

**economics:** A social science studying the way in which individuals and societies choose among the alternative uses of scarce resources to satisfy wants.

**effective demand:** Demand that involves desire and an ability to pay. In other words, it is the demand that can be measured by actual spending.

**efficient market hypothesis:** An investment theory that states it is impossible to 'beat the market' because stock market efficiency causes existing share prices always to incorporate and reflect all relevant information.

**endogenous variables:** These are economic factors that affect other aspects of a theory or model from within. For example, the level of unemployment will determine the amount of income tax collected.

**Energy Performance Certificate** (EPC) An official document that shows how energy-efficient a building is, in terms of its fabric and its services (i.e. heating, cooling, hot water, ventilation and lighting). The rating is stated on an A–G scale, and is similar to the colour-coded labels that are provided with domestic appliances such as refrigerators and washing machines.

**entrepreneur:** A factor of production involving human resources that perform the functions of raising capital, organising, and managing other factors of production and making business decisions. The entrepreneur is a risk-taker.

**equilibrium:** A situation in which the plans of buyers and sellers exactly coincide, so that there is neither excess supply nor excess demand.

**equilibrium price:** The price that clears the market, at which there is no excess quantity demanded or supplied; also known as the market-clearing price.

**equity:** See *horizontal equity* and *vertical equity*.

**equity withdrawal:** A term used, in property circles to represent the owner's fund. For example, if you buy a £100 000 house, of which £60 000 is borrowed 'potentially', you may be able to release the £40 000 that you own; hence the phrase, equity withdrawal.

**excludability:** See *principle of exclusion*.

**exogenous variables:** These are economic factors that impinge upon a theory or model from the outside, such as the weather. They are sometimes referred to as autonomous variables, and they contrast with endogenous variables.

**expenditure approach:** A way of measuring economic activity (see *gross domestic product*) by adding up the values of all spending on final goods and services.

**externalities:** The benefits or costs that are experienced by parties other than the immediate seller and buyer in a transaction. Also known as external costs or benefits.

**factor markets:** In this market, households are the sellers; they sell resources such as labour, land, capital and entrepreneurial ability. Businesses are the buyers of these resources to generate output (see Figure 8.1).

**factors of production:** Often grouped under four headings. See *resources*.

**financial account:** A record of flows of money into and out of the country for the purposes of investment or deposits into financial institutions.

**financialisation:** A process whereby financial markets, financial institutions and financial elites gain greater influence over economic policy and economic outcomes. Sometimes referred to as 'financialism'.

**financial instability hypothesis:** An idea central to Hyman Minsky's work that financial cycles are an inherent part of an economic cycle, as whatever is happening in the financial markets tends to be amplified in the broader economy.

**fiscal austerity:** Living within the constraints of the government's annual budget.

**fiscal policy:** A combination of government spending and taxation used to achieve macroeconomic management.

**free enterprise:** A system in which private business firms are able to obtain resources, to organise those resources and to sell the finished product in any way they choose.

**full repairing and insuring lease** (FRI lease): Rental terms under which the tenant bears most of the running and maintenance cost. Institutional investors favour such leases.

**Gini coefficient:** A measure of income distribution, devised by an Italian statistician Corrado Gini in 1912.

**golden rule:** A fiscal objective that constrains government only to borrow to finance investment not to fund current spending.

**government failure:** The concept that government policy intervention may not necessarily improve economic efficiency.

**government intervention:** Measures undertaken by the state to achieve goals not guaranteed by the market system.

**Great Moderation:** A term used to refer to the period 1986–2006, when many countries experienced relative calm and constant economic growth; a period that some regarded as the end of boom-and-bust economics.

**gross domestic product (GDP):** The most common measurement of a nation's income generated from resources within its own boundaries – the monetary value of its output of goods and services.

**gross national income (GNI):** A measurement of a country's wealth. It represents the total output of goods and services produced by the country in a year, in terms of residence of the owners of productive resources. In other words, it is GDP with the net value of overseas assets factored into the calculation.

**harmonised index of consumer prices (HICP):** A standard measure of consumer price inflation, that permits a comparison to be made between EU countries. The series commenced in January 1996 and became the official target of UK Government policy in 2004. It is usually referred to as the consumer price index.

**hereditament:** A legal term used to distinguish a non-domestic property asset that can be valued as a separate item for business rates. Broadly speaking, these are separately occupied business units within buildings.

**horizontal equity:** The concept that all people should be treated identically; an idea that informs policy directed towards equal opportunities.

**human capital:** Investment in education and training that enhances productivity of labour.

**ILO unemployment measure:** A rate of unemployment produced by the International Labour Organisation. It defines unemployment as being concerned with people who are without work yet actively seeking employment. Data is gathered through labour force surveys.

**IMF:** See *International Monetary Fund*.

**income approach:** A way of measuring gross domestic product by adding up all factor rewards – that is, the sum of wages, interest, rent and profits.

**index numbers:** A way of expressing the relative change of a variable between one period of time and another. This involves setting a base year number at 100; the value of the variable in subsequent years is then expressed above or below 100, according to its percentage deviation from the base.

**inflation:** A sustained rise in prices, which is officially measured by the consumer price index.

**inheritance tax:** Makes a compulsory transfer of funds from an individual estate to the government at the time of death. It only applies, however, if the taxable value of the estate on death is over a certain amount.

**institutional model:** a new approach to understanding property markets by focusing on the rules, norms and regulations by which society functions. It emphasises how changes to the political, social, legal, financial and professional framework affect the nature of markets over time.

**interest rates:** These are the payments made as the cost of obtaining credit, or the rewards paid to owners of capital.

**International Monetary Fund:** A financial organisation established in 1944, primarily to standardise global relations and exchange rates. It has since evolved into an international organisation broadly concerned with preventing crises in monetary systems. It offers financial assistance to nations in need of correcting balance of payments discrepancies and other debt problems.

**investment:** Spending by businesses on things like machines, buildings, and research, which can be used to produce goods and services in the future.

**investor-developer:** A property company that retains completed schemes as part of its own asset portfolio.

**joint-stock bank:** See *commercial bank*.

**Keynesian economics:** A branch of economics characterised by a belief in government intervention to correct the sluggish nature of labour markets. It is based on the ideas of John Maynard Keynes and has formed a central part of economic and government thinking for many years following the Second World War.

**labour:** The human factor of production; in other words, the mental and physical contributions to economic activity.

**lagging indicators:** Economic statistics (such as unemployment and investment) that change approximately 12 months after a change in overall activity.

**land:** The factor of production that is virtually fixed in quantity. In the economic sense, it includes both the physical space and natural resources, such as coal, oil and water, natural vegetation and climate.

**land value tax:** An idea dating back to 1879 to suggest that all public expenditure could be raised from a tax on land. More than a hundred years later, however, land taxes still only account for a small share of government revenue.

**law of demand:** Quantity demanded and price are inversely related – more is bought at a lower price; less at a higher price (other things being equal). Also known as the *theory of demand*.

**law of supply:** The relationship between price and quantity supplied (other things remaining equal) is a direct one. For example, as price increases, so does the quantity supplied.

**leading indicators:** Economic statistics (such as retail sales and consumer credit) that change approximately six months in advance of gross domestic product and are used to predict changes in the economic cycle.

**lender of last resort:** A function of each central bank is to back up the nation's financial system whenever the going gets tough. For example, the Financial Services Compensation Scheme guarantees deposits of up to £85 000 in UK authorized banks, building societies and credit unions.

**liabilities:** The legal claims for payment that can be made on an institution or company – in short, the amount owing to others.

**liquidity:** This describes the ease with which an asset can be used to meet liabilities. Cash is the most liquid asset.

**Lorenz curve:** A geometric representation of the distribution of income, developed by Max Lorenz in 1905. For an example, see Figure 8.1.

**macroeconomics:** The study of economy-wide phenomena, such as total consumer expenditure.

**macroeconomic objectives:** Targets relating to the whole economy, such as employment, price stability and the balance of payments.

**market:** An abstract concept concerning all the arrangements that individuals have for exchanging with one another. Thus, we can speak of the labour market, the car market, the commercial property market, the housing market, the building materials market, the credit market and so on.

**market-based instruments:** These involve various incentive systems designed to operate through the price mechanism to encourage environmentally friendly behaviour. Examples include carbon taxes, the climate change levy and landfill tax.

**market-clearing price:** See *equilibrium price*.

**market economy:** An economy in which prices are used to signal the value of resources to firms and households.

**market failure:** A situation in which the free forces of supply and demand lead to either an under- or over-allocation of resources to a specific economic activity.

**market mechanism:** See definitions for *market economy* and/or *price mechanism*.

**market structures:** The characteristics of a market that determine the behaviour of participating firms, such as the number of buyers and sellers and the ease of entry into (and exit from) a market.

**merit good:** A good that has been deemed socially desirable by politicians. If left to the private market, these goods may be under-consumed.

**microeconomics:** Study of the economic behaviour of individual households and firms, and how prices of goods and services are determined.

**MITR:** See *mortgage interest tax relief*.

**modelling:** Simplified representation of the real world used to aid understanding and predict economic phenomena.

**monetary policy:** Policy implemented by the central bank to maintain financial stability. This broadly involves monitoring and managing: inflation rates (through interest rates and quantitative easing); credit growth (by setting reserve requirements and

running stress tests); and stating minimum mortgage requirements (such as limits on loan to value ratios).

**monetary policy committee (MPC):** A Bank of England committee, established in 1997, to set interest rates independently of HM Treasury, in order to achieve the UK Government's predetermined target rate of inflation.

**money multiplier:** See *credit creation*.

**monopoly:** A market structure where a single supplier dominates the market.

**moral hazard:** A phrase used to describe a situation where a financial agent (or an insured party) may take on greater risks than they ethically should, on the basis that someone else will pick up the tab if things go awry.

**mortgage-backed securities:** These are a collection of loans, initially agreed on individual residential and commercial properties, that have subsequently been parcelled up as investment bonds. This process enables illiquid mortgage loans to be traded – passed on – as new financial securities.

**mortgage interest tax relief (MITR):** A government subsidy paid to mortgage holders. Provided in several OECD counties, where governments allow the interest payments on mortgages to be deducted from their taxable income.

**multiplier:** The number by which an initial injection into an economy must be multiplied to find the eventual change in national income.

**national accounts:** An annual record of an economy's performance.

**national income:** A generic term for all that is produced, earned and spent in a country during one year. Strictly speaking, it is defined as GNI minus capital depreciation. See *gross national income*.

**national income accounting:** A measurement system used to estimate gross domestic product (GDP) and gross national income.

**national insurance contributions (NICs):** A type of tax that entitles one to social security benefits and a retirement pension. The amount of contribution depends on how much you earn and whether you are employed or self-employed.

**negative equity:** This describes a situation in which the value of someone's home has fallen below the value of their mortgage.

**neo-classical economics:** A traditional school of thought that believes in free competitive markets to maximise national output.

**net present value:** A mathematical procedure by which the value of a sum or a stream of sums due to be received at specific dates in the future is expressed in terms of its current value.

**new economy:** A term coined in the late 1990s to describe a way of restructuring economies through the use of information technology.

**normal profit:** The minimum level of reward required to ensure that existing entrepreneurs are prepared to remain in their present area of business.

**Office for National Statistics (ONS):** The government agency responsible for compiling and distributing official statistics on the UK's economy, demography and society at a national and local level.

**official rate of inflation:** Typically, in most industrialised countries, this is the mid-point of a target range allowed for consumer price increases. For example, in the UK, the current official target rate of inflation is 2% (i.e. between 1% and 3%), as measured by the consumer price index.

**offshoring:** A process where certain functions of a company are moved overseas, where they can perform at a lower cost.

**oligopoly:** A situation in which a large part of the market is supplied by a small number of firms. The firms may behave as if they are interdependent.

**opportunity cost:** The highest-valued alternative that has to be sacrificed for the option that is chosen. In other words, the true cost of something is what you have to give up to get it.

**output approach:** A way of measuring gross domestic product by adding up the value of the output produced by each sector of the economy.

**outsourcing:** The provision of business services and accommodation by third parties, in exchange for rent and income.

**particulars delivered (PD forms):** These are official instruments used to administer any transfer or sale of land or property. The relevant 'particulars' of the transaction must be 'delivered' to the HMRC Stamp Duty Office and Land Registry within 30 days of the transfer.

*per capita* A Latin phrase meaning 'per head of the population'.

**perfect competition:** A theoretical model in which the decisions of buyers and sellers have no effect on market price.

**perfectly inelastic:** Describes a situation where the quantity of a good or service is fixed, regardless of its price (see *price elasticity*).

**planning regulations:** Each local authority has a set of plans on how its area will develop, and a committee responsible for deciding what is allowed to be built and where. The terms of reference are determined by centrally produced planning policy statements and guidance.

**post-occupancy survey:** These involve questioning tenants about experiences relating to their property's performance. The survey is carried out after the tenants have been resident for a short period of time.

**price elasticity:** A measurement of the responsiveness of the quantity demanded/supplied due to a change in price.

**price index:** The cost of today's basket of goods, expressed as a percentage of the cost of the same basket during a base year.

**price mechanism:** A signalling system between firms and households, concerning the use of resources. Where the price mechanism operates, there is a market economy; consequently, the terms 'price' and 'market' are interchangeable.

**price system:** The process by which (relative) prices are constantly changing to reflect changes in supply and demand for different commodities.

**primary income:** This forms part of the current account of the balance of payments, and consists of compensation of employees and investment income.

**prime yield:** A benchmark level of rental income earned on a property of the best physical quality, in the best location, and with a tenant who has good financial credentials.

**principal-agent:** A concept used to highlight market failure caused by a conflict of interests due to the lack of knowledge between a consumer (the principal) and a supplier (the agent).

**principle of exclusion:** This means that anyone who does not pay will not be allowed to benefit from consuming a particular good or service.

**principle of rivalry:** The principle that private goods cannot be shared. If person A uses a private good, then that prevents the possibility of person B using that good. Persons A and B cannot eat the same apple simultaneously.

**private commercial:** A category used to consider privately funded commercial developments such as shops, offices and leisure facilities.

**private finance initiative (PFI):** A form of procurement devised to encourage private investment in public sector projects. PFI consortiums are typically responsible for the construction, finance and management of a facility and, thereby, provide support services for a period of years following construction.

**private goods:** A product that can only be consumed by one individual at a time. Private goods are subject to the *principle of exclusion and rivalry* – see above definitions.

**privatisation:** The transfer of assets from the public sector to the private sector.

**procurement:** A generic term used by professionals within the built environment to describe the general process of obtaining, acquiring or securing some property or land.

**profit:** The income generated by selling something for a higher price than was paid for it. For example, in construction it would represent the difference between total revenues received from purchasers or tenants, and the actual cost of building the property.

**progressive income tax:** A tax system in which, as one earns more income, a higher percentage of the additional income is taxed.

**public choice theory:** A relatively new concept to mainstream economics, which seeks to explain how government policy is selected.

**public goods:** Goods and services that can be consumed by everybody in society, or nobody at all. In technical language, for goods in this category, the principles of exclusion and rivalry do not apply.

**public sector:** The simplest definition is to include all forms of ownership by central and local government.

**quantitative easing:** The purchase of financial assets by a central bank, with the expressed objective to increase the supply of money in the economy and ease conditions in credit markets.

**quasi-public goods:** Goods or services which, by their nature, could be made available for purchase by individuals, but which the state finds administratively more convenient to provide for all the nation (e.g. roads).

**real estate investment trusts (REITs):** A property fund based on tax incentives designed to improve the flow of funds into commercial and residential property. Several models exist around the world, the longest standing being in the USA and Australia. The UK Government introduced them in January 2007.

**real rate of interest:** The rate of interest obtained by subtracting the rate of inflation from the nominal rate of interest.

**real value:** Measurement of economic values after adjustments have been made for inflation; also referred to as real terms.

**recession:** A period of time during which the rate of growth of business activity is consistently less than its long-term trend (i.e. negative).

**recovery:** The phase of a business cycle when output begins to rise towards the long-term trend.

**refinancing rate:** The rate of interest at which the European Central Bank lends on a short-term basis to the Euro banking sector.

**registered social landlords:** A group of private organisations that manage homes for tenants on lower incomes with support from the government. There are around three million such units owned by charitable companies, housing associations and so on.

**rental value:** The periodic return (monthly/yearly) that a property might reasonably be expected to command in the open market at a given time.

**repo rate:** The rate of interest at which the central bank lends funds on a short-term basis to the banking sector.

**residual land value:** A valuation method used to estimate the site value of a proposed development. It involves identifying *all* market costs of the development – the so-called 'gross development costs' – to establish how much can be viably allowed for the land component.

**residual method:** A procedure used to estimate the land (site) value of a development – see *residual land value*

**resources:** Inputs used in the production of goods and services; commonly categorised as land, labour, capital and entrepreneur (see separate glossary entries for details). 'Factors of production' is another way to refer to resources.

**retail price index (RPI):** A statistical measure of the change in the prices of goods and services bought for the purpose of consumption by the vast majority of households in the UK.

**Royal Institute of British Architects (RIBA):** The principal professional body in the UK concerned with architecture; established in 1834.

**Royal Institution of Chartered Surveyors (RICS):** The main UK professional body concerned with surveying in its various guises; founded in 1868.

**right to buy (RTB):** Government legislation that was passed in 1980 to allow council tenants of two or three years' standing the legal power to acquire their houses at a discount of the market value. In 2015, this idea was extended to housing association property.

**sale and leaseback:** The splitting up of a trading company into an operating company and a property company; the so-called 'opco-propco' structure.

**scarcity:** A reference to the fact that at any point in time there exists a finite amount of resources, while people have an infinite amount of 'wants' for goods and services.

**seasonally adjusted:** A process of estimating regularly occurring effects caused by weather and holidays, and removing them from the data.

**secondary income:** This forms part of the current account of the balance of payments, and consists of transfers of money for which there is no corresponding return of an item of economic value.

**secular stagnation:** This hypothesis was a term revived by Larry Summers in 2013, to distinguish the problem of the changing pace in economies in the post-crisis world from 2010 inwards.

**secured loans:** Credits backed by collateral; sometimes referred to as 'secured lending to households'. This includes things like credit cards, loans from retailers and (increasingly) other forms of consumer borrowing, such as payday loans

**selling-off plan:** The concept involves buying a property at current prices before it has actually been built, based on the proposed floor plan and site layout, as it is not possible to inspect units that do not yet exist. When the development is completed, however, the capital appreciation may make the risk worthwhile.

**serviced office:** A commercial property where the landlord provides a complete range of services such as furniture, cleaning, IT, reception and secretarial support, and so on.

**shadow banking system:** A term coined in 2007 to highlight the range of financial intermediaries that were operating below the official radar at the height of the financial crisis. The classic examples were hedge funds, pension funds and insurers. Since 2007, many of these have been reined into the traditional sector, and are now regulated by the central bank.

**sick building syndrome:** Defined by the World Health Organisation as a general feeling of malaise caused by working in certain modern buildings. No definite causes have yet been identified, but references to mechanically ventilated buildings do seem to be prevalent in the literature reporting this syndrome.

**social housing:** Dwellings provided for households in 'need' by Local Authorities and Registered Social Landlords. These are usually rented, but may be owned on a shared basis; in the majority of cases, the provision is below market cost, the difference being made up by government subsidy.

**stable equilibrium:** A situation in which, if there is a shock that disturbs the existing relationship between the forces of supply and demand, there will be a self-corrective counterforce that automatically remedies the disequilibrium.

**stabilisation policy:** Traditionally, such policy attempts to expand demand when unemployment is high, and to curtail demand when inflation accelerates.

**stamp duty land tax:** A property tax that is calculated at the time of purchase according to the price paid on the transaction. Different rates apply to residential, buy to let, and commercial property.

**statistical weights:** A factor by which a component is multiplied to reflect the level of consumers' expenditure on that component.

**substitute goods:** Goods and services are considered substitutes when one can be used in place of the other. A change in the price of one, therefore, causes a shift in demand for the other. For example, if the price of owner-occupied property goes up, the demand for rented property rises.

**supply curve:** The graphic representation of a supply schedule, which slopes upwards (has a positive slope).

**supply schedule:** A set of numbers showing prices and the quantity supplied for a specified period of time. In effect, the schedule shows a rate of planned production at each price.

**sustainable development:** There are several specific definitions but, in general terms, this represents progress that balances social, environmental and economic concerns.

**sustainable investment rule:** A fiscal rule stating that public sector net debt as a proportion of GDP should be held over the economic cycle at a stable level – say, below 40% of GDP.

**tax bracket:** A specified interval of income to which a specific and unique marginal rate of tax is applied.

**tax burden:** The distribution of tax incidence within society.

**total expenditure:** The total monetary value of all the final goods and services bought in an economy during the year.

**total income:** The total amount earned by the nation's resources. National income, therefore, includes wages, rent, interest payments and profits, received respectively by workers, landowners, providers of capital and entrepreneurs.

**total output:** The total value of all the final goods and services produced in the economy during the year.

**trade balance:** The difference between the value of goods and services one country sells to other countries, and the value of the goods and services it buys from other countries.

**trader-developer:** A property company that disposes of completed schemes (often to institutional fund holders) in order to raise collateral for the next project.

**transaction costs:** All of the costs associated with exchanging, such as the costs of finding out price, quality, service record, durability, and the cost of enforcing any contract.

**transmission mechanism:** The process by which a central bank's change to the official interest rate is passed on through financial markets to businesses and households, and subsequently determines the general level of prices, output, and employment in the economy.

**unsecured loans:** Credits provided to individuals that are not attached to collateral. It is sometimes referred to as 'unsecured lending to households'. It includes things like credit cards, loans from retailers and (increasingly) other forms of consumer borrowing, such as payday loans.

**upwards-only rent review:** This is a standard clause of a commercial property lease, which prevents the contracted rate of rent from falling. In other words, landlords can raise the rent at set intervals – say, every five years.

**vendor:** A seller of land and property.

**vertical equity:** Measures to achieve social justice or fairness by providing benefits targeted at people with specific needs. The concept accounts for policies such as means-tested benefits, and taxing the rich more heavily than the poor.

**viability:** A sufficient rate of return to allow the property project to proceed.

# Webnotes

## Introduction

1. BBC News item relating economic health to the sales of men's underpants: http://www.bbc.co.uk/news/business-20975333
2. 'Designer pawn': a new breed of high-end moneylenders: http://www.dailymail.co.uk/home/you/article-2225811/The-rise-designer-pawn.html

## Chapter 1

1. Regulatory Policy and Behavioural Economics (Lunn, 2014): http://www.oecd-ilibrary.org/governance/regulatory-policy-and-behavioural-economics_9789264207851-en
2. World Development Report, 2015: http://www.worldbank.org/en/publication/wdr2015
3. List of OECD member countries: http://www.oecd.org/about/membersandpartners/list-oecd-member-countries.htm

## Chapter 2

1. Types and names of local authorities in England and Wales: http://centrallobby.politicshome.com/fileadmin/epolitix/stakeholders/stakeholders/Factsheet_-_types_and_names_of_local_authorities_in_England_and_Wales_2010.pdf
2. Agencies involved in the development of 22 Bishopsgate etc: http://at22.co.uk/what-next

*New Economic Thinking and Real Estate*, First Edition. Danny Myers.
© 2016 John Wiley & Sons, Ltd. Published 2016 by John Wiley & Sons, Ltd.

3. CORE – Curriculum Open-access Resources in Economics: http://core-econ. org/
4. OECD wellbeing project: http://www.oecd.org/statistics/how-s-life-23089679. htm

## Chapter 3

1. Land Registry: www.nethouseprice.com
2. *The Economist* house price indicators: http://www.economist.com/blogs/ dailychart/2011/11/global-house-prices
3. Annual number of property transactions in the UK: https://www.gov.uk/ government/collections/property-transactions-in-the-uk
4. Number of property completions in the UK: https://www.gov.uk/government/ uploads/system/uploads/attachment_data/file/428608/LiveTable209.xlsx
5. State of the Estate: https://www.gov.uk/government/uploads/system/uploads/ attachment_data/file/419451/State_of_the_Estate_13-14.pdf
6. 'Right to contest': https://www.gov.uk/government/uploads/system/uploads/ attachment_data/file/269720/131216_Right_to_Contest_application_form_ final.odt
7. Government property finder: https://www.epims.ogc.gov.uk/government-property-finder/Home.aspx
8. JLL: http://www.jll.co.uk/united-kingdom/en-gb/
9. CBRE: http://www.cbre.eu/uk_en

## Chapter 4

1. Bank of England: http://www.bankofengland.co.uk/research/Documents/ workingpapers/2013/wp471.pdf
2. European Central Bank: http://www.ecb.int/home/html/researcher.en.html
3. Federal Reserve: http://www.federalreserve.gov/pubs/feds/1996/199642/19 9642pap.pdf
4. Magazine interview with Professor Steve Keen: http://evatt.org.au/news/445. html
5. The Resolution Foundation: http://resolutionfoundation.org/
6. McKinsey Global Institute reports: http://www.mckinsey.com/insights/ global_capital_markets/debt_and_deleveraging_the_global_credit_bubble_ update
7. Bank of England statistical interactive database: http://www.bankofengland. co.uk/statistics/Pages/bankstats/current/default.aspx
8. A three minute video clip that presents a synopsis of the paper by Burrows *et al.* (2015): https://www.youtube.com/watch?v=Jlq5hm7oSew
9. Signatories petitioning against the Fiscal Charter of 2015: http://www. theguardian.com/politics/2015/jun/12/osborne-plan-has-no-basis-in-economics
10. Proceedings of the Jackson Hole economic policy symposiums of 2011, 2012 and 2013: http://econpapers.repec.org/article/fipfedkpr/

11. Bank of England monetary and financial statistics: http://www.bankof england.co.uk/statistics/Pages/bankstats/2014/nov.aspx
12. European Central Bank macroeconomic and sectoral statistics: https://www. ecb.europa.eu/stats/acc/html/index.en.html
13. Bank Underground, a blog where Bank of England staff and academics) enter into an open debate about research output: http://bankunderground.co.uk/

## Chapter 5

1. Bank of England five minute video clip concerning money creation in the modern economy: https://www.youtube.com/watch?v=CvRAqR2pAgw
2. Positive Money: http://www.positivemoney.org/issues/debt/
3. Data from the Bank for International Settlements: http://www.bis.org/statistics/derstats.htm
4. Launch of Maine Tower in July 2015: https://www.youtube.com/watch?v=L7xPdrOSG4s
5. Bank for International Settlements list of central banks: https://www.bis.org/cbanks.htm
6. Bank of England macroeconomic model (MPC, 1999): http://www.bankofengland.co.uk/publications/Documents/other/monetary/montrans.pdf
7. An online net present value calculator: http://www.miniwebtool.com/pvif-calculator/?

## Chapter 6

1. The Great Recession, as defined by the National Bureau of Economic Research in the United States: http://www.nber.org/cycles.html
2. Royal event at the London School of Economics in November 2008: http://www.lse.ac.uk/study/meetLSE/pdf/focus/FocusNewsLetter10.pdf
3. Rogoff and Reinhart (2009) on banking crises 1800–2008: http://scholar.harvard.edu/files/rogoff/files/banking_crises.pdf
4. A Podcast of an interview between Paul Dolan and Richard Thaler, recorded on 9 June 2015 at the LSE: http://www.lse.ac.uk/newsAndMedia/videoAndAudio/channels/publicLecturesAndEvents/player.aspx?id=3127

## Chapter 7

1. World Bank Development Indicators: http://wdi.worldbank.org/table/4.2
2. World's central bankers annual conference at Jackson Hole, Wyoming, 2014: https://www.kansascityfed.org/publications/research/escp
3. *Private Eye* 2015; map of land and property registered in England and Wales in the name of offshore companies: http://www.private-eye.co.uk/registry
4. Transparency International: https://www.transparency.org/
5. Transparency International Corruption Perception Index, 2013: http://www.transparency.org/cpi2013/results
6. Newcastle at risk of financial collapse: http://johnharris.me.uk/?m=201411

# Chapter 8

1. Detailed UK quarterly real GDP on average income per head: http://www.ons.gov.uk/ons/datasets-and-tables/data-selector.html?cdid=IHXW&dataset=ukca&table-id=X11
2. World Development Indicators: http://data.worldbank.org/products/wdi
3. International Labour Organisation: http://www.ilo.org/global/about-the-ilo/history/lang--en/index.htm
4. Data about overseas investors (Knight Frank, 2013): http://www.knightfrankblog.com/global-briefing/news-headlines/assessing-foreign-demand-for-london-property/
5. Data about overseas investors (Savills, 2013): http://www.savills.co.uk/research_articles/141285/168751-0
6. The Great Recession as defined by the National Bureau of Economic Research in the United States: http://www.nber.org/cycles.html
7. OECD quarterly national accounts database: http://stats.oecd.org/index.aspx?queryid=350
8. OBR Economic and fiscal outlook, 2015: http://cdn.budgetresponsibility.independent.gov.uk/March2015EFO_18-03-webv1.pdf
9. Pew survey on Americans' opinions of the internet: http://www.pewinternet.org/2014/02/27/the-web-at-25-in-the-u-s/

## Critics of the internet

10. Jaron Lanier: http://bookshop.theguardian.com/who-owns-the-future.html
11. Doc Searls: http://tinyurl.com/ngawoys
12. Astra Taylor: http://bookshop.theguardian.com/people-s-platform.html
13. Ethan Zuckerman: http://bookshop.theguardian.com/catalog/product/view/id/273303/
14. Nicholas Carr: http://bookshop.theguardian.com/glass-cage.html
15. Andrew Keen: http://www.amazon.co.uk/The-Internet-Is-Not-Answer/dp/0802123139
16. *Guardian* articles on Instagram: http://www.theguardian.com/technology/instagram
17. Prologis, global provider of industrial real estate: http://www.prologis.co.uk/about/

# Afterword

1. Report on conference at Kings College Cambridge in April 2010: http://ineteconomics.org/community/events/the-economic-crisis-and-the-crisis-in-economics
2. First symposium of the Institute for New Economic Thinking: http://ineteconomics.org/
3. Adair Turner: http://ineteconomics.org/community/experts/aturner
4. Joseph Stiglitz: http://ineteconomics.org/community/experts/jstiglitz
5. Anatole Kaletsky: http://ineteconomics.org/community/experts/akaletsky
6. Ha-Joon Chang: http://ineteconomics.org/community/experts/hjchang

7.  Robert Schiller: http://www.nobelprize.org/nobel_prizes/economic-sciences/laureates/2013/shiller-bio.html
8.  Andrew Haldane: http://ineteconomics.org/community/experts/ahaldane
9.  List of winners of Nobel Prize in Economics: http://www.nobelprize.org/nobel_prizes/economic-sciences/laureates/index.html
10. Role of students: http://ineteconomics.org/community/young-scholars
11. Post-Crash Economics Society (PCES): http://www.post-crasheconomics.com/
12. Paul Krugman's *New York Times* column: http://www.nytimes.com/column/paul-krugman

**Webnotes**

# References
# and Recommendations

Adrian, T. and Shin, H.S. (2010). *The Changing Nature of Financial Intermediation and the Financial Crisis of 2007-09*. Federal Reserve Bank of New York Staff Reports, No. 439.

Akerlof, G. (1970). *The Market for Lemons: Quality Uncertainty and the Market Mechanism. Quarterly Journal of Economics*.

Allen, K. (2013). Subterranean building boom. *FT Weekend, Financial Times*, 15 March.

Alston, L.J. (2008). New Institutional Economics. In: Durlauf, S. and Blume, L. (eds). *The New Palgrave Dictionary of Economics* (2008). Palgrave Macmillan Ltd: London.

Archer, T. and Cole, I. (2014). Still not plannable? Housing supply and the changing structure of the housebuilding industry in the UK in 'austere' times. *People, Place and Policy* 8(2), 97–112.

Baker, D., DeLong, B. and Krugman, P. (2005). As*set Returns and Economic Growth*. Brookings Papers on Economic Activity 2005:1.

Bank of England (2015). *Stress testing the UK banking system: key elements of the 2015 stress test*. Bank of England: London, March.

Barker, K. (2003). *Review of Housing Supply: Securing our Future Housing Needs. Interim Report and Analysis*. HMSO: London.

Barker, K. (2004). *Review of Housing Supply – Delivering Stability: securing our future housing needs*. Final Report – Recommendations. HM Treasury and ODPM: London. Available at www.barkerreview.org.uk.

Barratt Development PLC (2011). *Annual Results Announcement for the year ended 30 June 2011* [online]. Last accessed on 30 November 2013 at http://www.barrattdevelopments.co.uk/barratt/en/investor/results.

Basu, K. (2006). Globalization, Poverty, and Inequality: What is the Relationship? What Can Be Done? *World Development* 34(8), 1361–1373.

Basu, K. (2010). *Beyond the Invisible Hand: Groundwork for a New Economics*. Princeton University Press.

Berkeley Group Plc. (2011). *Preliminary Results Announcement 24th June 2011* [online]. Last accessed on 18 June 2014 at http://www.berkeleygroup.co.uk/investor-information/results-and-announcements.

Bezemer, D.J. (2009). No One Saw This Coming: Understanding financial crisis through accounting models. *Munich Pesonal RePEc Archive* 16 June.

Bill, P. (2013). *Planet Property*. Matador: Leicestershire.

Bishop, M. and Green, M. (2010). *The Road from Ruin: How to Revive Capitalism and Put America Back on Top*. Crown Business: New York.

Blinder, A.S. (2013). *After the Music Stopped*. The Penguin Press New York.

Borio, C. and Disyatat, P. (2011). *Global Imbalances and the Financial Crisis: Link or No Link?* BIS Working Papers, No. 346. Bank for International Settlements: Basle, Switzerland.

Brockmeijer, J. Nier, E. and Osiński, J. (2013). *Key Aspects of Macroprudential Policy*. IMF: Washington, D.C.

Burrows, O. and Low, K. (2015). Mapping the UK financial system. *Quarterly Bulletin (Q2)*, 114–129. Bank of England: London.

Burrows, O. Low, K. and Cumming, F. (2015). Mapping the UK financial system. *Bank of England Quarterly Bulletin* **Q2**, 114–129.

Cabinet Office (2015). *The State of the Estate in 2013/14*. H.M. Government: London.

Callcutt, J. (2007). *The Callcutt Review of housebuilding delivery*. DCLG: London.

Cecchetti, S. and Kharroubi, E. (2012). *Reassessing the impact of finance on growth*. BIS Working Papers No 381. Bank for International Settlements: Basel, Switzerland.

Cecchetti, S. Mohanty, M.S. and Zampoll, F. (2011). *Achieving growth amid fiscal imbalances: the real effects of debt*. Proceedings of the Economic Policy Symposium – Jackson Hole, pp. 145–196.

CGFS (Committee on the Global Financial System) (2012). *Operationalising the Selection and Application of Macroprudential Instruments*. Paper No. 48, Committee on the Global Financial System: Basel.

Chang, H. (2011). *23 things they don't tell you about capitalism*. Penguin Books: London and New York.

Chang, H. (2014). How an economic fairy tale led Britain to stagnation. *The Guardian*, 20th October, p. 27.

Chang, Ha-Joon (2011). *23 Things They Don't Tell You About Economics*. Penguin: London and New York.

Chang, Ha-Joon (2014). *Economics: The User's Guide*. Pelican, an imprint of Penguin: London and New York.

Cheshire, P. and Hilber, C.A.L. (2008). Office space supply restrictions in Britain: the political economy of market revenge. *Economic Journal* **118**(529), F185–F221.

Coase, R. (1988). *The Firm, the Market, and the Law*. University of Chicago Press: Chicago.

Coase, R.H. (1991). Nobel Prize Lecture: The Institutional Structure of Production. Available from http://www.nobelprize.org/nobel_prizes/economic-sciences/laureates/1991/coase-lecture.html

Coleman, C., Crosby, N., McAllister, P. and Wyatt, P. (2013). Development appraisal in practice: some evidence from the planning system, *Journal of Property Research* **30**(2), 144–165.

Conaghan, D. (2012). *The Bank: Inside the Bank of England*. Biteback Publishing: London.

Construction Industry Council (2009). *The Impacts of the Recession on Construction Professional Services: A View from an Economic Perspective*. CIC: London.

CORE (2013). *Curriculum Open-access Resources in Economics*. Project funded by INET and led by Professor Wendy Carlin. Oxford University.

Coyle, D. (2012). *The Public Responsibilities Of The Economist*. Tanner Lectures, Brasenose College, Oxford, 18–19 May.

Coyle, D. (Ed, 2012). *What's the Use of Economics? Teaching the dismal science after the crisis*. London publishing partnership.

Dorling, D. (2014). *All That Is Solid: The Great Housing Disaster*. Penguin.

Easterlin, R. (2001). Income and Happiness: Towards a Unified Theory, *The Economic Journal* **111**, 465–484.

Evans, A. (1991). Rabbit Hutches on Postage Stamps: Planning, Development and Political Economy. *Urban Studies* **28**(6), 853–870.

Farag, M. Harland, D. and Nixon, D. (2013). Bank capital and liquidity. *Bank of England Quarterly Bulletin* (Q3).

FCIC (2011). *The Financial Crisis Inquiry Report*. Financial Crisis Inquiry Commission: U.S. Government Printing Office.

Fox, S. and Rainie, L. (2014). *The Web at 25 in the US*. Pew Research Centre: Washington, DC.

FSB (2010). *Reducing the moral hazard posed by systemically important financial institutions*. Report to the G20 Group, Financial Stability Board: Basle.

Friedman, B.M. (2009). The Failure of the Economy and the Economists. *New York Review of Books*, **LVI**(9), 42–45.

Geithner, T. (2014). *Stress Tests: on Financial Crises*. Crown Publishers: New York.

GLA – Greater London Authority (2012). *Barriers to Housing Delivery*. Molior: London.

Godley, W. (1999). Money and Credit in a Keynesian Model of Income Determination. *Cambridge Journal of Economics* **23**(4), 393–411.

Godley, W. and Lavoie, M. (2007). *Monetary Economics: An Integrated Approach to Credit, Money, Income, Production and Wealth*. Palgrave/Macmillan: London.

Grimsey, B. (2013). *The Grimsey Review: An alternative future for the high street*. Independent review: London.

Haldane, A.G. (2009). *Rethinking the financial network*. Speech delivered at the Financial Student Association in Amsterdam, 28 April.

Haldane, A.G. (2013). *Macroprudential Policies: When and How to Use Them?* IMF Rethinking Macro Policy II Conference.

Haldane, A. (2014). *The age of asset management?* Speech delivered to the Asset management conference at the London Business School 4th April and the Institute for New Economic Thinking conference – Human after all – Toronto, 10th April. All speeches are available online at www.bankofengland.co.uk/publications/Pages/speeches/default.aspx.

Harford, T. (2014). *The Undercover Economist* Abacus: London.

Harman, J. (2012). *Viability Testing Local Plans: Advice for planning practitioners*. Local Housing Delivery Group, CLG: London.

Harrison, F. (2005). *Boom Bust: House Prices, Banking and the Depression of 2010*. Shepheard-Walwyn, London.

Harrison, F. (2005). Want to get rid of boom and bust? Tax land, not income. *The Guardian*, 11 April.

Herndon, T., Ash, M. and Pollin, R. (2013). Does High Public Debt Consistently Stifle Economic Growth? A Critique of Reinhart and Rogoff. *Working paper number 322, Political Economy Research Institute*, University of Massachusetts, Amherst.

Hill, S. and Lorenz, D. (2011). Rethinking professionalism: guardianship of land and resources. *Building Research and Information* **39**(3), 314–319.

House of Lords (2013). *Ready for Ageing*. Select committee on 'Public Service and Demographic Change', Chaired by Lord Filkin, Report Session 2012–13, HL paper 140. The Stationery Office Limited: London.

Hudson, M. (2006). The Road to Serfdom: An Illustrated Guide to the Coming Real Estate Collapse. *Harper's Magazine*, April.

Jakab, Z. and Kumhof, M. (2015). *Banks are not intermediaries of loanable funds — and why this matters*. Working Paper No. 529, Bank of England.

Jorda, O., Schularick, M. and Taylor, A.L. (2014). *The Great Mortgaging: Housing Finance, Crises, and Business Cycles*, Federal Reserve Bank of San Francisco, Working Paper 2014-23.

Kahneman, D. (2003). Maps of Bounded Rationality: Psychology for Behavioural Economics. *American Economic Review* **93** (5), 1449–75.

Kahneman, D. (2011). *Thinking, Fast and Slow.* New York: Farrar, Straus and Giroux.

Kaletsky, A. (2010). *Capitalism 4.0: the birth of a new economy.* Bloomsbury: London, New York and Berlin.

Keen, A. (2015). *The internet is not the answer.* Atlantic books: London.

Keen, S. (2006). *The Lily and the Pond.* Interview reported by the Evans Foundations, at http://evatt.org.au/news/445.html.

Keen, S. (2011). *Debunking economics.* Zed books: London and New York.

King, M. (1999). *MPC Two Years On.* Speech given at the Queens University, Belfast, May.

Kothari, S., Lewellen, J. and Warner, J. (2014). *The behaviour of aggregate corporate investment.* MIT Sloan School of Management Working Paper.

Krugman, P. (2009). How Did Economists Get It So Wrong? *New York Times*, 2 September.

Krugman, P. (2009). *The Return of Depression Economics and the Crisis of 2008.* W.W. Norton Company Limited. ISBN 978-0-393-07101-.

Lanchester, J. (2014). *How to speak money.* Faber and Faber: London.

Layard, R. (2005). *Happiness: lessons from a new science.* Penguin Press: New York.

Lewis, M. (2014). *Flashboys: cracking the money code.* Penguin, Random House: UK.

Lin, L. and Surti, J. (2013). *Capital Requirements for Over-the-Counter Derivatives Central Counterparties.* IMF Working Paper 13/3, Monetary and Capital Markets Department: Washington D.C.

Lo, S. and Rogoff, K. (2015). *Secular stagnation, debt overhang and other rationales for sluggish growth, six years on.* BIS working paper 482. Bank for International Settlements. Basle.

Lorenz, D. and Lützkendorf, T. (2008). Sustainability in Property Valuation: theory and practice. *Journal of Property Investment and Finance* **26** (6), 482–521.

Lorenz, D. and Lützkendorf, T. (2011). Sustainability and Property Valuation – Systematisation of existing approaches and recommendations for future Action, *Journal of Property Investment & Finance* **29**(6), 644–676.

Lucas, R. (2009). In defence of the dismal science. *The Economist*: New York and London, 6 August.

Lunn, P. (2014). *Regulatory Policy and Behavioural Economics.* OECD: Paris

Mankiw, G. (2009). That Freshman Course Won't Be Quite the Same. *New York Times*, 24 May.

Mankiw, G. (2014). *Principles of Economics* (7th Revised Edition). South-Western College Publishing: Mason, Ohio, USA.

Marshall, P. and Kennedy, C. (1993). Development valuation techniques. *Journal of Property Valuation and Investment* **11**, 57–66.

Marx, K. (1847). *The poverty of philosophy.* Download available as a .pdf from: https://www.marxists.org/archive/marx/works/download/pdf/Poverty-Philosophy.pdf

McLeay, M., Radia, A. and Thomas, R. (2014). Money creation in the modern economy. *Bank of England Quarterly Bulletin* (March).

McKinsey (2015). *Debt and (not much) Deleveraging.* McKinsey Global Institute.

Meins, E. Wallbaum, H. Hardziewski, R. and Feige, A. (2010). Sustainability and Property Valuation: a risk based approach. *Building Research and Information* **38**(3) 280–300.

Milanovic, B. (2013). Global income inequality in numbers. *Global Policy* **4**(2), 198–208.

Milne, S. (2015). The Davos oligarchs are right to fear the world they've made. *The Guardian*, 22 January.

Minsky, H.P. (1974). The Modelling of Financial Instability: An introduction. *Proceedings of the Fifth Annual Pittsburgh Conference.* Instrument Society of America: University of Pittsburgh (Hyman P. Minsky Archive. Paper 467).

Minsky, H.P. (1992). *The Financial Instability Hypothesis*. The Levy Economics Institute of Bard College, Working Paper No. 74 (May). Prepared for *A Handbook of Radical Political Economy*. Edited by Arestis, P. and Sawyer, M. Edward Elgar: Aldershot, 1993.

Minsky, H.P. (2008). *Stabilizing an Unstable Economy*. McGraw-Hill: New York. (Originally published in 1986 by Yale University Press: New Haven, CT.).

Molior (2014). *Who Buys New Homes in London and Why?* British Property Federation: London.

Monbiot, G. (2015). How the universities allow a corporate cult to capture and destroy their best students. *The Guardian*, 3rd June.

Monbiot, G. (2015). 'The City's stranglehold makes Britain look like an oh-so-civilised mafia state'. *The Guardian*, 9th September.

MPC (1999). *The transmission mechanism of monetary policy*. Bank of England: London. Available on the Bank's website: www.bankofengland.co.uk.

Murgatroyd, G. (2014). *BCO Specification for Offices: Quick guide to key criteria 2009–2014 comparison*. Gardiner and Theobold: London.

Myers, D. (2005). A review of construction companies attitudes to sustainability. *Construction Management and Economics* **23**, 781–785.

Myers, D. (2006). *Economics & Property: the Estates Gazette guide*. EG books (2nd edition).

Myers, D. (2012). *Economics and Property*. 3rd Edition, Routledge: London and New York.

NBER (2010). *Business Cycle Dating Committee*, National Bureau of Economic Research: Cambridge MA. Announcement, September 20.

Neate, R. (2014). Scandal of Europe's Empty Homes. *The Guardian*, 24th Feb, pp 1–2.

OBR (2014). *Economic and Fiscal Outlook*. Office for Budget Responsibility, December, Cm 8966.

OBR (2015). *Office for Budget Responsibility: Economic and fiscal outlook*. HMSO: London. Presented to Parliament by the Economic Secretary to the Treasury by Command of Her Majesty (Cm 9024, March).

OECD (2015). *Focus on inequality and growth*. Organization for Economic Coordination and Development: Paris.

Orlowski, L.J. (2015). From pit to electronic trading: Impact on price volatility of U.S. Treasury futures. *Review of Financial Economics* **25**, 3–9.

Osman, M. (2004). An evaluation of dual-process theories of reasoning. *Psychonomic Bulletin & Review* **11**(6), 988–1010.

Ostry, J.D., Berg, A. and Tsangarides, C.G. (2014). *Redistribution, Inequality and Growth*. IMF: Washington. Staff Discussion Note, April.

Palma, J.G. (2009). The revenge of the market on the rentiers – Why neoliberal reports of the end of history turned out to be premature. *Cambridge Journal of Economics* **33**(4), 531–538.

Piketty, T. (2014). *Capital in the Twenty-First Century* (translated by Arthur Goldhammer). Belknap Press.

Private Eye (2015). 'Selling England by the offshore pound', 1st September, Issue 1400.

Rajan, R. (2010). *Fault Lines*. Princeton University Press: New Jersey.

Resolution Foundation (2013). *Squeezed Britain*. Available from: http://squeezedbritain. resolutionfoundation.org.

Resolution Foundation (2014). *Mortgaged Future: Modelling household debt affordability and access to re-financing as interest rates rise*. Researched by Matthew Whittaker for Resolution Foundation: London.

RIBA (2011). *The Case for Space: The Size of England's New Homes*. London.

RICS (2002). *Green Man Red Man*. A report authored by Cox, J. Fell, D. and Thurstain-Goodwin, M. for RICS Foundation: London.

**References**

RICS (2009). *Sustainability and Commercial Property Valuation*. Valuation information paper 13, September. Royal Institute of Chartered Surveyors.

Robbins, L. (1932). *An Essay on the Nature and Significance of Economic Science*. Macmillan: London.

Rogoff, K.S and Reinhart, C.M (2009). *This time is different*. Princeton University Press: Princeton and Oxford.

Rogoff, K.S. and Reinhart, C.M. (2010). *Growth in a Time of Debt* NBER Working Paper No. 15639. National Bureau of Economic Research: Cambridge, MA.

Roubini, N. and Mihm, S. (2011). *Crisis Economics: a crash course in the future of finance*. Penguin Books: London and New York.

Roxburgh, C., Lund, S., Wimmer, T., Amar, E., Atkins, C., Kwek, J.H., Dobbs, R. and Manyika, J. (2011). *Debt and deleveraging: The global credit bubble and its economic consequences*. McKinsey Global Institute: Washington, DC.

Samuelson, P.A. (2010). *Economics*. Tata McGraw-Hill Education.

Samuelson, P.A. and Nordhaus, W.D. (2010). *Economics* (19th Edition). McGraw-Hill/ Irwin: New York.

Sandel, M.J. (2012). *What Money Can't Buy: The moral limits to markets*. Farrar, Straus and Giroux: New York.

Schiller, R. (2012). *Finance and the good society*. Princeton University Press: New Jersey.

Shapps, G. (2011). *Think outside of 'identikit Legoland homes'*. Ministerial announcement, 9 March. DCLG: London.

Sharpe, S.A. and Suarez, G.A. (2014). *The insensitivity of investment to interest rates: Evidence from a survey of CFOs*. Finance and Economics Discussion Series Divisions of Research & Statistics and Monetary Affairs Federal Reserve Board: Washington, D.C.

Skidelsky, R. (2010). *Keynes the return of the master*. Penguin: London and New York

Smith, G. (2012). Why am I Leaving Goldman Sachs. *New York Times*, 14 March (letters page).

Snowdon, C. (2014). *Closing Time: who's killing the British pub?* IEA: London.

Solow, R.M. (2009). How to understand the disaster. *The New York Review of Books*, LVI. 8, May 14–27, 4–8.

Stevens, M. (2015). *Competitive goods market*. Unit 8 in *The Economy* Curriculum Open-access Resources in Economics, CORE: Ebook.

Stiglitz, J. (2010). *Freefall: free markets and the sinking of the global economy*. Penguin Books: London and New York.

Stiglitz, J. (2013). *The Price of Inequality: how today's divided society endangers our future*. W.W Norton and Company: New York and London.

Stiglitz, J. and Akerlof, G. (2009). A new economics in an imperfect world. *The Guardian*, 28 October.

Sutherland, D. and Hoeller, P. (2012). Debt and Macroeconomic Stability: An Overview of the Literature and Some Empirics, *OECD Economics Department Working Papers*, No. 1006, OECD Publishing: Paris.

Taylor Wimpey (2011). Results for the year ended 31 December 2010 [online]. https://www.taylorwimpey.co.uk/corporate/investor-relations/reporting-centre/2011.

Thaler, R.H. (2015). *Misbehaving: The making of behavioural economics*. W.W. Norton and Company: New York.

*The Economist* (2014). Fast Times. *The Economist*, April 5th.

*The Economist* (2014). Rise of the place-makers, *The Economist*, 16 August: 21.

*The Economist* (2015). The Never-Ending Story: first America, then Europe, now the debt crisis has reached emerging markets. *The Economist*, November 14th.

*The Economist*. (2015a). Watch Out. *The Economist*, 13th June.

*The Economist*. (2015b). What's wrong with finance? *The Economist*, 1st May.

Tucker, P. (2009). *The repertoire of official sector interventions in the financial system – last resort lending, market-making, and capital.* Presented at the Bank of Japan 2009 International Conference Financial System and Monetary Policy: Implementation. Bank of Japan: Tokyo, 27–28 May.

Tucker, P. Hall, S. and Pattani, A. (2013). Macroprudential policy at the Bank of England. *Bank of England Quarterly Bulletin* (**Q3**), 192–200.

Turner, A. (2010). *After the Crises: Assessing the Costs and Benefits of Financial Liberalisation.* 14th Chintaman Deshmukh Memorial Lecture, Reserve Bank of India, Mumbai, 15 February.

Turner, A. (2012). *Economics after the crisis.* MIT press: Massachusetts.

Turner, A. (2015). *Between Debt and the Devil: money, credit, and fixing global finance.* Princeton University Press.

United Nations (2013). *World Population Ageing.* United Nations: New York.

United Nations (2014). *Financial Production, Flows and Stocks in the System of National Accounts.* United Nations: New York.

United Nations, Department of Economic and Social Affairs, Population Division (2013). United Nations: New York.

VOA – Valuation Office & Agency (2012). *Business Floorspace (Experimental Statistics).* Release Notes – 17 May.

Wellings, F. (2006). *British Housebuilders: History and Analysis.* Blackwell: Oxford.

WEO (2010). World Economic Outlook: Rebalancing Growth. IMF: Washington, DC.

WEO (2014). World Economic Outlook: Legacies, Clouds, Uncertainties. IMF: Washington, DC.

World Bank (2013). *Inequality in Focus.* Vol. **2**, No. 3: October. Poverty Reduction and Equity Department. World Bank: Washington, DC.

World Bank (2014). *World Development Report: Risk and Opportunity – Managing Risk for Development.* World Bank: Washington, DC.

World Bank Group (2015). *Global Monitoring Report 2014/2015: Ending Poverty and Sharing Prosperity.* World Bank: Washington, DC.

World Development Report (2015). *Mind, Society, and Behaviour.* World Bank: Washington, DC.

World Population Ageing (2013). ST/ESA/SER.A/348.

Wyatt, P. (2013). *Property Valuation*, Second Edition. Wiley Blackwell: Oxford

# Index

---